COMMONWEALTH MIGRATION

Flows and Policies

CAMBRIDGE COMMONWEALTH SERIES

Published in association with the Managers of the Cambridge University Smuts Memorial Fund for the Advancement of Commonwealth Studies

General Editor: E. T. Stokes, Smuts Professor of the History of the British Commonwealth, University of Cambridge

Roger Anstey
THE ATLANTIC SLAVE TRADE AND BRITISH ABOLITION, 1760–1810

John Darwin
BRITAIN, EGYPT AND THE MIDDLE EAST: IMPERIAL POLICY IN THE AFTERMATH OF WAR, 1918–1922

T. R. H. Davenport
SOUTH AFRICA: A MODERN HISTORY

B. H. Farmer *(editor)*
GREEN REVOLUTION? TECHNOLOGY AND CHANGE IN RICE-GROWING AREAS OF TAMIL NADU AND SRI LANKA

Partha Sarathi Gupta
IMPERIALISM AND THE BRITISH LABOUR MOVEMENT, 1914–1964

R. F. Holland
BRITAIN AND THE COMMONWEALTH ALLIANCE, 1918–1939

Ronald Hyam and Ged Martin
REAPPRAISALS IN BRITISH IMPERIAL HISTORY

W. David McIntyre
THE RISE AND FALL OF THE SINGAPORE NAVAL BASE

T. E. Smith
COMMONWEALTH MIGRATION: FLOWS AND POLICIES

B. R. Tomlinson
THE INDIAN NATIONAL CONGRESS AND THE *RAJ*, 1929–1942
THE POLITICAL ECONOMY OF THE *RAJ*, 1914–1947

John Manning Ward
COLONIAL SELF-GOVERNMENT: THE BRITISH EXPERIENCE, 1759–1856

Further titles in preparation

COMMONWEALTH MIGRATION

Flows and Policies

by T. E. Smith

with contributions from Charles Price,
L. W. St John-Jones, William Gould
and R. Mansell Prothero

First published 1981 by
THE MACMILLAN PRESS LTD
London and Basingstoke
Companies and representatives
throughout the world

Printed in Hong Kong

British Library Cataloguing in Publication Data

Smith, Thomas Edward, *b. 1916*
    Commonwealth migration
    1. Commonwealth of Nations – Emigration
    and immigration – History
    I. Title
    301.32   JV7615

    ISBN 0–333–27898–4

Contents

Preface

This book seeks to examine the post-war movement of peoples between countries of the Commonwealth. It studies the way in which policies have evolved in individual countries to control or encourage such movement. In other words it is a book about a particular aspect of population policy in Commonwealth countries.

My own interest in population policy arose from earlier study of the demography of developing countries over a period of three decades. In the early 1970s a volume of mine was published on the politics of family planning in developing countries which used the case-study approach and looked in detail at the development of policy relating to fertility control in six countries. The same country case-study approach has been used in this volume for the reasons given in the introductory chapter. Necessarily this study of migration and migration policy involves the more developed countries of the Commonwealth rather more than the less developed countries, although the latter are by no means ignored and three of the six case-study chapters relate to them.

Bearing in mind how widely dispersed are the countries of the Commonwealth, I was fortunate to secure the co-operation of a number of professional colleagues prominent in the study of international migration. Charles Price, who contributes the chapter on Australian migration, is a Professorial Fellow of long standing in the Department of Demography in the Australian National University. L. W. St John-Jones, who contributes the chapter on Canada, has divided his time in the last fifteen years between working for the United Nations in various capacities and for the Canadian Government's Statistical Office. He is now engaged on a study of the demography of Cyprus. William Gould and R. Mansell Prothero, who contribute the chapter on Commonwealth countries of Africa, are Lecturer in Geography and Professor of Geography respectively at the University of Liverpool. The former has been a Consultant to UNESCO and the World Bank and the latter to WHO, the World Bank and the UK Ministry of Overseas Development. In addition to these contributors, invaluable assistance was given by Lynne Iliffe in the compilation of the chapter on Jamaica.

After obtaining her M.Sc. in Medical Demography in 1975 at the London School of Hygiene and Tropical Medicine, she continued for a time to work in the demographic field but is now a youth worker employed by the Inner London Education Authority.

I have also received helpful documentation on migration from a number of people in different Commonwealth countries. Here I would mention particularly Mr Brian Lythe of the University of Auckland. I have to thank Mr David Morgan for reading and commenting on the first draft of the chapter on Jamaica and Mr Lino Delia for performing a similar function in respect of the first draft of the chapter on Malta. There are others who have assisted me in one way or another but prefer not to have their names mentioned.

The Institute of Commonwealth Studies in the University of London provided me with an academic base and an office from which to operate. The Social Science Research Council provided a generous grant without which the project could not have been undertaken. Last, but far from least, I must thank very warmly Mrs Pamela Oldroyd, who typed the whole of the final draft of the book as well as an earlier draft of some of its chapters, in the course of which she spotted a number of errors and inconsistencies in the text. The book is better for the work that she has put into it.

London, August 1979   T. E. SMITH

1 Introduction

Much greater interest has been taken in the international migration policies of national governments in the last twenty years than ever before. For countries of immigration the questions that have been debated have included those relating to the desirability of retaining preferences for immigrants of designated ethnic or national origin, with a view to retaining the homogeneity of the host population, and to the alternative of disregarding ethnic or national origin and concentrating instead on the professional, occupational, linguistic and other skills of immigrants. The debate has also covered the question of numbers of immigrants; in some quarters within countries of immigration the view has been expressed with growing force that new immigrants are no longer required, or at most are required in much reduced numbers. Both trade unionists and conservationists, among others, have expressed such views from time to time.

Countries of emigration have also had their own heart-searching, for international migrants in these days are not the unemployed and the down-and-outs in their own countries, but rather people who often possess valued skills and on whom relatives left behind frequently rely for financial support. There has been considerable, if inconclusive, public debate over the 'brain drain' and in some countries, where young people are professionally trained at public expense, there is a require-ment that, on completing their qualifying examinations, they should serve their own countries for a period of a few years before considering emigration. On the whole, however, non-communist countries accept the right to emigrate as a human right, and the restraints on emigration tend to be related more to the ability to obtain an entry permit into another country and to the personal constraints involved in financing one's own and one's family's migration.

Migration between Commonwealth countries is an important part of the total international migration picture. The pattern of movement of peoples in the late nineteenth and early twentieth centuries between countries that are now or have until recently been members of the Commonwealth consisted of a web with two major and several minor strands. The first major strand, subdividing into several individual lines of communication, was the net migration from the British Isles to Canada, Australia, New Zealand and South Africa. The second major strand, also subdividing, was the movement, initially under indenture and later under less undesirable forms of recruitment, from the Indian sub-continent to British colonies and protectorates which required unskilled labour for the development of primary industries and for public works. The destinations for these flows of migrant labourers included Malaysia, Sri Lanka, Fiji, Mauritius, South and East Africa, Trinidad and Guyana. The Indian sub-continent also provided clerks, policemen, artisans and merchants in many British colonies.

These two major strands were largely independent of one another. Europeans, and particularly British and Irish, were welcome immigrants in Canada, Australia and New Zealand, but coloured British subjects were, with some exceptions, not wanted in these countries. The British Empire, as it was, never even approximated to an area of unfettered movement for British subjects of all races and colours. Only the British Isles were, at least on paper, open to all British subjects, and that freedom was never put to a real test in terms of large influxes until after the Second World War.

Migration from the Indian sub-continent brought short and medium-term economic gains to the British colonies which were able to make good use of the labour and other services provided by the immigrants. Initially the Indian labourers were regarded as transients, due to return to their native India at the end of the period of indenture, but largely male labour forces gradually gave place to mixed labour forces, and the permanent settlement of ethnically Indian populations in many of the colonies became certain. The official sponsors of these movements clearly failed to envisage the long term political difficulties which Indian settlement in territories with a very different native ethnic population would bring. The political difficulties have proved to be as acute in countries such as Trinidad, Guyana and Mauritius in which Indian indentured labour replaced black slave labour, and both ethnic groups remained as quite separate communities in the same country.

In contrast migration from the British Isles to the 'White Dominions' led to relatively few political problems and undoubtedly helped to strengthen Commonwealth relations. British and Irish emigrants to Australia, New Zealand and Canada integrated readily into the white host population and were usually young and adaptable enough to accept the changes in ways of life involved in living in the new environment. India did not seriously protest at the restrictions on entry of its peoples into countries such as Australia and New Zealand; indeed the Indian delegation moved a resolution at the 1918 Imperial Conference insisting that each member government, including India, should be free to restrict immigration from other Commonwealth countries, and this position was reaffirmed in later Imperial Conferences in 1921 and 1923. Indian anger was directed very much more at the exploitation of Indian labour in some of the colonies, and at the refusal to grant racial equality to Indians abroad, most particularly to the Indians in Natal. Indian labour emigration to South Africa was stopped before the First World War, and the whole indenture system of recruiting labour ceased to be valid as from the beginning of 1920.

The removal of indenture did not stop the flow of freely recruited Indian labour to destinations such as Malaysia and Sri Lanka, but the 1920s was the last decade until after the Second World War when net emigration of Indians took place on a substantial scale. The world depression reversed the flow, just as it reversed the direction of the flow from Britain to Australia, New Zealand and Canada. The war put a stop to the beginnings of a revival in international migration, and every country had to work out its own migration policy anew once peaceful conditions had been restored.

In most of the developing countries of the Commonwealth a 'population explosion' started within a few years of the end of the war as a result of rapidly falling mortality and maintained high fertility. In such countries further immigrants were not wanted unless they possessed particular qualifications needed for development. As a rule, when less developed countries of the Commonwealth became independent, restrictions on new immigration became even tighter and, in some cases, external outlets were actively sought for 'surplus' population. In defence of their own immigration policies Commonwealth governments generally were able to subscribe to the principle established earlier in the century that all countries should be free to restrict immigration as their governments saw fit. Pressures were sometimes put on pre-war immigrants by newly independent Commonwealth countries to return to their country of origin. The extreme example of such pressure was the summary expulsion of Asians from Uganda, but there are a number of other instances such as the phased move of 'Indian Tamils' (as opposed to 'Ceylon Tamils') from Sri Lanka to India under the agreement signed by the two governments concerned.

Pressures on particular sections of a country's population, resulting in emigration, must be carefully distinguished from a general encouragement to emigrate with the aim of reducing population pressure. In this book two of the detailed case studies, Malta and Jamaica, are examples of Commonwealth countries which have at times since the Second World War positively encouraged emigration from among the general population to alleviate population pressure.

Another small Commonwealth country, Mauritius, has gone through a phase of implicit encouragement to emigrate, although the acceptance of such encouragement has been largely confined to one section of the country's population, the so-called 'Franco–Mauritians'. Mauritius had a population estimated at 894,000 at the end of 1977; a further 28,000 lived in Rodrigues and other Mauritian dependancies. As the area of the island of Mauritius is only 732 square miles, the density of population is very high. The economy of the island is highly dependent on cane sugar production, although there has been some industrial diversification in the last ten years. Some 68 per cent of the population are descended from immigrants from the Indian sub-continent who moved to Mauritius, mostly as indentured labourers, in the nineteenth century; they are mainly Hindu but include a substantial Muslim minority. About 29 per cent of the population are Roman Catholic Franco–Mauritians, including Creoles. Most of the remainder are ethnic Chinese.

Until the end of the Second World War the rate of population growth did not present a problem. Suddenly in the immediate post-war years the rate of population growth accelerated with the eradication of malaria, and throughout the 1950s sustained high birth rates and low death rates gave Mauritius a rate of natural increase of population averaging about 3 per cent a year. In the already overcrowded island the colonial officials and local politicians at first sought to find relief for the island's population problems by trying to obtain outlets for Mauritian emigration in other less developed countries such as Madagascar. It was only when it became clear that the search was not bearing fruit that a prolonged public discussion over family planning commenced. A Mauritian family planning programme ultimately came into being and has had considerable success in bringing down the rate of population growth. Nevertheless the island does not provide sufficient occupational opportunities for the well-educated population of Mauritius. With the approach and arrival in 1968 of independence the Franco–Mauritians in particular, uneasy about their future as a minority community, looked increasingly for new countries in which to exercise their talents. The search for a new living was however directed towards the more developed countries of the Commonwealth and to France, and not as before to less developed countries.

It is to Australia, the United Kingdom and France, in that order, that most Mauritian emigrants have gone in recent years. The migratory link with France is fully explained by the cultural links that Mauritius has retained with that country ever since the island was ceded to Britain during the Napoleonic wars. French is still more widely spoken than English by Mauritians. Bearing in mind the relatively small size of the Mauritian population, emigration has been as substantial as emigration from the United Kingdom. Moreover, the official figures for emigration do not tell the whole story, for the many students who go overseas for higher education are not included in the statistics of emigrants, although a considerable number of such students do not return to Mauritius but instead settle in the United Kingdom, Australia and North America. The Mauritian community in Australia is now estimated to number about 30,000, mainly in the vicinity of Sydney, Melbourne and Perth, and this despite the fact that Australia has never extended the assisted migration scheme to Mauritius.

There is a policy of limited encouragement to emigrate in so far as the Mauritian government is willing to guarantee bank loans to pay for the passages of 'official' emigrants – that is those emigrants who have registered with the government their permits to enter other countries. The 'brain drain' does not unduly worry the Mauritian authorities who admit that they have lost some of their best doctors and other professional people but do not have undue difficulty in finding replacements. Mauritius in fact takes some pride in being able to provide other countries, particularly in Africa, with technical assistance in certain fields, predominantly in sugar production and processing.

Malaysia is another Commonwealth country from which there has clearly been considerable emigration in the last two decades. There has been no official encouragement to emigrate, either for the general population or for the major minority groups contained in the population. Nevertheless the net migrational loss of population in West Malaysia between the 1957 and 1970 censuses was, according to the data, over half a million. Whilst data deficiencies may conceivably contribute to an exaggerated figure, it is absolutely clear that there has been very substantial net outward migration since Malaysia attained independence in 1957. It is well established that many of the positions in the civil service and in quasi-government organisations in Malaysia to which non-Malay Malaysians might earlier have hoped to aspire are now virtually reserved for Malay Malaysians, and that a number of Chinese and Indian Malaysians who go overseas to complete their education or to receive professional training do not now return to their native country. It is also well-established that there has been substantial net migration of Chinese Malaysians from West Malaysia to Singapore since the end of the Second World War, though this flow appears to have declined since Singapore separated from Malaysia in 1963. Whatever the real volume of net emigration, it is clear that Malaysia is an example of a country from which there has been outward movement of a particular section of the population, not so much because of direct pressure as because of lack of satisfactory opportunities for those with a good education.

In another Asian Commonwealth country, Sri Lanka, there has been net emigration every year since 1950. Negotiations between the Governments of India and Sri Lanka resulted in a formal agreement being reached in 1964 for the repatriation of over half a million people of Indian origin, mainly estate labourers and their families, over a period of fifteen years. Total net migration between 1963 and 1971 is estimated to have reached only 156,000, but the number of Indian estate labourers leaving Sri Lanka increased very considerably after 1970. It seems unlikely however that the target contained in the agreement will be achieved. Natives of Sri Lanka do not appear to have migrated outside Asia on a sizeable scale, judging by immigration statistics and place of birth statistics of countries such as the United States, Canada and the United Kingdom. United Nations estimates are that some 30,000 persons born in Sri Lanka were living outside Asia in 1974.

Numerically far more persons born in India live outside Asia than persons born in all other Commonwealth countries of Asia and Pakistan combined. Persons born in India and now living outside Asia are, however, only about 0.1 per cent of the total population of that country. Most of the population of Indian ethnic origin now living in other less developed countries of the Commonwealth have of course been born in those countries, and Indian migration within the Commonwealth now largely consists of movements to and from the more developed countries. The United Kingdom alone contained 322,000 persons born in India at the time of the 1971 census, though some of these would not of course have been ethnically Indians. Emigration from India to other continents, politically important as it has been, has had no significant effect on the rate of population growth of the country, and such emigration has never been a plank in the population policy of independent India. The absence of a clear-cut migration policy on the part of the Indian government, combined with the apparent paucity of Indian migration statistics, explains the omission of India from the country case studies in subsequent chapters of this book. The Indian government has of course been concerned about the immigration policies of the United Kingdom, Canada and Australia, countries to which many of her nationals migrate, but this is more a matter of discussion in the chapters dealing with those three countries of immigration. Here it need only be said that the United Kingdom's immigration policy has from time to time since 1961 led to a pronounced cooling of relations between the two countries. Before the 1962 Commonwealth Immigration Bill was enacted, there was a debate in the Lok Sabha in New Delhi at which concern was expressed in no uncertain way about the lack of consultation on the part of the British government over its plans for immigration control in the United Kingdom. It was, however, the future of the Indian residents of East Africa following the Commonwealth Immigration Act of 1968 which led to the sharpest exchanges. In general the Indian government has been readier to criticise the British government on issues relating to its policy of immigration control than it has the governments of less developed Commonwealth countries about their treatment of residents of Indian descent.

Emigration cannot take place unless there are countries willing to accept immigrants. After the war Australia, New Zealand, Canada, Rhodesia and South Africa opened their doors once again to British immigrants and other Europeans with needed occupational qualifications. Australia was the only country in this group of five to have a defined numerical target for immigration, at an annual average of 1 per cent of the country's population, and there was a consistently aggressive selling policy by that country's representatives in the United Kingdom and in parts of Europe to obtain migrants with suitable qualifications and experience. The post-war migrant inflows and migration policies of Australia and Canada are examined in two of the central chapters of this book. South Africa and Rhodesia are covered, though in less detail, in the chapter on Commonwealth Africa.

New Zealand[1] is the one major Commonwealth country of immigration which is not the subject of a detailed case study in this volume. Quite apart from the small size of the immigrant stream in absolute terms when compared with its Commonwealth neighbour Australia, immigration policy in New Zealand has shown less change in the post-war period than is the case with Canada, Australia or the United Kingdom. Historically New Zealand has concentrated on admitting immigrants who will be quickly accepted and absorbed by the host community. The government's assisted passage scheme, in line with this policy, concentrated from 1947 on the provision of free passages to immigrants who had served in the United Kingdom armed forces in the

Second World War and nearly free passages to other single United Kingdom residents who were willing to accept employment in selected occupations. From 1950 the scheme was extended to Dutch, Danish, Swiss, Austrian and German nationals, and assisted passages were also provided to certain categories of married British immigrants with up to two children. The great majority of European assisted immigrants have, however, always been British. In 1970 a new assisted immigration policy was announced which covered the United States as well as Britain and some European countries. However, it seems that a would-be immigrant, even if from a country covered by the scheme, who is not of completely European origin would not be eligible for an assisted passage.

Unassisted immigration is not, however, restricted to persons of European origin. People of the Cook Islands, Niue and the Tokelaus have the status of New Zealand citizens and may enter the country freely. Substantial numbers of Samoans are admitted every year, either on a three-month permit which cannot be renewed without returning to Samoa or on a six-month permit which can be renewed and can lead to permanent residence. The six-month permits are, however, subject to a quota and the applicant must have guaranteed employment in New Zealand. Samoa is of course a country for which New Zealand once had responsibility as the colonial power. For the inhabitants of other Pacific Commonwealth countries, such as Fiji and the former Gilbert and Ellice Islands, entry for permanent immigration as opposed to short-term work permits is difficult to obtain.

Immigration statistics for recent years show that some 80 per cent of permanent and long-term arrivals admitted into New Zealand come from five English-speaking countries, namely the United Kingdom, Australia, Canada, the United States and South Africa. Well over three-quarters of these are British and Australian nationals. Movement between New Zealand and Australia is not subject to quotas or permits and has been showing a rising trend since the Second World War with each country at different times being the net beneficiary. Nearly half of the remaining 20 per cent of permanent and long-term arrivals come from the South Pacific area. The majority of the remainder come from Commonwealth Asian countries, and these include significant numbers of students who, although staying in New Zealand for over a year and thus qualifying as long-term arrivals, will not for the most part settle permanently.

New Zealand, like Australia, has had a very much reduced intake of fresh immigrants during the recession starting in the mid-seventies, and for the first time since the war there have been annual figures of emigrants in excess of the corresponding annual figures of immigrants. It is not that former immigrants are returning to their native countries in very large numbers so much as the departure of young native New Zealanders for long-term sojourns in geographically less isolated and economically more industralised countries that has led to this excess of emigrants.

In the post-war period general inter-continental migration, as opposed to short-term travel of businessmen and holiday-makers, has been on a more modest scale than in the early decades of the twentieth century. The large volume of labour migration within Europe replaced part of the flow of migrants from Europe to overseas destinations. The diminution in migrant flows from the United Kingdom has, however, been much less marked, in part because United Kingdom citizens have not as yet taken any appreciable part in the migratory movements in Europe. Moreover, movement between certain Commonwealth countries other than the United Kingdom, for instance between New Zealand and Australia and between the West Indian countries and Canada, has grown in volume since 1960. There have however been some recent indications to suggest that migration between Commonwealth countries, like international migration generally, will in future be on a much reduced scale, and this is a topic discussed in the concluding chapter.

This book is concerned more with migration policies than with the precise size of migration flows. Nevertheless some knowledge of the flows of immigrants and emigrants is crucial to an understanding of migration policy-making and legislation. Unfortunately the measurement of international migration is, for many countries, very imprecise. Some countries with otherwise sophisticated statistical systems collate no statistics on emigration. Some countries still make inadequate attempts to differentiate between immigrants and short term arrivals and between emigrants and short-term departures. Figures for immigration have on the whole been becoming more satisfactory in the industrialised countries except where there is substantial illegal immigration, but it is clear that policy decisions relating to migration have to be based on imprecise data.

The three chapters that follow describe the factors which enter into the decision-making process in three Commonwealth countries of immigration, namely Australia, Canada and the United Kingdom. They are followed by two chapters which indicate the way in which two densely-populated Commonwealth countries, Malta and Jamaica, have with mixed success actively searched for countries to which their own peoples could emigrate. Then a chapter on Africa discusses the climate for intra-continental migration between former British colonies, which has become much less favourable with the coming of independence.

2 Migration to and from Australia

by Charles Price

From the beginning of settlement until quite recently Australia was thought of as one of the main countries where families from the over-crowded British Isles could find room to make new homes and develop a new British society. Indeed, it could be argued that with the American colonies achieving independence, Canada treating the French culture and people as equal with the English, South Africa becoming increasingly Afrikaner, the East African highlands becoming more and more African and New Zealand being limited in size, Australia has for long been the major British ethnic home overseas. Certainly up to the Second World War some 90 per cent of the population was of British ethnic descent; in 1947 they numbered about 6.8 millions in a total population of 7.6 million. It is sometimes forgotten, though, that British families do not always migrate directly from the United Kingdom to Australia: an appreciable number come after some years, or even generations, in other British countries, notably New Zealand. Moreover, particularly in recent years, Australia has received numerous settlers of non-British ethnic descent from other parts of the Commonwealth, notably Malta, Mauritius, India and Malaysia. Contrariwise, many British settlers with their Australian-born children, as well as numerous persons of Australian parentage, have left Australia to settle permanently in other parts of the Commonwealth. In short, though not so important as the United Kingdom, Australia has become, as both importer and exporter, an increasingly significant centre of Commonwealth migration.

THE EARLIER DECADES: 1788–1940

The story begins soon after Captain Philip arrived with the first fleet of convicts and soldiers in 1788, with plans later to develop the Australian

11

colonies with free settlers drawn from the British Isles. It soon became apparent, however, that the voyage was so much longer and more expensive than the trans-Atlantic crossing to the Americas that few settlers would come without assistance; hence the colonies' practice, continued by the Australian Commonwealth after federation in 1901, of assisting newcomers of the right health, age, sex, marital status and occupation with passage costs and settlement expenses. In colonial days (1788–1900), in addition to more than 155,000 convicts, about 740,000 persons arrived in this way and another 955,000 or so under their own resources (many of these being drawn by the gold rushes of the 1850s) – about 1,850,000 in all. From 1901 to 1940 a further 422,000 arrived with government assistance and 493,000 unassisted, about 915,000 in all. Of the grand total of 2,765,000 approximately 324,000 or 11.7 per cent were non-British, 0.8 per cent of the assisted total and 21.7 per cent of the unassisted.

It should be remembered that many of those assisted in the 1920s were receiving help from Britain as well as Australia. The mother country had always approved of Australian efforts to attract immigrants but, once the colonies were established, had rarely given financial help. The First World War, however, greatly strengthened the hands of Lionel Curtis and others who had been arguing for a positive policy of strengthening the British Empire by transferring population from the overcrowded mother country to the underpopulated dominions; hence the Dominions Royal Commission of 1917 and the Empire Settlement Act of 1922. Australian governments responded enthusiastically, implemented various land settlement schemes in the early 1920s and then negotiated the '£34 Million Loan Agreement' of 1925 whereby Australia agreed to find cheap money for development schemes and the United Kingdom agreed to contribute £150,000 for every 10,000 assisted British migrants. Though many of the schemes proved disappointing the whole programme succeeded in moving nearly 200,000 British settlers to Australia between early 1922 and late 1929 when the depression brought everything to a halt. The agreement continued however, with Britain contributing monies when assisted migration started again in the late 1930s.

These special arrangements with the United Kingdom go far to explain why there were relatively so few non-British immigrants, especially in the assisted sector. In another sense they represented the immigration priorities gradually worked out by the Australian colonies and federation. First were settlers from the United Kingdom and the Old Commonwealth; these were generally regarded as so much akin to native Australians that they warranted government assistance with passages, jobs and accommodation. Second were northern Europeans, who could enter virtually without restriction but usually without government help. Third were southern Europeans, who could enter in limited numbers (in the 1920s they were restricted to a few thousand a year by administrative quota) and without government assistance; some preference, though, was at times given to British citizens (Maltese and Cypriots) both in terms of entry and occasional assistance. Fourth were non-Europeans who, because of the White Australia Policy, could only enter the country for any length of time if they were government officials, ministers of religion, students, merchants or relatives or employees of already established Asians, and then normally on a temporary basis only. For immigration purposes Lebanese were counted as Europeans.

Here it should be noted that the White Australia Policy – introduced in the 1850s to check the rapid influx of Chinese gold-diggers and extended to Indian hawkers and farmers, and to Japanese, Malay and Pacific Island sugar labourers and pearlers at the turn of the century – took scant notice of British nationality or membership of Empire. In many ways Australians were very proud and conscious of their British ties, but so afraid were they of being taken over by the 'teeming millions' of Asia, and so set were they on creating a racially homogeneous white nation, that they severely restricted the entry not only of non-European races from outside the Empire but also of British Indians, Sinhalese, Burmese and Malays, of Chinese from Hong Kong and Singapore, of black British nationals from the Caribbean, of Melanesian British subjects from Fiji and the Solomon Islands, and of natives of the British–French condominium of the New Hebrides. They even barred the permanent entry of natives from Australia's own territories in New Guinea, though Papuans were recognised internationally as Australian citizens.

On the whole the British imperial governments of those days (1850–1940) were agreeable to this Australian division of British subjects into the acceptable and the unacceptable, though at the turn of the century they strongly pressed Australians to abolish the old restrictive laws spelling out the races deemed undesirable and to introduce instead an education test which would not be so offensive to the Indian peoples Britain was then trying to cultivate. The new Australian Parliament of 1901 somewhat reluctantly agreed; hence the introduction of the dictation test, which ostensibly operated as a means to exclude the illiterate but which in practice was directed against coloured races in that it was seldom given to Europeans and was administered to non-Europeans in a way designed to make them fail; a Chinese scholar, say, would fail because he was tested in Norwegian, or a black Jamaican because he was tested in Russian. The other main concession Australia made to Westminster was – in the glow of good-will to India following the First World War and in the light of opinions expressed at Imperial Conferences 1917–21 – to remove from Indians and Sinhalese certain disabilities they had hitherto shared with other Asians in Australia: no voting rights, no invalid or old-age pensions, no right to bring in wives unless a merchant or government official, no staying on by students, merchants and others without obtaining a periodic extension of entry permit, etc. But these concessions were basically concerned with living conditions, not right of entry, and made little difference to numbers coming for settlement.

The statistics of Tables 2.1 and 2.2 show the effects of all these policies and movements. Table 2.1 shows that the appreciable number of Asians and Pacific Islanders in the country in 1901, who had come in before the restrictions began to hit hard at the turn of the century, declined noticeably between 1901 and 1947, even though their numbers were being reinforced by births in Australia. Some groups declined not only from restrictions on new immigration but also from substantial re-migration home; Pacific Islanders, mostly sugar labourers from the New Hebrides and Solomon Islands, also declined because of repatriation measures in 1906. Table 2.2 showing the countries of birth of the Australian population in various census years, indicates clearly some of the changes in the European immigration programmes and policies: the dominance of north European immigrants, notably German and Scandinavian, in the continental European movements in the nineteenth century, then the gradual switch to Italian and Greek migration in the decades before the Second World War, and a rise in the numbers of Yugoslavs, Poles and other east Europeans. These totals, however, were small compared with immigration from England, Scotland and New Zealand (by 1947 there were 43,000 New Zealanders by birth in Australia); immigration from Wales, like that from Canada and South Africa, was relatively slight though still noticeable.

An important change was the Irish component: it had been about one-quarter of British immigration for most of the nineteenth century but fell away in the depression years of the 1890s and failed to recover thereafter. This was largely because the total population of Ireland had fallen so much, as had Irish fertility, so there was much less incentive to emigrate. In contrast, immigration from England and Scotland

TABLE 2.1. Ethnic origin of the overseas-born population (estimates)

	1901 No.	%	1947 No.	%	1977 No.	%
Asia						
West Asian (Arab, Turk etc.)	1750	0.2	3796	0.5	63696	2.3
Indian (peoples of sub-continent)	4400	0.5	2230	0.3	24351	0.9
Chinese	30000	3.5	5210	0.7	38781	1.4
Japanese	3550	0.4	82		5138	0.2
Other Asian	1950	0.2	914	0.1	26484	0.9
Eurasian	200		321		17362	0.6
European	5164	0.6	10862	1.5	82678	3.0
Total	47014	5.5	23415	3.1	258490	9.3
Rest of World						
European	802484	93.4	719709	96.7	2489410	89.4
Part European	50		213		11440	0.4
African	250		130		5200	0.2
Mauritian	50		10		6520	0.2
Pacific Islander	9300	1.1	140		10400	0.4
Other	350		570	0.1	2626	0.1
Total	812484	94.5	720772	96.9	2525596	90.7
Total						
European	807648	94.0	730571	98.2	2572088	92.4
Part European	250		534	0.1	28802	1.0
West Asian	1750	0.2	3796	0.5	63696	2.3
Other	49850	5.8	9286	1.2	119500	4.3
Total overseas-born	859498	100.0	744187	100.0	2784086	100.0

Estimates are based on the Race Tables of censuses of 1901, 1947 and 1971 and net migration and deaths 1971–7. In 1971 the race question was changed to exclude mixed race answers and most persons of part European, part Other returned their race as European. The above estimates of part Europeans derive from the 1966 census and information of immigration categories.

TABLE 2.2. Birth places of the Australian population

	1901 No.	1901 %	1947 No.	1947 %	1961 No.	1961 %	1977 No.	1977 %
England	384321	44.7	381592	51.3	556478	31.3	873641	31.4
Scotland	101753	11.8	102998	13.8	132811	7.5	15806	5.6
Ireland	184085	21.4	44813	6.0	50215	2.8	67232	2.4
Wales	10000	1.2	11864	1.6	15898	0.9	26593	1.0
Total UK and Eire	680159	79.1	541267	72.7	755402	42.5	1123272	40.4
New Zealand	25788	3.0	43610	5.9	47011	2.6	106726	3.8
Canada	3159	0.4	4061	0.5	5990	0.3	13952	0.5
South Africa	1500	0.3	5866	0.8	7896	0.4	17053	0.6
Mauritius	740		236		1000e	0.1	10182	0.4
Fiji	585		1508	0.2	2674	0.2	7522	0.3
Other British*	16437	1.9	4621	0.6	10847	0.6	41739	1.5
Total Non-UK British*	48209	5.6	59902	8.0	75418	4.2	197174	7.1
Germany	38152	4.4	14567	1.9	109315	6.1	107924	3.9
Netherlands	594	0.1	2174	0.3	102083	5.7	94282	3.4
Scandinavia and Finland	16644	1.9	8365	1.1	18035	1.1	22227	0.8
Other northern Europe	7598	0.9	8669	1.2	35580	2.0	47294	1.7
Total northern Europe	62988	7.3	33775	4.5	265013	14.9	271727	9.8
Poland	300e		6573	0.9	60049	3.4	57796	2.1
Yugoslavia	800	0.1	5866	0.8	49776	2.8	137429	4.9
Other eastern Europe	3148	0.4	10527	1.4	108193	6.1	100285	3.6
Total eastern Europe	4248	0.5	22966	3.1	218018	12.3	295510	10.6

Italy	5678	0.7	33632	4.5	228296	12.8	276287	9.9
Greece	1000e	0.1	12291	1.7	77333	4.3	152279	5.5
Cyprus	20		681	0.1	8576	0.5	22856	0.8
Malta	200	0.1	3238	0.4	39337	2.2	55223	2.0
Other southern Europe	826	0.1	2470	0.2	6262	0.4	25958	0.9
Total southern Europe	7724	0.9	52312	7.0	359804	20.2	532603	19.1
Egypt	108		803	0.1	16287	0.9	30615	1.1
Turkey	200		252		1544	0.1	20121	0.7
Lebanon and Syria	1500	0.2	1886	0.3	7481	0.4	48271	1.7
Other Levant	150		1958	0.3	4471	0.3	12158	0.5
Total Levant	1958	0.2	4899	0.7	29783	1.7	111165	4.0
Indian sub-continent	8250	1.0	8170	1.1	18810	1.1	58907	2.1
Commonwealth Southeast Asia (except Singapore)	490	0.1	1285	0.2	7315	0.4	30066	1.1
Hong Kong and Singapore	367		1515	0.2	6303	0.3	22619	0.8
Total British Asia	9107	1.1	10970	1.5	32428	1.8	111592	4.0
China	29907	3.5	6404	0.9	14488	0.8	23523	0.8
Other Asia	6150	0.7	1945	0.3	10068	0.6	38825	1.4
USA	7448	0.9	6232	0.8	10810	0.6	32893	1.2
Other Non-Commonwealth America	770	0.1	1010	0.1	1421	0.1	34770	1.2
Total America	8218	1.0	7242	1.0	12231	0.7	67663	2.4
Other†	830	0.1	2505	0.3	6127	0.3	11032	0.4

TABLE 2.2 (continued)

	1901		1947		1961		1977	
	No.	%	No.	%	No.	%	No.	%
Total foreign born	859498	100.0	744187	100.0	1778780	100.0	2784086	100.0
Australia	2914303		6835171		8729406		11030822	
Grand total	3773801		7579358		10508186		13814908	

ᵉ estimate.
* Channel and Falkland Islands, Isle of Man, Gibraltar, unspecified Commonwealth countries in Africa, America and Oceania.
† Other Europe (Monaco, Andorra, Iceland, etc.); Africa excluding Egypt, South Africa, Mauritius and Commonwealth Africa; Oceania, excluding Fiji, New Zealand, Other British; At sea; birthplace not stated.

recovered during the large inflows of 1909–14 and 1919–29: the effect of this was to raise the English share of Australians born in the British Isles from 56 per cent in 1901 to 71 per cent in 1947, and the Scottish from 15 to 19 per cent. The Welsh remained steady at 2 per cent but the Irish share fell from 27 to 8 per cent. In other words, in the two large immigrations of the early twentieth century the English and Scottish peoples of Australia received considerable reinforcement and kept many family connections with 'home' alive. The Australian Irish received little reinforcement and gradually lost close friends and relatives in the old country. Nevertheless, their fierce support for Irish nationalist ambitions and their fury at English attempts to stamp out independence kept strong their love of the Irish country and church, an issue of some importance in Australian politics and education. It should be noted that even the large-scale immigrations of 1909–14 and 1919–29 were insufficient to replace the considerable numbers of earlier settlers from the British Isles who by the Second World War were reaching old age and dying off; as Table 2.2 shows, persons born in the British Isles fell from 680,000 in 1901 to 541,000 in 1947.

As some small counter to this large-scale movement from England, Scotland and New Zealand there was an outflow of Australian-born persons, mainly to Britain and New Zealand but also to Canada, the United States and South Africa, with a trickle to the Indian subcontinent, the Pacific Islands (mainly Fiji) and Latin America. Some of those moving were Australian-born children of British families who had spent several years in Australia and then moved back to Britain or on to other parts of the Empire. Others were Australian professional, business and technical men working abroad, especially in places such as Papua New Guinea and Fiji where Australia had considerable political and economic interests; there were 1000 native Australians in Fiji in 1946 and 4200 in Papua New Guinea in 1947. Yet others were casual travellers or other families scattered around the world; for example a few in South America were survivors of attempts by families from Australia to find Utopian settlements in Paraguay. Four movements, however, were more substantial. First, the 30,000 or so settled in the United Kingdom (30,472 in 1931 with about 2000 visitors) included some native Australians who had gone to Oxford or Cambridge for their university education or to London for advanced work in medicine, dentistry, law or the arts and then stayed or, if female, to do nursing or be with the British-born husbands they had married in Australia. In a sense this is the inevitable back-flow that accompanies any big migration: children or grandchildren visit their ancestral home to see relatives, discover the country or complete their education; a number then stay permanently. In another sense the movement reflects Australia's isolation and distance from the great centres of European art and culture: Australian singers, musicians, artists and writers often felt home circles too narrow and moved to more congenial circles in Britain, France, Italy or Germany.

The Australian migration to New Zealand, nearly 50,000 residents in 1921 and still 35,000 or so in 1951, was a very different phenomenon. Apart from the tourist element it represented a continuation of the early movement from Australia to New Zealand, dating back to convict and gold mining days, whereby many persons settled in Australia–whether born in Australia or elsewhere–later decided to try their luck in New Zealand, especially during the South Island gold rushes of the late 1850s and 1860s. Such persons have always been important in New Zealand, finding jobs in many areas and occupations and at times, as with Richard Seddon ('King Dick'), providing outstanding political leadership. For many decades, though, the Australian settler stream to New Zealand has been less numerous than the New Zealand flow to Australia; the latter's greater size and resources exert considerable attractive power over the smaller population and, at the end of the Second World War, there were about 45,000 New Zealanders in Australia compared with 35,000 or so native Australians in New Zealand.

The movement to southern Africa, though considerably smaller, also represents a well established exchange system. Though the Cape route took second place after the Suez Canal was opened, Capetown nevertheless remained an important port of call and numbers of South Africans took the chance to try out Australia: contrariwise, Australians sometimes stopped in South Africa on their way to Europe and stayed there. A much larger movement occurred in the 1890s when many Australians were attracted away from their recession-ridden country by the gold and diamond developments in southern Africa. Later they were attracted to Rhodesia and East Africa by the opening of land for European settlement; later still a small-scale development of Australian commercial and industrial interest in South Africa maintained a small but steady movement. In the mid-1930s there were over 6000 native Australians in South Africa (and about 1000 in Rhodesia and East Africa) and about the same number of southern Africans in Australia.

A similar though older exchange system developed with the west coast of North America. This movement dated back to the days when British and American whalers and sealers were accustomed to visit Sydney and

San Francisco and when the young Australian colonies imported much of their supplies, notably liquor, from across the Pacific; it increased considerably with the Californian gold-rushes of the late 1840s, went into reverse when gold was discovered in eastern Australia in the early 1850s, and then turned back again, towards British Columbia, when the Cariboo and other gold-fields opened up in the late 1850s and early 1860s. Some Australians later settled east of the Rockies, notably in Toronto and New York, but British Columbia and California were the main areas. This flow and reverse flow across the Pacific has continued ever since, not on a large scale but sufficient to place about 6000 Americans and 3000 Canadians in Australia and about 10,000 Australians in the USA and another 3000 in Canada by the First World War. In the 1920s and 1930s, while American numbers in Australia stayed fairly steady and Canadians increased somewhat, to 4000 or so, Australian numbers across the Pacific increased substantially; when the Second World War broke out there were some 15,000 Australians in the USA and 3000 in Canada.

The results of all these movements were that by 1940 well over 100,000 native Australians were settled overseas, as against some 800,000 overseas-born persons settled in Australia. Though the country was clearly attracting far more persons than it was losing, there were sufficient natives abroad to act as some sort of counter-flow and to pave the way for the larger emigration of later years.

THE SECOND WORLD WAR AND ITS AFTERMATH:1940–66

On this fairly clear and simple system of migration to and from Australia the Second World War fell with considerable force. First, Australians experienced a wave of fear at the Japanese capture of Singapore, air-raids on Darwin, submarine raids on Sydney, and steady military advance down through the islands until stopped by the naval battle of the Coral Sea; they very quickly realised that their small population could not by itself effectively defend a whole continent and determined to build up the white population as quickly as economic and social resources would permit. Second, during the war politicians became aware that the birth-rate had fallen so low during the 1930s that by 1945 the number of young persons entering the workforce was actually declining, so endangering all development programmes. Third, the Australian Labor Party, sometimes opposed to immigration pre-war, lest it produce competition between native and immigrant worker, became confident from its experience in war-time administration that it could successfully combine large-scale immigration with full employment; on its side the Liberal–Country Party opposition had for long wanted more immigration, to keep down the cost of labour and ensure industrial expansion by constant enlargement of home markets. These factors all combined to produce a two-party agreement to support a policy aiming at a 2 per cent population increase per annum, 1 per cent from the post-war baby boom surplus of births over deaths and 1 per cent from a determined and far-reaching immigration programme; this meant a net immigration of 70,000 persons a year in 1945, rising each year with population growth to 130,000 a year in 1970. For this no special legislation was necessary; the pre-war acts gave the federal government ample powers to make international migration agreements and spend public monies on assisting immigrants with passage costs, jobs and accommodation.

At first the energetic and vocal Arthur Calwell (Labor Minister for Immigration, 1945–9) hoped to maintain the tradition of ten Britons for every foreigner – and made a series of agreements with the United Kingdom based on the old Empire Settlement Act. A severe shipping shortage, however, hindered the movement and, in any case, it was far from certain that Britain could cover nine-tenths of the 1 per cent target for very long; certainly not when the initial rush was over and Britain's own shortage in the younger part of the workforce made itself felt. The Labor government thereupon decided quite consciously to abandon pre-war reluctance about providing non-British persons with assisted passages and to make strong efforts to find European alternatives – with the provisos that assistance be less than that given to Britons, that preference be given to northern Europeans, and that the outcome, when taken in conjunction with unassisted migration, be a reasonable 'balance of nationalities'.

The first alternative was approved Allied and Empire ex-servicemen, 'of pure European descent', who were not eligible under the Australia–Britain agreements; in this Australia hoped to get numerous Americans but in practice the programme – 1947–56 – gained mostly Dutch from Indonesia. The second alternative consisted of the one million or more Displaced Persons housed in European refugee camps which after 1947 were under the control of the newly formed International Refugee Organisation (IRO) and its 1951/2 successors, the United Nations High Commissioner for Refugees (UNHCR) and the Intergovernmental Committee for European Migration (ICEM); from 1947 on Australia took well over 200,000 of these refugees, most under direct agreement between Australia and IRO but others under private arrangements between IRO and voluntary organisations such as International Catholic Migration, the World Council of Churches and various Jewish and Lutheran societies. The third alternative was the unsettled populations at home in war-torn Europe: migration agreements were made with Malta (1948), the Netherlands (1951), Italy (1951) and Germany (1952) while later on multilateral arrangements were made via ICEM with Greece, Spain, Sweden and other countries of Europe; the old priorities were well in evidence, though, as assistance was extended only to a minority of Greek and Italian immigrants. The fourth alternative consisted of various suitable settlers dotted about in the Americas, Oceania, Asia and Europe – some of British ethnic origin – who were not eligible for assisted passages under the intergovernmental agreements; hence the General Assisted Passage Scheme of 1954. Finally, the Australian government willingly admitted European persons – and some western Asians such as the Lebanese – who, although conforming to immigration requirements of health, occupational experience and so on were not amongst those selected for assisted passages but could raise or borrow enough to cover their own passage costs, especially if sponsored by friends or relatives already established in Australia.

The various arrangements came into force bit by bit, with the Liberal–Country Party coalition taking over and extending Labor Party policy when it won the election of late 1949. On the whole things worked smoothly, with special hostel arrangements for housing the large Displaced Persons intake of 1948–51 and with trade union leaders having considerable voice, via various advisory committees, in the size and composition of the actual intake. Over the fourteen-years period 1947–61 about 1,467,000 new settlers arrived and about 170,000 left again, giving a settler loss rate of 11.6 per cent and a net gain of 1,297,000 or 1.1 per cent of population increase a year. Though the 1 per cent target was thus being achieved on average, this achievement was somewhat fortuitous. During the years 1949–51, with the mass refugee programme under way, settler intake reached 160,000 a year, so encouraging both Labor and Liberal governments to raise the target from 80,000 (the then 1 per cent figure) to 200,000 a year. Then followed a rapid fall in wool prices, the depletion of Australia's overseas reserves and much talk of the inflationary pressures of large-scale immigration, and targets and recruiting efforts were cut sharply back, much to the annoyance of several countries with whom Australia had recently completed migration agreements. By 1953 the target was only 80,000 and net gain a mere 43,000. Eventually the movement recovered and the target raised to 125,000, staying round that mark even during the recession of 1961–2. This time the Australian government coped by reducing the proportion of immigrant workers and raising that of wives, children and aged dependants; so satisfying overseas governments yet not unduly alarming the Trade Union and Labor Movements with their ever present fears of labour competition.

Another lesson the Australian government learned during these years concerned the British proportion in total intake: if that fell very low there would be cries of dismay and anger from numerous Australians who, while only too ready to accuse their 'Pom' cousins of condescending ways and ridiculous accents and mannerisms, were nevertheless still wedded to the concept of a British-type Australian nation. Alarm here became pronounced in 1952–4 because, though no accurate statistics were available, it seemed as though the British proportion was falling well below a third; in fact later estimates suggested that, whereas in the calendar year period 1947–52 persons of British ethnic origin, including New Zealanders, Canadians and so on, had made up nearly 40 per cent of net intake, in the period 1953–5 they made up only 25 per cent, considerably less than the 44 per cent contributed by southern Europeans. To counteract this trend the Australian government in 1955 restricted the steadily increasing entry of southern Europeans (by confining sponsorship of friends and relatives to parents, children and brothers) and made fresh efforts to encourage British immigration by increasing advertising and recruiting activities in the UK and introducing the new 'Bring out a Briton' sponsorship programme in 1956–7. These measures had some effect; the British proportion rose to 36.7 per cent in the period 1957–60 while the southern European fell to 26.2 per cent. The others at this time were largely German, Dutch, Scandinavian, Polish, Yugoslav and American.

Over the whole period mid-1947 to mid-1961 the ethnic composition of settler immigration balanced out roughly as follows: 500,000 from the British Isles (34.0 per cent); 255, 000 from northwestern Europe (17.4 per cent); 363,000 from southern Europe (24.7 per cent), mainly Italian and Greek but including 42,000 Maltese; 256,000 eastern Europeans, predominantly refugees with Poles and Yugoslavs as the largest contingents; 93,000 others, some 18,000 being New Zealanders, 8000 Americans, 4000 Canadians and 4000 South Africans; total 1.47 millions of which the British ethnic component was approximately 37.7 per cent.

THE GREAT EFFORTS OF THE SIXTIES: 1961–71

The recession 1961/2, as it happened, was relatively short-lived and settler migration quickly recovered, from 84,000 in 1961/2 to 100,000 in 1962/3 and 121,000 in 1963/4.[1] Indeed, it continued to rise throughout the sixties reaching 142,000 in 1965/6 and then – after a short slump – about 180,000 in both 1969 and 1970. During this recovery the government decided to raise the settler targets (shifting in the process from targets based on 'permanent arrivals' to targets based on the new and more reliable figures of 'settler arrivals'); hence the rise from the long-standing target of 125,000 permanent arrivals, 1959–63, through 145,000 settler arrivals in 1965/6 to 175,000 in 1969/70. In most years the country either achieved or only slightly missed these targets. Over the whole period, mid-1961–71, settler immigration totalled some 1,406,500 and net gain about 916,600 or about 0.8 per cent of total population, i.e. a little under the 1.0 per cent target for net migration.

This substantial difference between settler intake and net gain, about 489,900, consisted of some 339,800 settlers changing their minds and leaving permanently (settler loss) and about 150,000 Australian-born persons leaving permanently, i.e. 34,000 and 15,000 a year on average. These were much higher figures than those of the earlier period, 1947–61 (12,200 a year settler loss and 5200 a year Australian-born loss) and represented a considerable change in the character of migration. First, the economic recovery of western Europe not only reduced the number of new settlers coming from that area but increased the number of earlier settlers drawn back to their countries of origin; Greece, being slower to recover, maintained a high level of emigration until the late sixties but its return rate increased markedly during the period. Table 2.3 illustrates this, and also the fall in refugee migration from eastern Europe.

A substantial increase in settler loss also caused an increase in Australian-born loss as a third of this latter consisted of Australian-born children going home with their former settler parents. Also, in the sixties, Australians in their late teens and early twenties started to travel abroad more, some to settle permanently and some to take part in the growing international movement of the skilled and highly qualified.

The net effect of all this was that during the sixties Australia became aware that it had to attract some 49,000 new settlers each year just to cover loss; only after that could settler intake contribute to the 1.0 per cent target of 115,000 or more. This caused considerable heart-burning and eventually produced two enquiries into settler loss, 1966/7 and 1971–3; these recommended changes in selection procedures in order to

TABLE 2.3. Settler arrivals and loss: annual averages

Birthplace	New Settlers (SAg)		Settler Loss (SLg)		SLg/SAg (%)	
	1947–61	1961–71	1947–61	1961–71	1947–61	1961–71
Germany	6690	3160	760	2320	11.4	73.4
Netherlands	8670	2100	1075	1940	12.4	92.4
Other northern Europe	2875	4340	230	1980	8.0	45.6
Italy	16100	12230	1550	4920	9.6	40.2
Greece and Cyprus	6485	12530	330	3050	5.1	24.3
Malta	3030	2530	175	790	5.8	31.1
Yugoslavia	4060	10620	315	920	7.8	8.7
Other eastern Europe	14260	2550	300	1170	2.1	45.9
British Isles	35680	61500	6680	12600	18.7	20.4
Other British (Old Commonwealth)	3830	10700	425	2000	11.1	18.7
Other	3120	18390	360	2310	11.5	12.6
Total (Australia)	104800	140650	12200 (5200)	34000 (15000)	11.6	24.2

reject families unlikely to succeed in adapting to conditions in a new country and also improvements in settlement and welfare arrangements to help suitable settlers who had happened to encounter difficult conditions in jobs, housing or health.

Likewise, on the recruiting front, Australia made strenuous efforts to replace western Europe with other source areas. First, she tried to increase the flow from southern Europe, even giving way to Italy's demands that Italian immigrants be given the same assistance as Britons with passages, jobs and accomodation; this eventually led Australia to abandon completely its old ranking – Britons, northern Europeans, southern Europeans – and to make new arrangements with Italy, Greece, Spain and Malta during 1967–70, giving their migrants virtually equal treatment with British immigrants. Though these concessions lifted the number of assisted migrants from Italy and Greece they did not arrest the decline in total immigration from these countries; they did, however, play some part in increasing migration from Spain and Portugal.

Second, Australia turned to source countries outside the ICEM area. Yugoslavs, though ethnically acceptable, derived from a country which was officially communist and which had from the beginning taken an anti-western line over refugees; those coming to Australia, therefore, were those entering Austria, Italy or Greece unofficially, claiming refugee status, and receiving help from ICEM or another emigration agency. In the mid-sixties, however, the Yugoslav government showed signs of thawing and, after protracted negotiations, in 1970 signed a migration agreement which enabled Australian officials to recruit migrants in Yugoslavia and arrange for their direct flight to Australia. An even more significant innovation was the Australian–Turkish agreement of 1967, which extended the Italian-type arrangement to Turkish citizens, principally peasant peoples from Anatolia in Asia Minor. This dent in the White Australia Policy arose from an attempt to divert some of the Turkish guest-worker movement from western Europe to Australia and brought some 14,000 Turkish assisted settlers before it faded away in 1974. Also in the mid-sixties Australia opened a migration post in Beirut (1965), not to organise assisted passages from the Lebanon but to process the numerous applications by sponsors in Australia to bring relatives and friends out through Beirut; these included Armenians and Coptic Egyptians as well as ethnic Lebanese. The opening of this post was followed by a greatly increased immigration from the Lebanon, from an average of 500 Lebanese settlers a year during the period 1959–63 to more than 3500 a year during 1969–71 as well as numerous Armenians and others. In 1971 the Australian government decided to restrict movement from the Middle East, partly because of economic troubles in Australia but also to maintain a 'reasonable balance of nationalities'.

Though these new ventures represented considerable effort by Australian migration and diplomatic officers, in the most important area of all – namely the British Isles – little new effort was needed. A period of economic malaise, combined with a very severe winter in 1962/3, led many Britons to heed Australian publicity about economic opportunity and sunny beaches; settlers of UK origin increased steadily from 37,000 in 1961 to some 79,000 in 1965 and, after a slight fall in 1967, to 79,000 again in 1969; over the whole period 1961–71 UK settler migration averaged 61,500 a year compared with 35,700 a year for 1947–61 (see Table 2.3). The immigration of other ethnic British settlers also increased: New Zealanders from an average of 1300 a year, 1947–61, to 5800 a year, 1961–71; Canadians from 280 to 1200; South Africans from 270 to 800; others from 1975 to 2885. Americans, though not strictly British ethnics, are in some ways treated as such in Australia; settler migration from the USA increased from an average of 550 a year to 2830. In all, and excluding Americans, ethnic British immigration totalled about 72,000 a year, 1961–71, compared with 39,000 a year 1947–61 (see Table 2.3).

This marked improvement in British immigration, now making up 51 per cent of total settler intake compared with 37 per cent for the earlier period, greatly cheered the pro-British element in Australia and quietened their fears that Australia would quickly lose its British character. This in turn made it much easier for the government to organise the Turkish agreement and to allow the entry of more settlers from the Middle East. It also made it easier for the government to tackle the more difficult question of migration from southern and eastern Asia. Here Australia was making heavier weather than Canada and the USA, both of whom had had restrictive policies very similar to Australia's but who were steadily modifying them, partly from a guilt reaction following their internment of their numerous Japanese settlers after Pearl Harbour, without adequate compensation for confiscated land and goods, and partly because they valued Kuomintang China as an ally and knew that easing of restrictions against Chinese immigration would remove a great obstacle to friendly relations. New Zealand, too, less troubled than Australia by fears of Asian invasion, decided early to modify its restrictions on coloured immigrants. Against these modifications of the late forties and fifties, summed up in the new Canadian and US immigration regulations and laws of 1962 and 1965 respectively, the White Australia Policy stood out in stark and unpleasant relief; moreover it steadily became more of a handicap in foreign relations and eventually at meetings of Commonwealth Heads of State.

Still very close to the Japanese war threat, the Labor Government of 1942–9 not unnaturally refused to change traditional policy; indeed, the Chifly–Calwell Government acted very toughly by refusing to let Australians serving with the army of occupation in Japan bring their Japanese brides back with them, or to permit Sergeant Gamboa, a Filipino member of the US army who had married an Australian girl while stationed in Australia, to return to Australia after the war to join his wife and family. They even took steps to deport numbers of Asians who had entered Australia during the war as refugees, married Australians or established themselves in business and wanted to stay on after hostilities ended; initial steps to deport them were blocked by the High Court but the special War-time Refugees Removal Act was only thwarted by the election of late 1949 and the advent of a more merciful Liberal–Country Party Government.

Though the Liberals allowed the refugees to stay, and the Japanese war-brides and Sergeant Gamboa to enter, they did not want to abolish restrictions altogether. Yet this is what events pushed them slowly towards. In the early fifties they reluctantly decided to give permanent status to those Chinese who were in Australia with temporary permits but refused to return to China lest the new Communist Government persecute them. In 1956 they agreed to grant permanent status not only to a few 'highly qualified and distinguished' Asians allowed in as oriental librarians, language teachers and so on, but also to any non-European of good character obviously well-established in the country; also to allow them to become naturalised citizens after fifteen years' residence, with the right of bringing in wives and children. In 1958 they abolished the dictation test, replacing it with a simple entry permit system, such permits to be issued by the Minister of Immigration or his deputy with no rights of appeal or redress. In the late fifties and early sixties they, and the state governments, quietly started to revise the old laws discriminating against non-Europeans with respect to land holding, mining rights, various barred occupations, pension rights and suchlike. By 1966 practically all the discriminatory laws had vanished from the statute books, the only exceptions being a few clauses apparently overlooked, such as South Australia's ban on Asians leasing irrigated land or Queensland's ban on Asiatic women living in a public lodging house. Then, in 1964, they eased entry conditions for persons of part European origin so that, no matter what their appearance might be, they could enter simply in terms of skill, family relationship and degree of persecution or discrimination. Finally, in 1966, after the more cautious and conservative Robert Menzies had retired as Prime Minister to be succeeded by the more liberally minded Harold Holt, the government abolished the special fifteen year naturalisation requirement and expanded the highly qualified category to cover persons with technical or professional skills in short supply in Australia or who, by former residence or service to Australia abroad, showed that they could identify with Australian life and be easily absorbed into the Australian community.

The result of all these changes was, first, a substantial increase in the number of Asians and Pacific Islanders granted citizenship (40,000 in the years 1956–71, over 8000 being from western Asia) and, second, a marked rise in the number of non-Europeans entering as permanent residents or acquiring permanent status after some time as visitors; by 1969–71 this was averaging nearly 10,000 a year and by 1971–3 nearly 15,000 a year. For the first five years of the new migration system, 1966–71, new settler arrivals totalled nearly 20,000 Indians, including a few Pakistanis and Sri Lankans, 8000 Chinese (from Malaysia, Singapore, Indonesia and Hong Kong as well as China proper), nearly 9000 other Asians, some 8000 Eurasians, about 15,000 Lebanese and Syrians, 11,000 Turks, some 7000 Mauritians and about 3000 other non-Europeans. In terms of total population this represented a substantial annual increase in Australia's non-European population and was a long step away from the ultra-restrictive policy of earlier years.

There were, however, some things the Liberal–Country Party Government would not do for persons of non-European race: grant them assisted passages, even if qualified on all grounds other than race; grant them equality in naturalisation, the residential period for them remaining five years after that for Europeans had been reduced to three; extend to them, unless they were New Zealand citizens of Maori origin, the non-visa system operating between Australia and New Zealand; grant to non-European students an automatic right to stay in Australia after completing their course, even if they were acceptable in terms of language, social intermixture and a secure job. Nor would they extend to non-European refugees the same easy entry and post-settlement benefits granted to European refugees such as the White Russians from China or the Czechoslovaks fleeing the 1967 Russian invasion. Though proud of their refugee record (Australia accepted well over 350,000 European refugees, 1947–71), and active in refugee organisations such as UNHCR and ICEM, they were most reluctant to become involved in resettling any of the 1.5 million refugees in Africa, the 2.5 million refugees in Asia, or the 2.2 million refugees in the Middle East, though they did allow voluntary agencies and relatives to sponsor some of the Armenian, Assyrian and Lebanese refugees from western Asia. Hence Australia's slowness to do anything much for Asians being forced out of East Africa by discriminatory policies: even when Idi Amin forced Asians from Uganda at short notice in 1972, Australia, in marked contrast to Canada's immediate offer to accept 5000, responded to Britain's appeal for help by agreeing to accept only those few who were eligible for entry anyway, a number estimated at some 300 cases.

The Ugandan Asian crisis gave Australia yet another chance to reveal its traditional reluctance to make any but very minor concessions to persons of non-European race coming from other parts of the Commonwealth; though British nationality might give them certain privileges once resident – right to vote, right to become a permanent officer in the public service or mercantile marine, and so on – it gave very little advantage for purposes of entry. It did not even help much with short-term visits: while British nationals of European race had advantages over other Europeans with respect to visa procedures and re-entry permits, British nationals of other race had as much difficulty in obtaining visitor permits as anyone. This was particularly so for peoples such as Fiji Indians and Hong Kong Chinese, some of whom in earlier years had entered as visitors ostensibly to see relatives or business contacts and then shown great skill in delaying or avoiding departure long after their entry permit had expired. As a response to this, immigration officers developed the practice of examining all such applications very carefully, and of issuing visas to a few only, and then only after some delay. These delays not only interfered with the growing tourist trade but greatly angered some Fijians, Malaysians and others affected, as well as some Filipinos and other aliens undergoing the same treatment. Japanese, be it noted, received easier treatment, not simply because Japan was rapidly becoming Australia's major trading partner but also because relatively few wished to settle permanently while those coming on visits were most punctilious about observing entry conditions.

It is important to note here that not even Australian citizenship always guaranteed free movement in and out of the country. Australian Aborigines and natives of Australia's Papuan territory in New Guinea, though legally Australian citizens, experienced severe restrictions if wanting to travel, partly because of traditions of paternalistic control but also, so far as Papuans were concerned, because most Australians completely refused to accept the notion that half a million coloured persons could enter Australia whenever they wished.

It is also important to remember that despite all these restrictions on non-European persons, both within and without Australia and its territories, the short-term movement to and from Australia increased very greatly during the sixties; short-term visitors rose from 99,300 arrivals in 1961 to 432,400 in 1971 and residents leaving on short-term journeys overseas from 89,900 to 413,900. Much of this increase reflects Australia's growing business dealings with countries overseas – with consequent increase in business trips – and the country's growing tourist trade as air fares were reduced and package tourist trips improved. But much of it reflects the continuance of the main immigration programme and the resulting growth of the settler population: anything up to a third of the short-term resident movement were settlers with well established homes in Australia making short visits to their families in their country of origin, while many short-term visitors were persons visiting relatives and friends settled in Australia. Some of these then stayed on as permanent settlers, as did some tourists, businessmen and students who had no close relations in Australia but after a few months visiting decided to stay on permanently.

THE WHITLAM LABOUR GOVERNMENT: 1972–5

On the whole the Liberal–Country Party coalition had a good run in immigration matters from the time it took office in 1949 until 1970/1. Apart from minor economic downturns in 1951, 1958 and 1966, conditions were relatively prosperous and, despite an occasional economist complaining about the inflationary effects of immigration, the economy was well able to absorb the more than 2.6 million new settlers arriving. Certainly many influential persons and organisations, both business and trade unionist, continued to support the immigration programme and the government's measures to reach targets, even if these meant switching recruitment to new countries.

Nevertheless there were some signs of strain, particularly at the end of the period. First, the government was caught, somewhat irresolute, between liberal humanitarian groups on one side, urging the abolition of the last relics of the White Australia Policy and an increased intake of non-Europeans, and on the other a small militant group (including some disgruntled whites moving out of black controlled countries in East Africa) who wanted to 'keep Australia white' and formed the Immigration Control Group to press their views and mount anti-government campaigns in marginal electorates. Second, a number of welfare and local government organisations were complaining that continued large-scale immigration was starting to put considerable strain on housing, schools, hospitals, welfare organisations and so on. Here a number of immigrant societies took up the cry, demanding less public expenditure on new immigration (except for family reunions) and more on helping those already here with welfare, interpreting services, teaching English, ethnic schools, ethnic broadcasting and the like; though the government went some way to meet these demands – including abandonment of the old concept of 'assimilation' in favour of 'integration' and 'multi-culturalism' – some agitation still remained. Third, a growing number of persons were becoming interested in environmental and pollution control, and in checking the rapid acceleration in the use of non-replaceable natural resources; these, and others, sometimes became advocates of ZPG (zero population growth) and of moves to restrict both natural increase and net immigration.

These stresses and questionings all came to a head in 1971, in a time of recession, and led the Government to reduce the new settler target from 180,000 to 140,000 a year, to make various placatory gestures to immigrant organisations, and to take a firmer line against South African racism in the hopes of rendering more plausible its own efforts to maintain the last defences of White Australia. These difficulties and manoeuvrings gave Gough Whitlam, Don Dunstan, Al Grassby and other thinkers of the 'new' Australian Labor Party a tremendous opportunity. Bordering on the chauvinistic, very sensitive to Australia's image among Third World countries, and most hostile to the Liberals' 'sycophantic dependence' on the USA and Britain, they set about creating a 'forward-looking' migration policy which involved wiping the slate clean of the Calwell–Chifley heritage, changing traditional Labor migration policy and establishing a programme that would fit with their more aggressive Australian nationalism. They first persuaded the Party to delete the eighty-year-old reference to White Australia (1965) and then to add a plank that immigration policy be based on the 'avoidance of discrimination on any grounds of race or colour of skin and nationality' (1971). They also laid much stress on developing Australia as a multi-cultural society, on encouraging ethnic groups and cultures to play their full part in such development, and on giving more help to immigrants with problems of settlement and welfare. They also decided that large-scale immigration did indeed produce severe social and cultural strains, as well as over-hasty depletion of natural resources, and announced that Labour's immigration policy would no longer be directed towards increasing population.

It was with this programme that Labor entered the election of December 1972; after a resounding victory, and with Gough Whitlam as Prime Minister and Al Grassby as Minister of Immigration, the policy went rapidly into operation. By July 1973 Grassby and his officers had introduced a less discriminatory selection procedure, extended the assisted passage scheme to all races, abolished discrimination in migration to and from New Zealand, eliminated inequalities in naturalisation, made things easier for non-European students, allowed unimpeded travel overseas for Aborigines, and abolished all race statistics and special records of non-European migration. (The problem of Papuan immigration was resolved by Whitlam announcing a definite date for Papuan–New Guinea independence as a separate country.)

Grassby also agreed to take a few more Ugandan Asians and additionally, in July 1973, introduced an easy-visa system whereby tourists and other short-term visitors fron non-European countries could, like most Europeans, obtain visas without the careful checks heretofore prevailing simply by producing a pre-paid return ticket, a valid passport, a declaration that they had enough funds to support their stay and a written promise not to take a job while in Australia. Some senior administrators feared that these concessions would encourage numerous non-Europeans to enter as visitors and then stay on after their permits expired by going underground and taking jobs illegally. Grassby was compelled, in fact, to abolish the concession to Fiji in February 1974 – visas from there had jumped threefold and overstays greatly increased – and also to deport numbers of Latin Americans who had been misled by their travel agents into thinking a visitor's entry permit gave rights of permanent settlement. Eventually things became so difficult that Clyde Cameron, Grassby's successor after the election of May 1974 and a much more conservative Labor politician, abolished the easy-visa system altogether on the grounds that perhaps 50,000 short-term visitors were working illegally in the country, so taking jobs from unemployed Australians.

Partly as a result of these easy-visa overstayers but partly because of more relaxed conditions for permanent entry, the number of non-Europeans settling in Australia rose yet further, to nearly 20,000 a year during 1973–6; of these about 5500 a year came from western Asia (mainly Turkey and the Lebanon), about 7700 a year from British Commonwealth Asia (notably India), nearly 6000 a year from other countries in Asia, and a few hundred from countries such as Mauritius.

In the area of immigrant welfare Grassby was also active – providing more public funds for ethnic radio and interpreting services, and for immigrant welfare and education. He also placed much stress on removing all discrimination against immigrants, whether it be because of their ethnicity or newness; after his electoral defeat in 1974 (occasioned partly because of the special campaign against him organised by the Immigration Control Group) he was able to continue this work by becoming first Commissioner for Community Relations, charged with the responsibility of administering Labor's new statute against discriminatory practices.

In terms of Australian nationalism Grassby found himself close to Whitlam and the new independent Australian foreign policy; indeed, wherever immigration involved foreign affairs Whitlam saw that his own opinions carried great weight. Very early, for instance, he decided that Australia should withdraw from ICEM on the grounds that Australia could manage its migration affairs better alone than with other countries, that organisations existing to promote European emigration were irrelevant in the modern world and that ICEM was too much under American influence. Likewise his Cabinet felt that privileges for British Commonwealth countries were inconsistent with Australian nationalism and in 1974 abolished, first, the easy conditions whereby Britons obtained citizenship and, soon after, all British privileges in regard to visas, re-entry permits, naturalisation procedures, and the like. After some dismay expressed by traditional British supporters and annoyance amongst UK migrants settled in Australia the system settled down with little decrease in numbers travelling but with a marked rise in the number of UK citizens seeking Australian citizenship (three-year annual averages: 1971–3 = 6960, 1974–6 = 34,870). The old British Australian feeling, so strong in Sir Robert Menzies, Sir John Downer and other Liberal leaders, that historic ties with the 'Mother Country' deserved some special mark in migration and settlement policy, clearly weighed very little with the Labor Government.

In refugee matters the Whitlam Government was much less definite, partly because the old Liberal convention – that the Department of Immigration could normally take European refugees without delay – was replaced by a vagueness as to how a non-discriminatory refugee policy should work and which government departments should be responsible. Thus, despite urging from various voluntary societies concerned with refugees, the Government dithered for quite a time over the Chilean crisis of 1973; only when the emergency was over was a recruiting team sent to Chile to help recruit refugee survivors and then not as refugees but as ordinary immigrants. Likewise the Timorese troubles found the government perplexed, not only in choosing between Fretelin and the Indonesians but also about Timorese seeking refuge in Australia; the 1600 or so hurriedly arriving by boat or plane in 1975 were admitted, somewhat uncertainly, as 'visitors' and their final status left undefined. The Vietnamese crisis of April 1975 also caught the government uncertain. Whitlam, partly because he so strongly disapproved of American involvement in Vietnam and partly because he did not want to damage his hard-won relations with Hanoi, refused outright to help with the 130,000 refugees evacuated by the USA to Guam and the Philippines, and so long delayed his own decision to admit a few hundred Vietnamese, mainly those with close relatives permanently settled in Australia, that the Embassy could process only a few before Saigon fell. Later, however, he agreed to help UNHCR (United Nations High Commissioner for Refugees) with refugee families outside the American area of influence; he subsequently sent some migration officers to select 500 or so persons stranded in Hong Kong and Singapore. Though somewhat belated this marked a big step forward from the Liberals' timid little move over Ugandan Asians. It was not, however, enough to satisfy the voluntary agencies; they continued to press the government for a clear-cut refugee policy and for easier entry conditions for Lebanese and others from western Asia.

Finally there remains the matter of total target and intake. Influenced by the severe economic recession as well as by official party policy, the Labor government immediately reduced the new settler target from 140,000 to 110,000 in December 1972 and again to 80,000 in late 1974, about half to be assisted by the Government. With the 'anti-inflationary' budget of August 1975, Labor made further cuts still, allocating funds to cover only 20,000 assisted passages and indicating a total settler intake for the financial year 1975/6 of no more than 50,000; as 32,000 or so of these were required to replace a loss of 15,000 former settlers and 17,000 native Australians, the resulting net gain of 28,000 was the lowest in any financial year since the immigration programme had gotten under way in 1947. In line with this general running down of immigration, Whitlam agreed to reduce the importance of the Department of Immigration: after Grassby's departure in mid-1974 the department lost passport control to Foreign Affairs, migrant welfare to Social Security and migrant education to Education; its rump was then amalgamated with the Department of Labor. These changes greatly upset a number of immigrants who, though often critical of the department, nevertheless regarded it as 'their' department, existing to look after 'their' interests. Likewise some immigrants, notably refugees from communist countries, were greatly angered by Whitlam's recognition of Russia's annexation of the Baltic States.

In sum, in the hectic first eighteen months of Labor rule, Grassby had shown some support for continued migration and had made clear his concern for migrant welfare and his wish deeply to involve ethnic minorities in helping build a new Australia. The second eighteen months gave an impression that the Government was losing interest in immigration and refugees and that its concern for migrant rights and welfare might suffer the same fate, particularly in view of its narrow manpower-employment perspective.

THE NEW LIBERALS: 1976–

Members of the Liberal–National Country Party opposition (among them Michael MacKellar, Shadow Minister for Immigration and Ethnic Affairs) were not slow to realise what was happening. They clearly understood that post-war immigrants and their children now made up some 30 per cent of the total population – over half being non-British in ethnic origin – and were quick to identify points of immigrant unease. They also realised that their predecessors' fears about abolishing the last relics of the White Australia Policy were unfounded; apart from a few last ditchers, such as those in the Immigration Control Group, the public seemed to be accepting the higher non-European immigration with relatively little hostility or fuss. Their policy document of August 1975 spelt out their conclusions and proposals in detail, together with their conviction that immigration was essential for economic recovery, continued development and 'broader national strategies'.

When somewhat unexpectedly flung into power in late 1975 – after the Governor-General summarily dismissed the Whitlam Government for failure to ensure supply and issued writs for a general election – the Liberals at once put their programme into operation. Firstly, they created a new Department of Immigration and Ethnic Affairs having most of its old functions plus a new responsibility of supervising 'ethnic affairs' and the operation of the anti-discrimination laws. Secondly, they gave strong support to migrant welfare and ethnic activities in areas such as broadcasting. Thirdly, they early tackled the refugee problem. In February 1976 MacKellar told the 1300 or so Timorese evacuees still in Australia that they need not worry about being expelled and in May announced that those who wished could apply for permanent status. (He also tidied up the loose ends of the easy-visa programme: in January 1976 he announced an amnesty for all immigrants illegally in Australia – except those involved in crimes of violence, drug pushing or other serious offences – and by mid-1976 had processed most of the 7000 who applied for permanent status under its provisions.) He also agreed for members of relevant government departments to meet together over refugee matters, and also to meet twice yearly with the voluntary societies dealing with refugee resettlement. Then, in May 1977, he announced a comprehensive refugee policy that recognised Australia's commitment to the Convention on the Status of Refugees and helping UNHCR, either by contributing funds for work overseas or else by giving special assistance to resettle certain persons and families in Australia.

The first step under this policy was to send officers to Thailand and elsewhere to select a regular intake of refugees from political upheaval in southeast Asia; this considerably extended Whitlam's somewhat tentative moves earlier. Things started well but in late 1977 struck difficulties from the 'Boat Refugees', mainly Vietnamese who hired or seized fishing or other small vessels and arrived in northern Australia after much hardship and often in considerable distress. Though experiencing some adverse criticism from Labor leaders, and limited strikes by the Waterside Workers in Darwin, MacKellar refused to slow down the official recruiting or take hurried measures against the boat arrivals, though the latter now have to undergo normal medical and security checks before receiving an immigrant status. By mid-1978, including the 1200 or so admitted by the Whitlam Government, about 8000 Indo–Chinese refugees were in Australia; 1000 or so from the boats, nearly 1000 students and other temporary residents allowed to remain, and about 6000 selected by Australian officers posted abroad.

Partly as a result of these refugees, but also because of continued refugee and quasi-refugee migration from western Asia and an increase in settler migration from countries such as Fiji, Korea and the Philippines, non-European settler intake rose still further, to some 35,000 in 1976/7 and almost as many in 1977/8. Of the 1976/7 immigration some 14,500 were from Egypt and western Asia (mainly the Lebanon), nearly 8000 from British Commonwealth Asia (Hong Kong, Singapore and Malaysia being most prominent), just under 10,000 from other parts of Asia, nearly 3000 from Fiji and other Pacific islands and a few hundred from Mauritius and Africa. Though there have been occasional grumblings, with articles in the press on 'Asian Ghettoes' and the like, the Australian public has accepted the disappearance of White Australia with remarkable equanimity. Certainly the efforts of extremist groups — notably the Immigration Control Group and the small recent offshoot of Britain's National Front — have done little more than make things difficult for police controlling the occasional protest march and for politicians with slender majorities.

Finally, in basic matters of target and intake, MacKellar early made clear his desire to raise intake well above the 50,000 gross and 20,000 net of 1975/6. Exact targets had to await the opinions of ministers involved in economic management and planning, and though the 1976/7 gross settler target was raised to 70,000 (which in the event achieved a net gain of 56,000) a firm announcement came only with the ministerial statement of June 1978. Here MacKellar restated the government's basic objectives, stressed that immigration would be non-discriminatory in nature, agreed to ease conditions for family reunion and announced a triennium net migration target, 1977–9, of 70,000 a year; to offset loss of former settlers and native Australians this would, he thought, involve a gross settler immigration of 90,000 a year.

The policy statement said little about source countries. It seems plain, however, that with Australia now more widely open to refugees from Asia and Latin America and more ready to accept family reunion requests by settlers of non-European ethnic origin, there will continue for some years the recent marked shift in areas of origin, from traditional European countries to Asian, Oceanian and Latin American. Table 2.4 illustrates this shift, especially when compared with those of Table 2.3. (The later years have been broken to coincide with, allowing for the time-lag involved in implementing new policies, the changes of government outlined earlier.)

REVIEW

The statistics of Table 2.4 provide a convenient entry to a general assessment of recent migration trends. First, they reveal very clearly the failure of migration from the UK and Eire to average more than 37.6 per cent, let alone the 90 per cent of earlier decades, the proportion aimed at by the original Calwell programme. Once or twice, as in 1964–6 and 1971–3 the proportion did, in terms of new settlers, creep up over the 50 per cent level but these periods did no more than offset others when the proportion fell well below 30 per cent, as in 1953–5 and 1966/7. To some extent this failure to average even 40 per cent was compensated by the increase in immigration from other parts of the Old Commonwealth, notably New Zealand. In 1976/7 New Zealand provided more immigrants than the UK, with other Commonwealth countries and South Africa making appreciable contributions. Even so, adding migration from Old Commonwealth countries to migration from the mother country still failed to lift the British proportion over 45 per cent for the whole period 1947–77.

Though at first reluctant to accept the hard fact that a large-scale immigration programme involved more persons of non-British origin than of British origin – hence the outcries of the mid-fifties, the Bring Out a Briton campaign, and so on – most Australians have now become reconciled to this situation, and to the slow stripping of British privileges in migration and settlement. Partly they have seen that non-British settlers, though of very different background and culture, can not only conform to British–Australian notions of acceptable life styles and standards but can also contribute much to the development of Australian culture and society; hence the widespread acceptance of the notion that Australia is now a multi-cultural nation which must permit ethnic groups to express and maintain their own values and customs. Not that conservative views and discriminatory practices have vanished – far from it – but Australia is now a very different country from the one which, in the shadow of the near Japanese invasion of 1941,

TABLE 2.4. Net migration: 1947–77 (annual averages)

Origin	1947–71 Annual average	%	1971–73 Annual average	%	1973–76 Annual average	%	1976–77 Annual average	%	Total 1947–77 Nos	%	Settler Arrivals	% Loss
UK & Eire	37288	37.9	29356	51.6	18892	32.5	11652	17.9	1021957	37.6	1341595	23.8
New Zealand	2564	2.6	2107	3.7	5008	8.6	12382	19.1	93186	3.4	120448	22.6
Canada	500	0.5	1043	1.8	−197	−0.3	171	0.3	13644	0.5	24023	43.2
South Africa	395	0.4	851	1.5	634	1.1	1721	2.6	14774	0.6	19756	25.2
Other British*	2154	2.2	3725	6.6	4182	7.2	5193	8.0	76910	2.8	83121	7.5
Total British	42901	43.6	37082	65.2	28519	49.1	31119	47.9	1220471	44.9	1588943	23.2
North Europe	10830	11.0	−437	−0.8	324	0.6	−190	−0.3	259823	9.6	387485	32.9
East Europe	14952	15.2	4320	7.6	2041	3.5	1708	2.6	375333	13.8	430044	12.7
South Europe	22406	22.7	−1979	−3.5	3450	5.9	1855	2.9	545991	20.1	724716	24.7
Total Europe	48188	48.9	1904	3.3	5815	10.0	3373	5.2	1181147	43.5	1542245	23.4
USA	1122	1.1	1594	2.8	796	1.4	−1735	−2.7	30760	1.1	55760	44.8
Other America	470	0.5	2701	4.7	4808	8.3	2987	4.6	34090	1.3	39162	13.0
Western Asia†	2363	2.4	5356	9.4	5037	8.7	13642	21.0	96174	3.5	104979	8.4
Commonwealth Asia	2000	2.0	5515	9.7	7470	12.9	7251	11.2	88996	3.3	94092	5.4
Other Asia	1230	1.3	2441	4.3	5692	9.8	7833	12.1	59319	2.2	64482	8.0
Other countries††	195	0.2	322	0.6	−7		466	0.7	5762	0.2	8794	34.4
Total	7380	7.5	17929	31.5	23796	40.9	30444	46.9	315101	11.6	367269	14.2
Total Foreign-born	98469	100.0	56915	100.0	58130	100.0	64936	100.0	2716719	100.0	3498457	22.3
Australia	−9298		−22075		−14062		−8589		−318081			
TOTAL	89171		34840		44068		56347		2398638			

* Commonwealth countries in Africa, America, Europe, Oceania and about two-thirds Commonwealth Asia 1947–61 to cover ethnic British.
† All countries south of USSR and west of Afghanistan.
†† Non-commonwealth Africa, Asia, Oceania.
Not stated: The 14510 persons whose origin was not stated or born at sea have been distributed pro rata to the foreign-born.

so energetically and optimistically embarked on the post-war immigration programme.

In a sense there was little that Australians could do about it. Just as in the UK, by the time the cumbersome machinery of politics and administration really faced up to the facts of the large-scale immigration of the 1950s there were so many persons of Indian, Pakistani and West Indian origin in the country that nothing short of large-scale repatriation could stop the UK becoming a multi-racial society, so many conservative British–Australians – of all political parties – became fully aware of large-scale new ethnic minorities much too late to stop their growth and consolidation. By mid-1978 post-war immigrants and their children made up some 30 per cent of the population, well over half being of non-British origin. A rough estimate suggests that whereas in 1947 about 90 per cent of the population was of British ethnic origin in mid-1978 that proportion was about 77 per cent, that is about 10.9 million of Australia's 14.2 million total. The remaining 3.3 million consists of some 600,000 persons of Italian origin, about 500,000 of German (over 300,000 being descendants of nineteenth century immigrants), some 300,000 of Greek, 200,000 of Yugoslav, 160,000 of Dutch (including Dutch families from Ceylon and the Netherlands East Indies), 150,000 of Scandinavian (two-thirds deriving from immigrants of the nineteenth century), 90,000 of Maltese, 90,000 of Polish origin (including Polish Jews), with smaller populations deriving from almost every other country. There are even small contingents from Iceland, Monaco and Lichtenstein.

Though persons of European racial descent make up 97.1 per cent of Australia's population, the last few years have seen persons of Asian and Oceanian origin become relatively more numerous. Table 2.1 shows how, under the impact of the White Australia Policy, the proportion of settlers of non-European race fell from some 6.0 per cent of the foreign-born population in 1901 to 1.8 per cent in 1947; and how, with the gradual easing of restrictions and the slow acceleration of non-European immigration after the Second World War, the proportion rose again slowly until by mid-1977 it had reached about 7.6 per cent or about 212,000 souls. Table 2.1 also shows that this non-European population was still largely Chinese but with appreciable numbers of Indians, Malays and other southeast Asians, and of Mauritians and Pacific Islanders. In this respect Australia differs markedly from the UK: in Australia there are few persons of African race, maybe, including those born in Australia, a total of 5000 from Africa and the West Indies; also relatively few Pakistanis, possibly 3000 in all; Indians, though much more numerous, total no more than 22,000. There are far more east and southeast Asians and these, with the 21,000 Pacific Islanders (including about 8000 descendents of the islanders brought in during the nineteenth century for tropical labour and another few thousand illegal immigrants of recent years) and the 140,000 or so Australian Aborigines and 15,000 or so Torres Strait Islanders, give a very different racial mixture to that developing in the UK.

It is here worth noting that information and statistics on race are now far less comprehensive than in earlier years. Immigration landing cards and lists ceased recording race in 1948 while the special race records kept by the administrative section controlling temporary entry permits have been largely abolished by policy changes since 1972. The census still asks persons to identify their race but in recent years has done no more with the answers than produce broad statistics of Aborigine, Torres Strait Islander, Chinese, European and Other. This means that, though Australia has better race information than the UK, it now has less comprehensive information than the USA.

The net result is that those interested in Australia's newer racial minorities – Vietnamese, Filipinos, Indians, Mauritians, Fijians and so on – have to make do with birthplace records; and these can be very confusing, as with birthplace 'Fiji' which combines in one category persons of Melanesian, Indian and European racial origin, or 'India', which combines in one category persons of Indian, Persian (Parsee) and Arab origin, persons born in India of English military or civil service parents, and children born in India of Anglo–Burmese parents who left Burma after the Second World War and, after some years in India, have been migrating to Western Australia in considerable numbers. It is even more difficult for those working with older racial groups, such as the descendants of the Afghan camel-drivers of the 1860s, of the Malay pearlers and sugar labourers of the 1890s, or of the Pacific Island tropical labourers of the 1880s and 1890s; they are all born in Australia and, if not recorded as distinct racial groups, are virtually indistinguishable from the rest of the Australian-born population. This can lead to difficult situations as when descendants of the Pacific Island labourers, now preferring to call themselves South Sea Islanders and claiming to total between 30,000 and 50,000, agitated for the special welfare and educational privileges recently granted to Aborigines and Torres Strait Islanders. Estimates based on earlier censuses, where more comprehensive race statistics were given, put the total at 7000 to 8000 as a maximum but the absence of more precise statistics in recent censuses makes the whole issue somewhat confused.

All these changes in the Australian population – both racial and cultural – naturally raise the question: what has happened to the original English, Scottish, Irish and Welsh peoples, the founders and pioneers of modern Australia? Aided by a net immigration of more than a million souls (see Table 2.4) they still make up three-quarters or so of the total population. But the balance between them has undergone further change. The decline of the Irish, from one-quarter of total immigration during the nineteenth century to less than one-tenth in the first four decades of the twentieth century, continued after the Second World War. About 8.0 per cent of net British Isles immigration during the period 1901–40, Irish intake has averaged only 6.2 per cent in the years since 1947, that is, about 2100 a year, with peaks of more than 3000 a year in the early fifties and later sixties. This immigration, about 64,000 in all, has derived not only from Northern Ireland and Eire: it has also come from Irish settlements in the Liverpool region of England where Australian advertising and migration officers have persuaded some Irish families to take the chance provided by the assisted passage schemes. It is of interest to note here that, like the United Kingdom, Australia has found difficulty in defining its allegiance and migration relationships with Eire and its people: while recognising that Eire is no longer British in terms of formal allegiance, Australia has given persons of Eireann descent and citizenship almost exactly the same migration privileges extended to British citizens from the UK.

The Scottish, too, have failed to maintain their pre-war level which was 19 per cent of British Isles immigration. They started quite well in the late forties with well over 5000 a year and then reached 6500 a year in the early sixties. They then fell away to 2200 a year in the seventies making a total of only 136,000 or 4500 a year, only 13.4 per cent of the British Isles total. The Welsh have done a little better than their pre-war average of 2 per cent, providing Australia with 25,000 settlers, that is 2.5 per cent of British Isles net migration. England has done best of all, contributing a net total of 796,000 or 26,200 a year. Though this intake was very uneven – 22,500 a year in the late forties, eventually up to 43,000 a year in 1966–71, then way down to 7000 a year or less 1975–7 – it was sufficient to keep the English average at 78 per cent of British Isles immigration, compared with 71 per cent 1901–40 and 56 per cent in the nineteenth century. In other words, net migration from Britain since 1947 has been overwhelmingly Anglo–Saxon with the Celtic fringe contributing relatively little. Indeed, English immigration has been the largest ethnic stream in immigration as a whole; the 796,000 English net total is far ahead of the next largest ethnic stream, the 273,000 from Italy (see Tables 2.2 and 2.4). Though native Australians may still criticise their English cousins for silly 'Pommy' ways and customs they recognise that, in terms of population and culture, England is still a major influence in Australian life.

This English total is, of course, the net total – the number remaining after numerous settlers changed their minds about staying permanently in Australia and either returned home or went on to New Zealand, North America or elsewhere; the original settler total was about 986,000 which means that nearly 24 per cent of English settlers decided to leave again. In practice this was not a particularly high rate of settler loss, at any rate compared with the German loss of 32 per cent, the Dutch loss of 30 per cent, the Spanish–Portuguese loss of 34 per cent, or the North American loss of 44 per cent (see Table 2.4, last column). It was in fact very close to the average loss – 22.3 per cent – the main peoples with significantly lower losses being refugees such as the Poles (6.6 per cent), peoples from unstable and unhappy conditions (Cypriots 7.8 per cent or Lebanese 8 per cent), or peoples from relatively undeveloped countries with living standards well below those of Australia (Latin America 13 per cent, India 5 per cent). Nor is it a conspiciously high loss rate compared with those of countries such as Canada or the USA.

During the sixties and early seventies this loss greatly worried Australian authorities and was one of the factors considered by the Whitlam Government when severely cutting targets in 1975/6. It certainly looms large in present immigration planning, as instance the government's immigration statement of June 1978 suggesting that the planned net gain of 70,000 migrants would require a gross settler intake of 90,000; this implies a loss of 20,000 former settlers and native Australians, equivalent to 22 per cent of settler intake. Some feel this is too low a loss margin: in the sixties settler loss alone equalled 24.2 per cent of settler arrivals with native Australian loss equal to another 10.7 per cent, i.e. a loss of nearly 35 per cent, while in the period 1973–6 the combined loss was even higher, 53.6 per cent of arrivals. Admittedly the early seventies were somewhat unusual, with depression conditions both reducing the number of new settlers and increasing the number of former settlers leaving. Nevertheless, unless Australia's new immigrants are nearly all refugees, and this is most improbable, it seems likely that long-term loss will stay well above 22 per cent, probably nearer 35 per cent, and that government planning is here somewhat unrealistic.

There are several reasons for the difficulty Australian authorities have in accepting the hard facts of settler loss. First is the amount of money spent on advertising and recruiting, on assisted passages, on reception hostels, on placing immigrants in jobs and seeing to their welfare and education; no one likes to admit that anything up to one-third of their investment is being wasted and it is noteworthy that Australia's assisted immigrants (nearly two-thirds of the post-war total) are just as ready to leave permanently as unassisted migrants. Second is the historic fact that until recently Australians have always looked upon immigration in terms of contribution to growth, development and defence, that is, in terms of building up the permanent population. Policy has never been geared to short-term labour schemes such as the guest-worker programmes of western Europe. Indeed, it has usually been most discouraging; one of the difficulties with the Turkish programme, 1967–74, was the conflict of outlook and interest between Australian authorities wanting Turks to settle permanently and the Turkish immigrants who had thought Australia was introducing a short-term worker scheme such as that of Germany or the Netherlands. With this background many Australians find it difficult to accept the fact of modern international mobility, of a large mobile population of skill and experience, which moves from country to country, spending several years in a place where its skill is needed and then moving on elsewhere. It is, as it happens, difficult to know how many fall into this category but the statistics suggest that about one-tenth of settler arrivals and maybe one-quarter of permanent departures could be involved; certainly the number of persons leaving Australia for permanent residence in the USA or Canada is often more than double the number of Americans and Canadians leaving Australia while those leaving for permanent residence in New Zealand are about three times the number of New Zealanders leaving Australia.

Nor are the foreign-born the only ones involved in this transilient mobility: native Australians are part of it. Again it is difficult to estimate how many of the 620,000 Australians who left their native land for long-term residence abroad during the years 1947–77, or of the 170,000 who departed saying they were leaving permanently, were in fact transilients; information about Australians employed abroad in professional, administrative and technical work suggests it is considerable, both in Commonwealth countries such as Fiji and in non-Commonwealth countries such as Indonesia or the Philippines. In many ways they cannot be distinguished from Australians settled in permanent jobs abroad, that is, the successors of Australians settling abroad in the nineteenth and early twentieth centuries. Here the main Australian settlements expanded considerably. The 30,000 or so in the UK in the 1930s had increased only to 33,000 by 1951 but during the next twenty years expanded to 57,000, still mainly in the London area but with 3900 in Scotland, 1300 in Wales, 3900 in the Southwest and the rest scattered in smaller numbers through other regions. Some, of course, were short-term visitors while others were children born in Australia to former British settlers (the British census of 1971 showed some 9000 children aged 0–9 as having been born in Australia to British parents). Australians of Australian parentage were concentrated more in the ages 20–34, and were predominantly women – many were in the UK as wives, nurses, teachers, secretaries and the like.

The Australian population of North America also increased noticeably after the Second World War. The 3000 in Canada in 1940 expanded to nearly 10,000, still mainly in Vancouver and Toronto, while the 15,000 in the USA grew to 24,000 (38,000 if including the second generation), again predominantly in California. The western Pacific also saw an expansion of Australian settlement. The 35,000 in New Zealand in 1951 had grown to 44,000 in 1971, again mainly settled in the Auckland and Wellington areas (21,000 and 9000) but with a scattering in every province. These were more than compensated for by the number of New Zealanders in Australia, which rose quite sharply from 44,000 or so in 1947 to 106,000 in 1977. The islands, too, saw more Australians, partly as a result of Australia's increasing economic involvement, especially in Fiji. The Australian population of Papua New Guinea, however, has lately decreased, notably with the advent of independence and the departure of many Australian civil servants, soldiers, teachers and others, and of some planters and businessmen fearing a take-over of property and enterprise. In like manner, and for somewhat similar reasons, there has been some reduction in the number of native Australians resident in South Africa and East Africa.

The movements just outlined are basically continuations or retractions of earlier movements. Elsewhere Australians have been moving into countries previously containing few or none. Many of these are Australian-born children of former settlers – probably a majority of Australian natives resident in Germany, the Netherlands, Italy, Greece and Malta are in this category. The 10,000 native Australians in Italy in 1971, for instance, were concentrated in the younger ages (7960 of the 10,300 were aged 0–20) and were living mainly in those Venetian, Campanian, Calabrian and Sicilian districts from which Italian migration to Australia had been most concentrated.

All in all, since 1947, some 320,000 native Australians have gone abroad and not come back, about half with the deliberate intention of settling permanently in other countries but the rest with the intention of travelling or working overseas for some years and then returning. Some of these, including many transilients in professional and commercial jobs abroad, will undoubtedly come back but others will almost certainly make permanent homes abroad and, if returning at all, will make only short visits to see family and friends. Such loss is a blow to many Australians, reared in the tradition that people come to Australia to help build a new nation, but in fact the 320,000 is small in comparison with Australia's net gain of 2.7 million foreign-born persons over the same period – less than 12 per cent.

The balance of all these movements in and out of the country appears in Table 2.2. This not only shows the growth of ethnic populations not given in other tables (English, Scottish, Irish, Welsh, Scandinavian, Polish, Cypriot, Egyptian, Turkish, Lebanese, Fijian, Mauritian, and so on) but also contrasts the size of these populations at the end of the nineteenth century, at the end of the Second World War, and at the end of the two main post-war migration periods, 1947–61 and 1961–77. Apart from the Irish every ethnic population has significantly increased since 1901, which means that even the great British immigration of the nineteenth century did not bring as many English, Scottish or Welsh settlers to Australia as has the immigration of the last thirty years – and so too with the other nineteenth century settler peoples, the Germans and Scandinavians. The only other grouping smaller in 1977 than in 1901 was the Chinese-born, though here, if we add persons born in Hong Kong and Singapore, the 1977 total exceeds that of 1901. In short, Table 2.2 reveals the very marked ethnic shift brought about by recent immigration policies and programmes.

Nor are these shifts ephemeral. The old Chinese population was almost entirely male (400 males to every one female) because before 1910 the villages of southern China discouraged the emigration of women and children; consequently, when Australian restrictions on Chinese immigration began to hit hard at the turn of the century, effectively preventing families joining their menfolk established in Australia, the Chinese population steadily declined as men either died or returned home. Since 1956, however, policy has permitted non-European families to join their menfolk in Australia, and often migrate as family units. By 1971 the sex-ratio for non-Europeans people in Australia was 141 males for every 100 females, moving still closer to parity by 1977; which means there are enough females to enable continued growth within Australia by natural increase. Persons of European origin did not suffer these restrictions and except for temporary episodes – as when Italian men settling in Australia between the wars left their families behind for some years until established, and when more Polish and Ukrainian refugee men than women arrived after the Second World War because the Nazis had put more men than women into war-time labour camps – maintained a more balanced sex ratio. Since 1961 the ratio for total immigration has been 111 men for every 100 women and, with recent government policy placing much stress on family reunion, this may well go lower in future. Even the Vietnamese boat refugees include numerous women and children.

Here, then, is the brief story of Australia as a country of immigration and emigration since the end of the Second World War. Undoubtedly Australia has continued to fulfil its function as a major country of settlement for families from the British Isles; by the early seventies there were somewhat more persons of British Isles birth in Australia than in either the USA or Canada. But these British persons have become of less numerical importance in total immigration, comprising only 40 per cent of the foreign-born in 1977 (Table 2.2) instead of the 90 per cent of the nineteenth century. Glad though Australians have been to have settlers of British origin, and willing though they have been to assist them with passage costs and initial accommodation, they have not since 1948 been willing to hold back plans for large-scale immigration and development if the British Isles could not provide the target numbers. Because of this, the earlier preferences and privileges extended to British immigrants have now been abolished and, though there is in practice some preference given, officially policy now makes no distinction between nationalities or races.

In contrast, with non-Europeans, Australia has not had to change policy to abolish discrimination; from quite early days the Australian colonies were determined to prevent any significant non-European settlement, whether migrants were from countries of the British Empire such as India or alien countries such as China or Japan: all were to be kept at bay in the interests of a White Australia. Moreover, as racial discrimination eased off gradually after 1949 all races benefited, not just those from Commonwealth countries. So, while Australia has received since 1947 considerable numbers of Indians, Malaysians, Hong Kong Chinese and Mauritians she has also received appreciable numbers of Japanese, Filipinos, Vietnamese, Indonesians, Turks, Lebanese and other peoples of non-Commonwealth background. Table 2.2 shows that whereas persons born in Commonwealth Asia totalled about 111,600 in 1977, persons from western Asia and other Asia totalled 170,000 or so. Likewise, in its present work with the United Nations High Commissioner for Refugees, Australia is drawing no distinction in terms of nationality; hence its special programme to select and settle refugees from Indo-China. Ironically enough, the thing that is testing this careful stance of non-discrimination in refugee work is the crisis in Rhodesia and the coming crisis in South Africa. Some Australians, now thoroughly wedded to the cause of 'anti-racism', dislike the thought of accepting hundreds of 'white racists' from southern Africa, even though such persons are refugees and often of British ethnic origin. The grumblings are slight at present but will undoubtedly increase greatly if such refugees become much more numerous. This is a strange swing indeed away from the old doctrine of White Australia and the white man's Australian paradise: unless, of course, the white backlash also increases strongly – and there are possibilities of this.

Whatever the outcome here, however, there can be no doubt that post-war migration, in both policy and intake, has seen a strong move away from older notions of Australia as a new home for the over-crowded families of the British motherland. As Australia grows in economic and political strength, and as its population becomes more diverse and less British, this move will be consolidated. That, together with Britain's own move away from Empire and Commonwealth into closer membership of the European Community, will mark the final end of a fascinating episode: Australia's special historic place in British migration.

3 Canadian Immigration

by L. W. St John-Jones

BACKGROUND

'All Canadians, unless they belong to the tiny minority descended from the country's original inhabitants, are immigrants or descendants of immigrants' states the Canadian Government's Green Paper on Immigration of 1974. The descendants of the original inhabitants – Indians and Eskimos – number about 1 per cent of the population today. As the history of the country is clearly linked to the story of immigration, a few salient points in Canadian history will help to suggest some earlier trends in immigration.

It was in 1534 that a French seaman, Cartier, arrived in the St Lawrence river and took possession of 'New France' for the French king. More than half a century later, Champlain, a fur trader, helped to found settlements at Quebec and Montreal. Colonisation was slow, however. War between England and France led to the former obtaining a considerable foothold in France's North American territory by the early 1700s, and then to the fall of Quebec in 1759 and the surrender of all New France to the British. The French population, numbering about 60,000, remained concentrated in the Quebec–Montreal area. Soon immigration from Britain became significant, and increased further after 1815. Other migrants came north over the border from the United States, particularly after American independence and, later, after the Anglo–American war of 1812. The period after 1815 was generally one of development and the opening up of the West. Confederation in 1867 brought four of the colonies established by Britain, including the French-speaking colony of Quebec, into union. Control of civil law and education was conferred on the provinces, and the right of use of the French language was safeguarded in Quebec and in the Federal Parliament and Courts. A Dominion from 1871, Canada takes a prominent role today in Commonwealth interests and affairs, as she always has. 'The Commonwealth is for many of us our window on the

world . . .' proclaimed the Canadian Prime Minister at the 1975
Commonwealth Heads of State meeting.

Between 1815 and 1840 an estimated half a million people left the
British Isles for Canada – more than went to the United States – and
between 1846 and 1854 another half million, mainly from Ireland. Apart
from a continuous interchange of population with the United States and
a few newcomers from Germany, the great majority of all immigrants in
that period came from the British Isles. In the 100 years from 1861,
about three and a half million people immigrated in the first half and
some five millions in the second, an average of about 1.6 per cent of the
population each year in the first half and 1 per cent in the second. This
division of the century masks two major changes in immigration history.
In 1902 and 1903, the annual totals of immigrants took a marked
upturn; high figures were maintained up to the year before the outbreak
of the First World War when the highest total of all time was recorded –
401,000 persons, or the equivalent of over 5 per cent of the population at
that time. After the war, the upsurge was maintained in great part up to
1929, and it was only the subsequent economic depression of the 1930s
followed by the Second World War which brought immigration back to
nineteenth century levels. It soared again in the 1950s, the second largest
intake of all time occurring in 1957 with 282,000 immigrants. With the
upturn of 1902/3 came the second major change in pattern, less obvious
but more significant – immigrants became more numerous than emigrants, instead of the net loss of population calculated for each decade
since 1861. Departures from Canada were, and are, not recorded, but it
was always known that many native-born Canadians as well as
immigrants moved to the United States. However, the balance became
favourable in the first decade of the century not because emigration fell
but because new arrivals increased. Only in the decade of the 1930s was
the balance ever negative again.

Minor restrictions on immigration were imposed in the first years of
confederation, notably an Act of 1885 limiting the immigration of
Chinese. The power to make immigration regulations, that is to impose
a selective policy, was taken in 1906. In 1922 a new regulation listed the
admissible classes for the first time – agriculturalists, farm labourers and
female domestic servants. After 1945 a review of the national attitude to
immigration was clearly needed, and the post-war mood was established
by Prime Minister Mackenzie King in May 1947, who said that the
government's policy was to foster the growth of population by
encouraging immigration – 'such numbers of immigrants as can be
advantageously absorbed in our national economy'. Immigration must

be related to the country's absorptive capacity, even though it was impossible to forecast that capacity in detail. Further, 'Canada is perfectly within her rights in selecting the persons whom we regard as desirable citizens'–entering Canada was a privilege, not a right; the Canadian people did not wish to make a fundamental change in the character of the population as a result of immigration. Later, the demands of the labour market led to a broadening of the admissible classes and to a new Immigration Act in 1952.

Up to the First World War immigrants continued to come mainly from Britain and the United States, with much smaller numbers from France and other countries of north and western Europe as well as a few groups from eastern Europe. In 1921 the preference for certain national groups was officially expressed in a requirement that all immigrants must obtain visas in advance of arrival, unless they were British or United States citizens. By 1926, some preference was allowed to citizens of various western European countries, and after the Second World War exemption from the visa requirement was extended to the French and Irish. A regulation of 1950 gave much wider discretion in admitting immigrants, while still maintaining preference for the British, Americans, Irish and French, and in the following year agreements were concluded to admit very small numbers of Indian, Pakistani and Ceylonese nationals annually. By 1960, eligibility was governed by a regulation made four years earlier, which listed as admissible the four preferred nationalities; citizens of western European countries coming for employment or as entrepreneurs; a wide range of relatives of Canadian residents provided they were living in a European country, the Americas, Egypt, Israel, Lebanon or Turkey; and those admitted under the agreements with India, Pakistan and Ceylon. This was a more precise definition than had existed earlier. Preference for people from certain countries was, then, a keystone of immigration policy. That Britain was the principal source was due not only to policy, but to tradition and to practical links such as shipping lines. The British, it was argued, should have preference because they could accommodate themselves to economic and social conditions in many lands and were akin racially and culturally to the majority of Canadians.

After the end of the Second World War, Canada played a major role in resettling European refugees, and by 1952 had admitted 124,000 refugees in a total of 800,000 immigrants. This refugee movement was in part responsible for a novel pattern of source countries in the first ten years of peace. Only 40 per cent of immigrants came from Britain (and the colonies) and the United States together in those ten years (Table

TABLE 3.1. Numbers and nationality of Canadian immigrants 1946–55

Nationality of Immigrants 1946–55	Numbers (thousands)
UK and colonies	396
Italy	133
Germany	132
Netherlands	108
Poland	104
USA	82
France	24
Other countries	243
	1222

3.1). The pattern proceeded to change yet further, as numbers from Britain, the Netherlands, the United States and Poland fell away, but increased from Italy, Greece, Hungary and Portugal. In 1958–61, Italians outnumbered British immigrants, and were the largest national contingent, and, by that time, few European countries failed to appear on the list of source countries – a far cry from the policy of only twenty years earlier.

The United Kingdom, or Britain, as a source of immigrants was virtually synonymous with the Commonwealth up to 1960. Certainly, small numbers came from Australasia and South Africa, and small but growing numbers from Hong Kong, India, the West Indies and Pakistan, but the overwhelming majority of the Commonwealth total was always from the United Kingdom. Even in 1960, when immigration from the United Kingdom was low, no more than 17 per cent of Commonwealth immigrants came from any other country.

What were the ethnic origins of the population of 1961, and what was the part of the Commonwealth in them? Of a little over 18 million, just under a half were of British ethnic origin, slightly under a third were French and almost all of the remainder stemmed from other European countries, chiefly Germany, Russia, Italy, the Netherlands and Poland. About one in every six persons in the population had been born abroad, but only one in twenty in the United Kingdom. The number born in France was so small – 36,000 – that it was not even given in most of the relevant census tabulations; it was even exceeded by the number born in China! While nearly half of the total population was of British stock, more than half of the immigrants from the United Kingdom were aged over 50, and nearly half of them had been in Canada for over forty years. Large majorities of the German and Italian immigrants, on the other hand, had arrived in the previous ten years, and almost half of them were aged under 30. Obviously the ethnic character of the population was in the process of changing, and the contribution to it of both Commonwealth and French stock was diminishing.

THE PERIOD 1960–7

The year 1960 was poor for immigration. Only 104,000 persons entered Canada, although the average in the previous ten years had been 154,000. Fluctuations in the annual totals of immigrants were very marked; if the 1960 figure is taken as 100, the years immediately before and after were in the following proportions: 1957 – 271; 1958 – 120; 1959 – 103; 1961 – 69; 1962 – 72; 1963 – 89. Such large variations were not found in the inflows of the other two major countries of immigration, the United States and Australia, where the ranges in the same period were 95–123 and 79–103 respectively. Immigration into Canada must have been subject to some factors that did not apply to the other two countries. No doubt the United States' system of annual quotas helped to stabilise inward flows there, and perhaps something of the same effect was obtained by Australia's assisted migration scheme. The fluctuations in Canada were due in part to the practice commonly referred to as 'tap on, tap off', involving adjustments of the immigrant intake, at short intervals, to what Prime Minister King had termed the 'absorptive capacity'; for instance, 'all stops were pulled to meet the labour market's apparently insatiable demand for workers of all kinds', the government's Green Paper of 1974[1] states in connection with the economic boom of 1956–7; and promotional activity in a number of European countries was intense in 1966, but ceased altogether within a few years, to cite another instance. Unlike both the United States, with its annual quotas, and Australia, with its target of an annual increase of population of 1 per cent through immigration, Canada has never expressed any numerical objectives for immigration, although one minister did express the idea in the 1960s of a total intake each year equivalent to 1 per cent of the population, and another, predicting that the 1966 total would reach that objective, hoped that the same trend would continue in the years to come.

It is convenient to divide the post-1960 period into two sections with the dividing line at 1967, because that year was one in which new regulations of importance were introduced. In the first period, an average of 127,000 persons arrived each year – still considerably less than in the 1950s; and a third came from Commonwealth countries. Table 3.2 gives details. It will be seen that huge variations in total numbers continued. Those of the mid-1960s were accentuated by an event which gave rise to concern – the eventual admission as immigrants of many thousands of people who came to Canada as visitors, applied to immigrate after their arrival, refused to leave, and thus presented the government with the awkward choice of either admitting large numbers who would not ordinarily have qualified or formally deporting them. As a compromise, many were permitted to stay – a specific solution to a particular problem, not to be repeated in the future.

TABLE 3.2.   Immigration into Canada, total and Commonwealth 1960–7

| | All countries | Immigrants from The Commonwealth | | |
		Total	UK	Other Commonwealth countries
1960	104111	25229	19585	5644
1961	71689	15121	11870	3251
1962	74586	20284	15603	4681
1963	93151	31407	24603	6804
1964	112606	39031	29279	9752
1965	146758	53783	39857	13926
1966	194793	79087	63291	15796
1967	222876	88984	62420	26564

At this point, the reader's attention is drawn to some definitions of the published data. The headings in Table 3.2 refer to the country of last permanent residence. These particular data of origin may not be the most informative, but out of a variety published in the annual 'Immigration Statistics', they are used because they alone are cross-tabulated by other characteristics. Data on country of birth or citizenship have the advantage that documentary evidence is usually available in support; and it may be noted that these two sets of data have, in fact, differed little when summarised annually. Immigrants coming from Britain as a country of last permanent residence, however, numbered from 1961 to 1967 8 per cent more than were actually born in Britain, and similar discrepancies occurred with the United States and

Australia; for some immigrants all three countries obviously served as no more than a stop on the way to Canada. On the other hand, Indian-born immigrants were about 50 per cent more than the number coming from India as their last residence – a figure which decreased later as more Indians immigrated and came from India itself. The discrepancy varies over time for all source countries. Unless stated to the contrary, the country of last permanent residence is used in this chapter, as no other available data can, in general, serve its purpose. Several groupings of countries inevitably contain minor inaccuracies, and, curiously, Hong Kong disappeared from the list for three years from 1966, immigrants from there being included under 'China'.

Ever since the start of immigration control, the occupations as well as the numbers of immigrants have been linked to the needs of Canada's economy. What, then, is known of the immigrants as workers? The available information is of new arrivals' *intentions* to work, as stated upon entering the country. Of course, the immigrant may change his mind about working or about the kind of work he does, or have a change forced on him by circumstances. The intentions cannot be related to later census data, because by the time of the census so many immigrants had left Canada that the comparison is meaningless. Nevertheless, the immigration data are – when viewed from one year to another and from one source country to another – significant.

From 1962 (when data on occupation, cross-classified by country of last residence, first became available) to 1967, 432,000 intending workers immigrated, in a total of 845,000 persons. This is a considerably higher proportion of workers than in the Canadian native population. Britain and the Commonwealth contributed an above-average proportion of workers, but, among Commonwealth countries, large variations were found: for instance, three-quarters of all Australian immigrants in-tended to work, but only 38 per cent from India, and 30 per cent from Hong Kong. Here, as in other ways, the Commonwealth immigrants were anything but a homogeneous group.

What the 1974 Green Paper terms 'the changing mix and pattern of demand' called for agriculturalists and domestics in the 1920s, for no additions at all to the labour force in the 1930s, and in the 1950s for a quite different type of immigrant – professionals and other highly-skilled workers. Consequently a marked change from any earlier occupational pattern was seen in the inflow of the 1950s, once the post-war urgency of reuniting families and aiding Europe's refugees had passed. Table 3.3 demonstrates trends before and during the period 1960–7. Because most of these headings comprise many individual

TABLE 3.3. Occupation groups of immigrants into Canada stating an intention to work 1946–55, 1960 and 1967

1946–55	%	1960	%	1967	%
Manufacturing	23	Manufacturing	18	Professional	26
Agriculturalist	22	Service	16	Manufacturing	24
Service	11	Labourer	14	Clerical	14
Labourer	9	Professional	14	Service	9
Construction	8	Clerical	11	Construction	9
		Agriculturalist	10		

occupations of varying degrees of skill, the apparent changes in the level of expertise are far from precise, but agriculturalists, labourers and service workers became fewer while the proportions of professional and clerical workers increased by leaps and bounds; a marked trend to higher skills seems clear. The best defined as well as the greatest change occurred in the professional group, which increased from 7 per cent in the early post-war years to a quarter of all working immigrants by 1967. In that year, the numbers of immigrants in certain professions, presumably accurately recognised by immigration officers, were impressive – 3700 professional engineers, 1300 doctors and dentists, 7300 university and school teachers and 4300 trained nurses, out of a total of 120,000 workers. While the Commonwealth supplied about the same proportion of workers, 30 to 40 per cent, as it did of all immigrants, over half of the professionals in each year came from Commonwealth countries. There were important differences among the major source countries in the percentage of professionals among immigrant workers as Table 3.4 shows. Differentials such as these certainly influenced the re-shaping of ideas about immigration which took place in the 1960s.

TABLE 3.4. Major source countries 1962–7: percentage of professionals among immigrants to Canada intending to work

USA	43
Britain	29
Germany	12
Italy	3
Greece	3
Portugal	3

The small inflow of trained domestic servants from the West Indies originated in arrangements begun in 1955 with certain West Indian governments to select and train a few persons locally with the object of their immigrating to Canada to work as domestic servants. Connections with the Caribbean had for long been closer than with other parts of the Empire except Britain itself. A century before, trade had been active, and in its wake, Canadian banks and a life assurance company opened for business before the turn of the century, and soon after, the first trade agreement was formally concluded. In 1955, then, 75 and 25 persons were to be admitted from Jamaica and Barbados respectively; the numbers soon increased, and Trinidad and British Guiana were added. A total of 280 persons came in 1960; in 1966, the quota was raised to 500. In 1966 a total of over 5500 West Indians immigrated, and the domestic servants quota became a small part of Caribbean immigration. These agreements between Canada and the West Indian governments were an example – unusual on the immigration scene – of co-operation between Commonwealth countries.

At first sight the provincial destination of immigrants does not seem significant in a study of immigration to Canada as a whole. The clue to the policy considerations involved lies in the fact that four-fifths of the population of French stock lived in Quebec Province, and that four-fifths of the Quebec population were of French origin – matters fundamental to Canada's dual culture and the deep-seated emotions which accompany it. People of the French culture were in political command of the second most populous province after Ontario. Was this powerful group indifferent to the fact that the numbers coming from France were tiny, that this was a trend which seemed unlikely to change and that consequently the immigrants who did go to Quebec were largely non-French-speaking? How many immigrants did, in fact, go to Quebec, and who were they?

In 1961, Quebec Province had 29 per cent of the country's population and Ontario 34 per cent, but 24 per cent of immigrants went to Quebec and 51 per cent to Ontario. By 1967 even this large differential had widened a little as Ontario continued to take half of the year's immigrants while Quebec's share fell steadily. In most years from 1962 to 1967, Italians formed the biggest national group of new arrivals in Quebec, followed by French, British, Greeks, Americans and Egyptians; in the later years, numbers of Portuguese, Germans and West Indians joined them. Of all Commonwealth immigrants, only single-figure proportions went to Quebec. Altogether, the province received not only a low proportion of immigrants compared with its size, but also, obviously, rather few persons likely to speak French.

Table 3.2 shows that, in 1967, four times as many immigrants came from Commonwealth countries other than Britain than in 1960, as a result of a reversal of earlier policy which allowed New Commonwealth sources to take a prominent part in Canadian immigration for the first time in history. The Immigration Act in force in 1960 was that of 1952. The Act was an instrument for control and enforcement, but contributed little to immigration policy. It dealt specifically with matters such as the rights of entry of Canadian citizens, examination procedures and deportation orders, but left the important issue of who might be admitted as an immigrant to regulations which were made by the Governor-in-Council, in effect by the Minister. The regulations in force were clear about the countries from which immigrants were admissible, but it was only natural that the startling changes which had recently occurred in the national composition of the newcomers – with Italians heading the list for four years and the British being heavily outnumbered by western and southern Europeans in the post-war period as a whole – should lead to some reconsideration by the policy-makers, even though the subject aroused little interest among the public. It was becoming an issue whether the range of immigrants was wide enough; whether, in fact, Prime Minister King's statement of 1947 that the Canadian people did not wish to make a fundamental alteration in the character of the population was still wholly valid.

The views of the Special Committee of the Senate on Manpower and Employment of 1961 were probably an important factor at this time. 'It is hardly an overstatement to say that a high level of employment is a goal deserving of the utmost priority' were among the first words of its report. Growing unemployment was 'of major concern both from the standpoint of lost human opportunities and lost production'; the growth in output of the economy had failed to match population growth, and the resulting unemployment was particularly heavy among young people, the unskilled and the inadequately educated. Whether by coincidence or not, the Committee's emphasis on skills and training and its complementary concern for unemployment among the unskilled and poorly educated was accurately reflected in the immigration practice of the 1960s. Linked to this issue was the sponsorship principle. Introduced in the 1920s, sponsorship was a sign of Canada's concern for the reunification of families; it assumes that an immigrant will settle down better – as well as be assisted in case of need – if he has close relatives who will sponsor him. The qualifications required of an independent immigrant, who, without family support, has to fend entirely for himself, are therefore relaxed for a sponsored immigrant. In the early 1950s nearly a third of all immigrants were sponsored, and as this proportion grew still further, it was seen that such immigrants did not necessarily match up with labour force requirements. Moreover they were numerous enough to hold up the processing of independent applicants who did meet these needs. In 1959 more than half of all immigrants were sponsored, and, after allowing for wives and other non-workers among the remainder, the numbers admitted to accord with the economic needs of the country were small. Although the proportion of sponsored immigrants fell after 1959, it was still 33 per cent in 1967, so the issue continued to be of concern. Indeed, the Minister was obliged to report to the Parliamentary Committee of 1966 that, in the previous year, unskilled immigrants represented some 40 per cent of the total.

Mention must be made here of an inflow of long standing, which probably exerted more influence on attitudes to immigration than its numbers would ever suggest. It was noted above that, in 1961, more immigrants resident in Canada had been born in China than in France. As the census found five and a half million people of French, but only 58,000 of Chinese, ethnic origin, it might be thought that the immigration of Chinese was a very recent occurrence. On the contrary, Chinese first arrived in the 1870s, and numbered 27,000 in 1911. Their reception was unhappy, and in 1885, the federal legislature, at the instigation of the British Columbia government, acted 'to restrict and regulate Chinese immigration' and imposed a head tax of $50 on each adult Chinese resident, a sum which had become $500 by 1905. In 1923, the Chinese Immigration Act virtually ended further immigration, and it was not until after the Second World War that the Act was repealed. In recent years the subject has been of interest for different reasons. Illegal immigration of Chinese from Hong Kong was on such a scale that in 1960 the government introduced the Chinese Adjustment Statement Programme which gave Chinese who had immigrated illegally the opportunity to declare the facts, and then in most cases be allowed to stay. From the 1880s until recently the topic of Chinese immigration was an uncomfortable one, as, first, the inflow was severely restricted in discriminatory fashion, and then an intake which had got out of hand was regularised after the event because no better solution to the problem could be found.

In February 1962 new Immigration Regulations were brought into force, section 31 of which permitted entry to anyone 'who by reason of his education, training, skills or other special qualifications is likely to be able to establish himself successfully in Canada', provided that he could maintain himself temporarily or had prior arrangements made for him. This signalled the end of discrimination on the grounds of race or national origin since such a change, once made, could never be reversed in the political atmosphere of the day. Being a regulation, the new provision received no prior sanction from Parliament. It aroused a minimum of either acclaim or criticism.

It appears that to most people, including Members of Parliament, the new regulation came as a surprise. Two years previously the Commonwealth had, exceptionally, been mentioned in Parliament in the context of immigration when a Member, noting that the Minister in a speech had extended a general invitation to United States citizens to emigrate to Canada, asked if the invitation was extended to all citizens of the Commonwealth too. When the Minister replied that the door was always open to qualified immigrants from the Commonwealth, he pressed his point by asking if that meant all citizens of the Commonwealth, and received the answer 'Qualified to enter'; in other words, the *status quo* as regards national origins remained, and at that time the concept of the Commonwealth was of little, if any, significance. In the supply debate of the same year, the Minister stated the views of the government on immigration: Canada needed immigrants in a steady flow, and had 'a responsibility to admit newcomers in accordance with our ability to provide opportunities for them'. Of course Canada would continue to choose from among available applicants those who would be most suitable to life in Canada; the key to the policy would be proper selection standards designed to bring the best possible immigrants to Canada. This prompted the next speaker, a former Minister of Immigration, to suggest that the present Minister might well have read out Prime Minister King's 1947 statement, since what she said did not deviate from it in any single particular that he could discover. In February 1961, twelve months before the 1962 regulations went into effect, the Minister told the House that the outline of policy she had given a year before was still valid, adding 'traditionally we look to the United Kingdom to supply a larger number of immigrants annually than we usually receive from any other country'. Nothing in the supply debate, the principal discussion of the subject in the year, gave any hint that a radical change in policy was imminent; nor was any such suggestion made at other times, despite mild hints from individual Members. One urged the removal of racial discrimination and another wanted a quota system, so that Canada could receive some immigrants from all countries, including those of the British Commonwealth. From one or two Members the hints were very restrained indeed, Mr Lester Pearson saying, for example, that the value of the agreements with India, Pakistan and Ceylon was not so much in the numbers concerned but in the point that they removed the feeling of discrimination that had existed before, because they put Canadians going to those countries on the same basis as nationals of those countries coming to Canada; and the former Minister, in urging an extension of the West Indian quota, said: 'I am not suggesting any large-scale immigration. I do not think the West Indian community in Canada or anyone else really wants to see mass immigration.' What seems surprising now is, first, that a stronger lead in abolishing discrimination by country of origin was not given in Parliament, since objection to it obviously existed and second, that the government gave no indication in advance that it was considering, let alone about to introduce, such a revolutionary change.

The announcement of the new regulation was undramatic. Made by the Minister in Parliament on 19 January 1962, it gave 1 February as the effective date. In a brief explanation of the new provisions, she said of the vital section 31: 'This means that any suitably-qualified person from any part of the world can be considered for immigration to Canada entirely on his own merits, without regard to his race, colour, national origin or the country from which he comes.' The chief beneficiaries, she continued, would be Asians, Africans, and nationals of the Middle East countries. She hoped that the new regulations would commend themselves to all Members of Parliament regardless of party, to all Canadians, and to prospective immigrants round the world. The Minister made no attempt to explain the reasons behind the changes, even though they ran contrary to age-long tradition and the deliberate practice of many decades. Even more surprising, in retrospect at least, was the immediate reaction – one which must have disappointed the Minister's hope that the regulations would commend themselves to all Members; the next speaker, the former Minister quoted earlier, noting the claim that section 31 abolished discrimination, commented: 'Of course, it does nothing of the sort. It substitutes one set of criteria for discrimination for another.'

Immediate reports in the press were, if anything, even more surprising, one newspaper recording that the new regulations shied away from opening the gates to increased immigration and left a subtle preference for immigrants from Europe and the western hemisphere, maintaining the long-standing barriers against Chinese, Japanese and other non-white persons.[2] If this statement is difficult to understand in view of the wording of section 31, it could perhaps have been inspired by remarks made by the Minister herself to a press conference, at which she was reported to have said 'we haven't opened up all the way . . . it's on a basis of maintaining special provisions for those countries which have traditionally supplied most of our immigrants'. A further remark reported – that for the time being there would be no change in the quotas on immigrants from India, Pakistan and Ceylon, but that nevertheless any qualified immigrant from those countries would be able to apply for admission regardless of the quotas if he could meet the new tests of skill, training and education – now appears ambivalent, and read together with a further reported remark that she did not think that the new regulations would change Canada's immigration pattern, leads to an impression that the pool of skilled, trained and educated people in the countries mentioned, and indeed in many others, had been underestimated. The more considered comment made over the next few days varied in tone, the *Ottawa Journal* remarking that it was true that the opportunity for immigration had broadened, but that in fact one form of discrimination had been substituted for another, because most would-be citizens from the tropical countries would continue to have difficulty in meeting Canadian standards; another, on the other hand, stressed the progress made in eliminating discrimination through the revised policy which ensured that everyone should have an equal chance of entering Canada and then an equal chance to succeed. The last comment, one must think, had a firmer foundation in section 31 than in the Minister's reported remark that it was on a basis of maintaining special provisions for those countries that had traditionally supplied most of Canada's immigrants.

What prompted the 1962 regulations, by which Canada led the way among the three great countries of immigration by several years in abolishing discrimination in the selection of immigrants on the grounds of country of origin? There may have been unofficial criticisms of the old policy from interested countries; if there were formal *démarches*, no record of them is available yet, and enquiry suggests that probably none were made. Minor pressures existed within Canada, we know, but in Parliament at least they were minor indeed. Consultation with the United States, which was shortly to follow the Canadian lead, is said to have played no part. To find the key to the mystery, it seems necessary to look outside the relevant department to the Prime Minister of the time, Mr John Diefenbaker, who had held that office for four and a half years when the 1962 regulations were tabled. Mr Diefenbaker has told the writer that it has been his life-long view that colour discrimination is the world's greatest problem. In his memoirs, he expands on this remark by stressing that the Commonwealth's most pressing problem, at the time of his assumption of office as Prime Minister, was the need to make that organisation colour-blind. He continually stressed in speeches and at conferences the need to subscribe to the principle of non-discrimination between human beings on the grounds of race or colour.[3] Mr Diefenbaker had, when in opposition, striven for a Canadian Bill of Rights. When such a Bill eventually received assent during his government, in 1960, it included the words: 'It is hereby recognised and declared that in Canada there have existed and shall continue to exist without discrimination by reason of race, national origin, colour, religion or sex the following human rights and fundamental freedoms . . . .' Today, the document is on display in the library of Parliament and is pointed out to every visitor by the guide. At the beginning of the 1960s, it would have been illogical for a Prime Minister who had successfully battled over many years for such a Bill not to have changed immigration policy in the way that section 31 of the new regulations did. In retrospect, it may be thought that Mr Diefenbaker acted in advance of the opinion of the public, of the House of Commons, even of his own Minister responsible for immigration; fifteen years later, it is hard to find any one concerned with immigration policy, in or out of Parliament, who does not support his convictions as a matter of course.

In further parliamentary comment, the essential importance of the change continued to be overlooked, or at least to evade comment. Some of the comment was probably fair party politicising – one Member protested against passing such an important measure by regulation at all – 'I point out that this is legislation by ministerial regulations – there is nothing more undemocratic.' Another Member indeed emphasised the importance of the new regulations – by quoting from a newspaper, which had stated 'The greatest change in immigration policy since Mackenzie King announced the resumption of immigration in 1947 has gone into effect without approval or even debate in parliament', but other comment suggested that the real significance of section 31 was not generally grasped. Some examples follow.

A Member who often joined in the generally scanty discussion of immigration said that the new regulations could only keep people out, and 'the very thought of the grading of applicants for admission to Canada as cattle are graded for exhibition will not encourage anyone to seek entry to our country'; it was a hypocritical statement that racial discrimination had been eliminated. Another Member enquired if the agreements with India, Pakistan and Ceylon could be cancelled so as to remove the restrictions on numbers from those countries, and drew from the Minister this reply 'In cases where we do have agreements we may try to increase the numbers of immigrants we receive from those countries in addition to the quota which has been established'. Yet, one may think, the very existence of the agreements was contrary to the intention of the new section 31. To readers of today, some of the contemporary comment seems, perhaps, uninformed; for instance, any selection means discrimination of a kind – of course, not racial discrimination – so objection to any form at all of selection would seem to imply that any number of would-be immigrants should be accepted. If the Members who objected to the new selection criteria on the grounds that they were a new form of discrimination really intended that to happen, one must conclude either that they had not understood section 31, or that they failed to recognise the risk of Canada being swamped by immigrants from all over the world, many of them with little or no education. As for the accusation of hypocrisy, section 31 was unequivocal, and it was hardly the Minister's fault if it was not read correctly; it was revolutionary, but far from hypocritical. It is true that the regulations left one vestige of national discrimination, relating to the admission of certain sponsored relatives; if it were this to which the Member referred, he failed to say so, or, better, to suggest how it might be rectified. Then one must wonder, further, how it came about that by March 1964, twenty-five months after the new regulations became effective, the Minister appeared able to adhere to the quotas for India, Pakistan and Ceylon by saying 'we may try to increase the numbers of immigrants we receive from those countries in addition to the quota'; today it seems that the agreements and the concept of the new section 31 were entirely incompatible, and that of the two it was unquestionably the agreements which had to give way. A lack of clarity concerning not only the implications but even the facts of the 1962 regulations was probably linked to the long time which it took for the regulations to have much effect on the immigration flow.

Although selection of unsponsored immigrants was now based on education and skills and not on origin, the new policy seemed to have little effect up to 1966. It could well have led to a much higher intake from the West Indies with its already established flow; Hong Kong, from which there had been illegal immigration for years; and from India, a source of many of the skills needed in Canada. However, the state of the Canadian economy was uncertain in the years following 1962, so a firm preference was still given to professionals and skilled workers, of whom many developing countries were themselves short; and it seems possible that if the Minister was still proclaiming in 1964 that immigrants from certain European countries were best suited to industrial development, immigration officers outside Europe and the United States may have been uncertain about how diligently to apply the new policy. Even so, within the greatly increased numbers entering in the years 1963–6, significant, if small, increases from certain countries did occur: 737 to 2233 persons from India; 2354 to 3935 from the West Indies; and 338 to 1434 from Hong Kong (birthplace). By the following year, 1967, the increases had become marked, even in the context of the biggest total intake for fifty years – 4000 persons from India, over 8000 from the West Indies, 6400 from Hong Kong and China and 3000 from the Philippines. In 1961, the final year of the old policy, only 2800 persons, or 4 per cent of all immigrants, came from Asia (including the preferred countries of Israel, Lebanon and Turkey) and 1090 from Africa (including the preferred country of Egypt and the 'Old Commonwealth' country of South Africa); by 1967 these numbers had risen to 21,000, or 9 per cent, from Asia and 4600 from Africa. In Asia, the chief contributors to the increase were Commonwealth members – India and Hong Kong. All these changes, together with growing numbers from Britain itself, resulted in 40 per cent of all immigrants coming from Commonwealth countries in 1966/7. As the total intake from the Commonwealth increased sharply Britain's share in it fell – naturally, as it was not affected by the change in Canada's policy, while the New Commonwealth countries were. In 1967 the UK share fell to 70 per cent of all Commonwealth immigration from 80 per cent in the previous year; and it went on to decrease much more in succeeding years. Despite these changes, the new immigration aroused little public interest.

As an immigrant was required to obtain his entry visa before reaching Canada, the facilities that Canada provided abroad for obtaining it formed an important factor in immigration practice. The existence of a visa office of the Canadian immigration service was necessary to make sizeable immigration from any particular country feasible. Consequently the siting of the visa offices is a matter of interest. Up to 1962, they were mostly to be found, naturally, in the preferred countries. The existence of an office in a particular country signified both a Canadian interest in immigration from that country and local interest in emigration to Canada. Table 3.5 shows how many offices were open and where they were, regionally, in 1961 and 1967. The offices newly opened between 1962 and 1967 were in the following countries: Europe – two in France, one each in Britain, Italy, Portugal and Spain; Asia and the Middle East – one each in Japan, Lebanon, Pakistan and the Philippines; North Africa – Egypt; West Indies – one each in

Jamaica and Trinidad; and one in Australia. One European office, in Oslo, was closed in the period. It was a clear indication of current trends that of fourteen new offices, no more than four were situated in the traditional source countries. Yet large parts of the world were still uncovered by the direct services of an immigration office – for example the whole of South America – and the practical difficulties of filling all the gaps was one reason why the 1962 regulations were not seen to have much immediate effect.

TABLE 3.5.   Number of Canadian Immigration Visa Offices, 1961 and 1967

	1961	1967
United Kingdom	6	7
Northern Europe	15	15
South and East Europe	3	7
Europe	24	29
Asia and Middle East	3	7
North Africa	—	1
Australasia	—	1
West Indies	—	2
	27	40

Despite a new immigration policy in 1962, apparently unrelated issues led to a further reconsideration of the immigration scene in the form of a White Paper in 1966, followed by a Special Joint Committee of the Senate and House of Commons which sat later that year. Among those issues, according to the Green Paper,[4] were high unemployment, particularly of unskilled and under-educated workers, the changing pattern of skills required and a consequent need for workers ready and able to be trained in them, the large volume of sponsored immigration, and the embarrassment of visitors seeking to become immigrants.

The White Paper, 'Canadian Immigration Policy', argued that in the new technology many people would need to master more than one occupation, so the productive worker would be the one with the education or training to learn new skills and profit from new opportunities. It was necessary to look again at the system by which a skilled person was permitted entry on his merits, and once admitted, to sponsor poorly educated or unskilled relatives, who could in due course sponsor their own unskilled relatives – and so on. To overcome this problem, a new class of 'nominated' relative was proposed – someone part way between sponsored and independent. In general, it was thought that

Canada would need as many immigrants as the country was likely to attract in the foreseeable future. The White Paper was not only expansionist but also non-discriminatory, the Minister said on introducing it in Parliament; it did not mean that geography would make no difference at all to people's chances in practice of coming to Canada, but in principle there would be no discrimination. The White Paper concentrated on current problems, at the expense, perhaps, of the long-term issues, and was not a document to arouse deep interest or lively discussion.

To the Special Joint Committee which began work a month after the White Paper appeared, the Minister emphasised the desirability of a closer relationship between immigration and economic, social and humanitarian considerations, the need for up-graded skills and for greater productivity in the labour force, and the expansionist, non-discriminatory, nature of all the Government's proposals. The problem of sponsored immigrants took up much of the committee's attention, and drew representations from the Minister of Industry and Commerce of Manitoba, which are of interest today when 'Canada appears largely to have overcome any *general* shortage of professional and highly-trained people'.[5] Manitoba had a relatively high requirement for unskilled and semi-skilled workers, and while official policy might be non-discriminatory in terms of geography and race, it did discriminate against the kinds of people Manitoba needed – not only highly skilled people, but those able and willing to undertake the jobs requiring lesser skills. Throughout, the committee took the policy of non-discrimination by country or race for granted; its origins were not discussed or questioned, and its possible implications went virtually unmentioned.

This deliberation resulted in new Immigration Regulations in 1967. They contained two important provisions. The first refined the procedure of seeking skills and training by setting out a system of points to be awarded by the immigration officer overseas in the case of independent applicants, under the following nine headings: education and training, personal qualities, occupational demand, occupational skill, arranged employment or occupation designated as in short supply in particular areas of Canada, knowledge of English and French, having a relative in Canada, and the destination proposed. Up to 20 points out of 100 could be obtained for education and training, and a minimum of 50 altogether was required to qualify. Occupational demand would be notified to visa officers at intervals from Ottawa; so would the designated occupations; so would the demand for labour in particular areas which affected the destination factor; at ages over 45, credit for age ceased. Guidelines for assessing the other factors would be issued to immigration posts. The second important provision was designed, in accordance with the White Paper's proposals, to reduce the numbers of sponsored immigrants with their exemption from the normal immigrant requirements: this class was now to be limited to close dependent relatives, and a new class, termed 'nominated' relatives, was to include the others – sons and daughters of 21 and over, brothers, sisters, etc. – and would be subject to most, although not to all, of the criteria now assessed by points and applied to independent applicants, including those of education and training, occupational demand and occupational skill. This was the government's solution to the problem of balancing the needs of the labour market and the claims of family relationship. It would not affect either the independent application or the close, dependent relative, but it aimed at ensuring that other relatives fitted into the economic scene almost as well as independent applicants. The new provision probably resulted primarily from the numbers of sponsored immigrants coming from the countries of non-traditional preference – at one point, the Green Paper mentions in this context 'an increase in sponsored relatives from southern Europe' – but it would also be a major factor in the future pattern of immigration from the new source countries, where equally strong family ties and equal pressure to emigrate existed, and where the population was, in some cases, far larger than Canada's.

The period 1960–7 was, all in all, a very exciting one in Canada's immigration history. Not only were there large numbers of immigrants, including the seventh highest annual total since records began 110 years earlier and the second highest for over 50 years, but the period saw a new approach to immigration, which could well change the composition of the population in time.

THE PERIOD 1968–75

After the huge total intake of 1967, the numbers of immigrants continued to fluctuate again, but at a generally higher level than earlier – an average of 166,000 against 127,000 annually from 1960 to 1967. The variations from year to year were again wide, the total in 1971 being, for instance, little more than half of that in 1967, while only three years later it was almost at the 1967 level again. Over the same years, immigration into the United States also was at a high level, but with far smaller variations; in Australia, on the other hand, numbers rose from 1961 to a peak in 1970 and then fell away again – almost the reverse of the Canadian pattern, at least in the later years. As in 1960–7, immigration into Canada continued apparently to be subject to factors that did not affect flows into Australia, or, to a lesser degree, the United States, in the same way. Canada's own 'tap-on, tap-off' policy, mentioned earlier, was certainly one. However, as the Green Paper points out, changes in the immigration movement were not all due to domestic causes. In the previous six years, that is 1968–73, the following four factors are cited in the Green Paper as having had a significant effect on both the size and composition of the immigrant movement: the Czechoslovakia and Uganda refugee movements, the job opportunities provided by the European Economic Community countries to Europeans who might have emigrated to Canada, the acceptance of thousands of persons who might not normally have been admitted but who exploited loopholes in the immigration law, and two special programmes which accepted, in similar fashion, large numbers of persons who arrived as visitors and sought immigrant status while actually in Canada.[6] The present writer suggests that a further factor was of fundamental importance – and, moreover, will continue to be so in the future, while three of those mentioned by the Green Paper were clearly of limited duration. One of the Green Paper's four factors, the inflow of Europeans seems, on examination of the figures, to have been less important than might have been supposed, judging by the totals of immigrants from Europe, for example – 83,000 in 1960, 81,000 in 1964, 52,000 in 1971 and 89,000 in 1974. To identify the additional factor, it is necessary to examine the composition of the immigrant movement, distinguishing the traditional sources from the new sources. In Table 3.6 Europe as a whole and the United States are listed separately for a reason which will become apparent later, but together they may be regarded as the traditional sources in this context; 'Other regions' include Asia, the West Indies and other non-traditional sources from which sizable immigration first became feasible in 1962. Several points may be observed in Table 3.6. First, the composition of the inflow up to 1960 was generally traditional. Second, different trends may be observed in the numbers coming year by year from the three different source areas; none of the trends was linked to the others; and only numbers from Europe followed, to any noticeable extent, the pattern of the annual totals. Third, the pattern of percentages, year by year, was different again – and unequivocal; in it may be found the important missing factor that helped to determine the annual totals. Some explanation of the second and third points follows.

The influences that lay behind the numbers coming in from Europe

TABLE 3.6. Immigrants into Canada by areas of origin 1968–76

	All immigrants	Immigrants from			% of Immigrants from		
		Europe	USA	Other regions	Europe	USA	Other regions
1946–60	2005230	1723685	145125	136420	86.0	7.2	6.8
1960	104111	82610	11247	10254	79.3	10.8	9.8
1968	183974	120702	20422	42850	65.6	11.1	23.3
1969	161531	88432	22785	50314	54.7	14.1	31.1
1970	147713	75609	24424	47680	51.2	16.5	32.3
1971	121900	52032	24366	45502	42.7	20.0	37.3
1972	122006	51293	22618	48095	42.0	18.5	39.4
1973	184200	71883	25242	87075	39.0	13.7	47.3
1974	218465	88694	26541	103230	40.6	12.1	47.3
1975	187881	72898	20155	94828	38.8	10.7	50.5
1976	149429	49908	17315	82206	33.3	11.5	55.1

were recognisable, were usually to be foreseen, and were effectively made subject to some control by Canada, notably through the use of the 'tap-on, tap-off' process. Probably the most important influence was the state of Canada's economy – as was seen by a medical officer at Canada House, London, who concluded that the numbers of medical examinations taken by prospective immigrants, that is by obviously serious applicants, varied over a ten-year period in accordance with the levels of unemployment in Canada a few months before – not with levels of unemployment in England.[7]

From the United States, however, the flow pattern and background factors were different. Numbers increased regularly from 1960 to 1974, quite contrary to the pattern of arrivals from Europe, and were characterised by large proportions of professionals and small proportions of sponsored and nominated immigrants. They were popularly associated to some extent at least with dissatisfaction with American foreign policy and with its Vietnam policy in particular. Moreover, immigration from the United States was far easier than from, say, Italy, both physically and psychologically. A peak of over 26,000 persons was reached in 1974; in 1975, however, there was a marked drop, the reason for which is not yet clear; it was repeated in 1976.

The third stream, 'Other regions', is mainly from Asia, the West Indies and Africa. It grew steadily year by year, being 10 per cent of the total intake in 1960, almost a quarter by 1968, and over a half in 1975. Most of the countries contributing to this stream were those from which immigration was first sanctioned by the 1962 regulations. Of course, only a small minority of the populations of the new source countries qualified for entry to Canada on any of the standards set since 1962. Nevertheless in absolute numbers the potential was considerable. This seems to explain adequately the ninefold increase from 'Other regions' sources since 1960. It was the major influence in the high overall level of immigration from 1968 on, the steady increase of immigrants from new source countries outweighing the continuing annual fluctuations in the numbers from Europe.

In 1971/2 the United States was first on the list of source countries, but in all other years since 1961 Britain continued to provide more immigrants annually than any other single country. But for the other Commonwealth countries a quite different pattern emerged. The year 1968 was the last in which Britain provided more than half of the Commonwealth total. Between 1960 and 1967 three-quarters of all Commonwealth immigrants came from Britain, as Table 3.2 showed; from 1968 to 1976 that figure dropped to an average of 43 per cent, and in the final year was no more than 33 per cent. In the days when immigrants still came primarily from the traditional sources (including all of Europe), the proportion from Britain generally rose as the overall total rose, probably because promotional activity was usually more energetic there than elsewhere, and because British immigrants comprised larger proportions of non-sponsored immigrants. However, the similarity of trends in British and overall immigration would logically become weaker as total numbers came to depend more and more on inflows from developing countries.

Many of the increasing numbers from 'Other regions' listed in Table 3.6 came from Commonwealth countries. Consequently the trends in the annual intake from Commonwealth countries other than Britain were quite different from the long-established, more stable, movement from Britain itself. Within the Commonwealth, figures for Asian and West Indian groups of countries are shown separately in Table 3.7 because they supplied the bulk of the Commonwealth total. The most important other Commonwealth sources were Guyana, Fiji, Tanzania, Kenya and Australia. A majority of immigrants from the less developed countries came from states which are members of the Commonwealth – about 60 per cent in 1975, for instance. Moreover entry from some non-Commonwealth countries in the developing world, notably the Philippines, South Korea and Vietnam, also increased. Where motivation to immigrate into Canada was concerned, little distinguished the Commonwealth from the non-Commonwealth developing countries; where there may have been a differential was, rather, in the opportunity of reaching Canadian immigration offices.

TABLE 3.7. Immigrants to Canada from the Commonwealth and from Non-Commonwealth countries 1968–76

| | All Countries | Immigrants from Commonwealth | | | | | Non-Commonwealth Countries |
		Total	UK	Asia	West Indies	Other Commonwealth	
1968	183974	65136	37889	12314	7563	7370	118838
1969	161534	68096	31977	14851	13093	8175	93438
1970	147713	59840	26497	12224	12456	8663	87873
1971	121900	45397	15451	11508	10843	7595	76503
1972	122006	51457	18197	12776	8233	12251	70549
1973	184200	87148	26973	28029	17178	14968	97052
1974	218465	101461	38456	30620	18870	13515	117004
1975	187881	90793	34978	26118	14350	15347	97088
1976	149429	64753	21548	21398	11592	10215	84676

Due to the division in 1967 of the old sponsored class into sponsored and nominated, the proportion of immigrants exempted from any selection criteria at all fell from 30–40 per cent in the early 1960s to a range of 21–27 per cent after 1967. Their numbers remained quite steady year by year, not fluctuating with the annual total intakes, but being governed, presumably, by the number of immigrants who had arrived in earlier years and now felt settled enough to bring their close relatives to join them. Numbers in the new class of nominated relatives varied very much as the annual totals did – naturally, since they were subject to most of the selection criteria spelt out in the points system. The result of these two trends combined was a general reduction in the proportions of independent immigrants, so much so that in 1971 and 1972 it actually dropped below 50 per cent. Great differentials between countries of origin existed according to data for 1967–73 included in the Green Paper,[8] and their pattern was unequivocal; inflows from the Western European countries and the United States and Australasia contained high proportions of independents; from southern Europe the proportion was small; from the new source countries it was high to begin with, but then fell rapidly to southern European levels. In the long term, therefore, a clear differential is found between western Europe, the United States and Australasia on the one hand and virtually all other countries on the other. Some examples are Britain 87 to 64 per cent independent in different years between 1968 and 1973; Portugal 27 to 4 per cent; India 62 to 29 per cent. Pakistan provides a good example of how the figures from a new source country progressed: in 1967 the percentage of independents was 65; in 1968, 48 per cent; in 1971, 34 per cent; in 1972, 29 per cent. Whether or not such proportions of independent immigrants formed a satisfactory outcome to the measure introduced in 1967 to reduce the numbers of sponsored relatives was obviously a question for consideration by the policy-makers.

Mention was made earlier of ambiguities in the data on country of origin because an individual's last permanent residence may differ from his country of birth. From 1968 on Britain became more important as a staging post as about one in ten persons immigrating from Britain had been born elsewhere. On the other hand, many more persons born in the new source countries were coming to Canada directly from those countries – for instance, in 1963–7 only two-thirds of Indian immigrants came direct from India, but from 1968 to 1973 nearly 80 per cent. Two apparently contradictory influences may be seen here: a trend to more second stage migration and the development of large migrant flows direct from the new source countries in addition to the continuing, far smaller, flows of Indians to Canada via Britain.

As in the former period, 51 per cent of immigrants intended to work – a proportion which remained remarkably steady from year to year regardless of the fluctuations in total numbers and their varying composition. Among immigrants from the Commonwealth as a whole, the percentage was a point higher; from individual Commonwealth countries or areas, the proportions again varied considerably, but the variations were becoming less marked; for example the very high proportions of workers in the flows from Australia and the West Indies fell and the extremely low proportions from Hong Kong rose. Small percentages such as 43 from Asia and 42 from Africa were probably due in part to unfamiliarity among women from those continents with the concept of 'going out to work'. About half of the arrivals from Britain intended to work. If the British intake remains steady or falls while that of Asians and Africans continues to rise, the overall proportion of intending workers is likely to fall.

The other major factor in the immigrant workforce – that of occupational skills – underwent a very marked change. First, the proportion of the skilled in all immigrant workers fell from 74 per cent in 1966 to 51 per cent in 1973.[9] The definition of 'skilled' is that of the Immigration Department, signifying from five to ten points out of a maximum of ten for occupational skill in the points system described earlier; to end many years of effort to obtain skilled immigrants with such a remarkable decrease seems bound to have led to reflection within the department. At the same time the proportion of professionals among working immigrants increased from 23 per cent in 1960–7 to 27 per cent after 1967. Again, the Commonwealth as a whole provided a slightly greater proportion of professionals, and Britain markedly more – 33 per cent of all workers. Among other Commonwealth countries except Australia, however, the proportions of professionals fell from the early 1960s on. For example, between 1963 and 1967 professionals were 63 per cent of all immigrant workers from India; in 1968–73 that figure fell to 39 per cent, and in 1974 it was actually 17 per cent! The Green Paper specifically associates the decline in skills with the new nominated class, 'members of which generally have been less skilled'. It points out that the movement of nominated immigrants has tended to be less responsive to swings in occupational demand. Accordingly during periods of lower economic activity the proportion of nominated immigrants has tended to increase. From 1968 to 1973, 29 per cent of nominated workers were classified as skilled, compared with 41 per cent of sponsored, and 72 per cent of independent working immigrants. According to the Green

Paper, it was reconciling two immigration imperatives – respect for the family unit and response to domestic manpower demands – that was the problem.[10] It is arguable that a third imperative, non-discrimination, arrived on the scene in 1962 and may not have been accorded the share it deserved in the reconciliation process.

A further decrease in the proportions of immigrants going to Quebec Province has set the background to a change of heart in the province over immigration. Although 28 per cent of Canada's population lived in Quebec in 1971, no more than 16 per cent of that year's immigrants intended to settle there, and that figure was itself part of a clear downward trend. In the 1960s, the birth rate also fell, and in 1971 Quebec's gross reproduction rate was 0.913 – less than replacement level. Not only did the long-term future of Quebec's population seem in jeopardy, but, worse, the French culture in particular was threatened on two fronts. First, not many French-speakers came to Canada. Few data on this point have been published, but from 1964 to 1975 it is known that less than 10 per cent of all immigrants spoke French. Even among immigrants to Quebec, only 30–37 per cent spoke French – about the same proportion as spoke neither French nor English. Not only did English-speakers outnumber French-speakers going to Quebec in every year for which data are available, but – and this is the second factor – a 'distinct tendency of immigrants to become assimilated with the anglophone rather than the francophone community', to use the Green Paper's words, was generally observed. According to one authority, about 95 per cent of those who are not of British or French origin adopt English as their home language.[11] For long, Quebec's attitude to immigration was either indifferent or hostile. Then, Members of Parliament began to refer to the danger facing the French culture: one, in 1964, thought that the Federal Government should see that the proportion of the French entity in Canada was maintained, and because 'it is very difficult to make a Frenchman leave his own country', immigrants should be brought in from northern Italy, with which the French entity had a considerable cultural affinity. The Federal Minister went to France in 1966 and agreed with officials there that 'further attempts should be made to increase the proportion of French immigrants coming to Canada'. The province itself then took action. A Ministry of Immigration was set up in 1968, a foreign service created a year later, and an agreement with the Federal Government in 1971 gave the province the right to post an orientation officer and an interpreter in federal immigration offices. In 1975, Quebec gained the right to see and give views on the applications of all prospective immigrants destined for the province. To encourage a proportionately greater intake in Quebec will be a hard task, and might conflict with the interests of other provinces which are less concerned with encouraging immigration. Henripin has no doubt that the relative significance of both the French and other language (i.e. neither English nor French) groups will decrease, and sees no prospect of halting the decline.

The years immediately following 1967 were a time of consolidation as the new regulations were put into practice, the network of Canadian immigration services spread further and further afield, and the inflow of immigrants continued in the new patterns described earlier. Parliamentary discussion of the subject was minimal. By 1969 some reaction to the broadened base of immigration was apparent, the Minister pointing out to the Commons in December that applications were down in Europe and up in Asia and the Caribbean. On the same day, a Member expressed his view that while race and colour were not grounds for judging the suitability of immigrants, it was legitimate to criticise a policy which 'concentrates on immigrants who by reason of climatic conditions in their country of origin and by reason of their standards of skill and training inevitably pose great problems for everyone concerned with their relocation in a radically different, highly sophisticated, industrialised urban society such as ours'. Fourteen months later, two of the few parliamentary references to the Commonwealth in the context of immigration were made, one in the form of an appeal by a Member that the Commonwealth Caribbean should be given a special place in foreign policy, and the other proposing a pilot project for bringing in a certain number of West Indians not up to Canada's strict immigration requirements, whom Canada would then provide with education and training. Nothing came of the proposal.

In 1973 the Minister announced to Parliament that, as a first stage in a review of immigration policy, he had appointed a small group to identify all the options open for the future, that he was inviting the advice of the provincial governments and over a hundred organisations, and that the results of this stage and of some special studies to be made would be a Green Paper, which should provoke further national discussion. In welcoming the Minister's statement, a Member wanted the goal to be an up-to-date policy based not on race, colour, sex or national origin, but on the ability of the immigrant.

The promised Green Paper on immigration appeared in 1974. 'From the outset, the approach to this review has emphasised the value of public discussion and the desirability of obtaining the widest possible cross-section of opinion' the preface states – entirely in contrast to the approach to the 1962 regulations, which included neither discussion among the public nor in Parliament. The Minister had invited national organisations and Canadians generally to submit whatever comments they might wish to offer. Briefs and letters submitted in response to this invitation together with exchanges with the governments of the provinces and the views of consultants had been studied, and within the department a team of officials had worked on preparing a series of discussion documents – the Green Paper. The Paper appeared in four parts entitled 'Immigration Policy Perspectives', 'The Immigration Programme', 'Immigration and Population Statistics' and 'Three Years in Canada'; the last three parts furnished background material, the preface stated, while 'Immigration Policy Perspectives' looked to the future, concentrating on challenges and policy choices in an effort to contribute to public understanding of the problems of forming a policy in a field where the economic, social and cultural interests of the nation intersected. The Paper neither made recommendations nor announced courses of action; rather, it was intended to serve as the basis for informed and constructive debate and to stimulate thinking.

After dealing with broad population considerations, the first part drew attention to the rapid growth of the non-British and non-French elements in the population and to the role that immigration might play in Canada's overall population increases in the future. It then proceeded to what we have seen to be the principal theme of immigration policy for many years – the link with economic policy and economic facts. 'As our ways to measure the present and future demand in Canada for immigrant workers improve, immigration policy must ensure that this capability is fully exploited and applied to the selection process.' General shortages of professional and highly-trained people had disappeared, but shortages persisted in unskilled or semi-skilled occupations; this reinforced the argument for a high degree of selectivity in admitting immigrants. Since the 1966 White Paper had concluded that 'Canada will need as many well-qualified immigrants as it is likely to be able to attract during the foreseeable future', strong forces round the world including high population growth rates, advancing standards of education in the developing countries, and generally higher population mobility in the industrialised countries had combined to give Canada an unprecedented drawing power. This led to the conclusion that 'Canada's appeal as a country of immigration is unlikely in future to call for deliberate stimulus from Canadian policy.' On the domestic front, by contrast, there were reasons connected with the labour market to question the wisdom of an expansionist policy.

The Paper, listing four striking features of the post-1967 immigration movement, namely the change in source countries, the increased proportions of workers found in the sponsored and nominated categories, the downward trend in skills and the accentuation of uneven patterns of settlement, commented that according to a departmental survey, economic, not family, reasons formed the motive to emigrate in the case of most nominated immigrants, and that there might be a case for a sharper distinction between immigrants filling Canada's manpower needs and those joining families. Four options for future policy were set out. They were, first, to retain the present system, which did not include any limitation of numbers; second, to relate immigration even more intensely to economic and labour market needs, drawing a very clear line between persons admitted because the labour market needed them and those accepted for other reasons – meaning, perhaps, the elimination of the nominated category; third, to set explicit targets for immigration annually, either global or regional targets, or even by individual immigration post, amounting to a quota system; fourth, to fix a maximum figure for all immigrants in a particular period and specify priorities for different categories of immigrants within the maximum. None of these options was ideal; however, they indicated the range of possible solutions, 'the merits and difficulties of which Canadians may wish to consider in debating how immigration policy should be fashioned'.

It was, perhaps, the mention of targets and maxima which prompted the press to report an intention to restrict immigration. Some comment was favourable in tone, some was critical. One newspaper thought the Green Paper a 'curiously bland and woolly document' which gave an impression that the Government was trying to say something but just what was not clear; there was a vague feeling that the department was not much in favour of immigrants and the basic attitude was negative.[12] Another thought it legitimate and necessary to stem the flow of immigrants.[13] A third newspaper interpreted the Green Paper as a basis for a more restrictive policy; ostensibly, discussion of it would be open-ended, but in fact it would simply be the prelude to action whose broad shape was already apparent.[14] A fourth saw the Green Paper as meaning one thing: the administration was going to stem the ever-increasing flow of immigrants, and to say that the Paper would allow Canadians to review operations and decide what policy the country would embrace in the next years brought to mind Henry Ford's maxim that one could buy any colour of Ford so long as it was black.[15]

Such comment appeared to overlook the fact that adequate means to control the flow of immigration existed already and that it was not necessary to prepare a Green Paper and call for public debate in order to institute such control. Certainly the total number of immigrants had risen rapidly in the four years before the publication of the Green Paper, but in the five years before that the figures had fallen equally sharply, so that in 1967 and 1974 the totals were almost the same. The emphasis in press comment on limitation and a negative attitude may have prompted some misunderstanding of the purpose behind the Green Paper and some public unease, since talk of restriction led naturally to ideas of discrimination. In March 1975, the Minister took the opportunity of announcing the appointment of a Special Joint Committee on Immigration of the Houses of Parliament to emphasise that the government was not flashing a red light on immigration. By embarking on this whole examination, it was not his intention to slam the door, he said; it had been suggested that Canada might be wise to consider controlled immigration in terms of numbers, but the examination was not a red light, but more a caution light, suggesting that the government should proceed with more policy consideration than previously.

The Special Joint Committee of the Senate and House of Commons on Immigration Policy was set up only a month after the issue of the Green Paper, in March 1975, and was empowered by its terms of reference to invite the views of the public on the issues which the Green Paper raised. It held nearly 50 public hearings in 21 cities, heard over 400 witnesses, and received more than 1400 letters and briefs from other individuals and organisations. Its report was submitted in November 1975.[16] In an appendix, it summarised public attitudes towards immigration policy, noting that a large proportion of the submissions received wanted all immigration, or all non-white immigration, to cease: however, while nearly 90 per cent of individuals' letters wanted tight or total controls on immigration, only a quarter of the briefs from organisations and oral witnesses expressed such opinions – a reflection of the tendency of those favouring stringent restrictions to write a private communication. Further, the committee noted, it was persons who were dissatisfied with the current policy who tended to address the committee, those who were comfortable with it being less likely to register any opinion at all.

Like the 1966 White Paper, the committee concluded that Canada needed immigrants, but its general tone was far less expansionist. The system should be capable of regulating the inflow, and the target must be based on criteria set by Parliament every year and open to public scrutiny. Immigration should be the control variable in a national population policy; the target would be adjusted to achieve an even rate of population growth, while taking changing economic conditions into account. The old assumption that immigrants would automatically balance with the economic capacity to absorb them was false; on the contrary, pressure on Canada to accept immigrants would exceed its capacity to absorb them. The nominated category of immigrant should be eliminated, and since the number of sponsored immigrants in any given annual total could be forecast fairly accurately, it would be possible to set a maximum figure for independent immigrants each year, resulting in a waiting list for the independents, who would be considered on a first-come, first-served basis. Less emphasis in selection should be placed on higher education and more on occupational skill and experience. Priority should be given to applicants contracting to go to a particular area and stay there for two years. Further, the principle that immigration policy should continue to be non-discriminatory on the basis of race, creed, nationality, ethnic origin and sex should be enunciated in the new Act. Nevertheless, the committee agreed that there was justifiable concern with the need to maintain a healthy, thriving French–Canadian presence, and thought that the government might take reasonable initiatives to help realise that objective, for example by encouraging immigration from Latin American countries because people with a Latin cultural background usually integrated easily into French language communities in Canada. The committee's conclusions were comprehensive and carefully explained, and it seems a fitting tribute to its thoroughness that the Minister was later able to report to Parliament that he had adopted some forty of the committee's recommendations.

An economic argument was put forward by the influential Economic Council of Canada that, if economic conditions really were likely to deteriorate over a long period of adjustment to lower birth rates, it might be necessary to view immigration specifically as a means of mitigating the declining rate of natural increase. An individual witness urged the creation of a Canadian population council or demographic commission; a number of others submitted the argument that general demographic policy should be studied before immigration policy, as doing otherwise was putting the cart before the horse. A provincial government gave the pragmatic view that its population should grow at a healthy 2 per cent a year and that a rate of immigration much like the present rate should be maintained to accomplish it. Other organisations went further and recommended rates of growth and eventual target populations, for instance an annual influx of 1 per cent of the population until the total population reached 40 millions. Many submissions were humanitarian in outlook. For example one church organisation urged the government to show that Canada was opting for the value of the person as a whole human being. Other suggestions were that immigration personnel should know the languages and customs of the regions from which large proportions of immigrants came, and Canada's International Development Agency should put more money into training in developing countries and compensate these countries for the loss of some of their professional workers to Canada. Criticism of the Green Paper was frequent; as one organisation said, the Paper viewed immigration as a problem, and, in contrast to the White Paper of 1966, it assumed a protectionist, restrictive attitude. Another organisation thought that the Government's professed policy of non-discrimination was imperilled by the very publication of the Green Paper.

Not everyone welcomed the public debate. An Asian group stated its belief that a government had to lead in many matters, and in immigration policy the opinion of the masses was bound to be one which was not enlightened. Linked to this view, perhaps, was a good deal of unease at the issues raised by the Green Paper concerning the sources of immigration; one organisation submitted, for instance, that the Paper insidiously showed that the recent increase in immigrants from certain Asian and Caribbean countries was larger than that from the traditional European sources and that such a statement appeared contrary to Canada's principle of universality; another thought that the Paper stimulated certain sentiments, mainly racial, which were undesirable in an open society such as Canada's. The Economic Council of Canada, on the other hand, thought that the racial question should be faced: a probably increasing proportion of future settlers would come from Asia, Africa, the Caribbean and Latin America, and many of them would be different from most Canadians in culture and life-style; as many of them should be accepted as could be satisfactorily absorbed. However, if there were a danger of significant conflicts within the indigenous community, the inflow should be tailored to a successful integrative process.

Another constantly recurring theme was that of the French language and culture. The Deputy Minister stated the official view. Quebec had a special position relating to the French language, but recognition of the interests of any province was limited by the fact that an immigrant was admitted to Canada, not a province, and, further, an immigrant was mobile and, after arrival, could easily decide to move. Even so, it was a national objective to recruit French-speaking people for Quebec. He proceeded to the other main aspect of Quebec's problem, the assimilation of immigrants after arrival. About two-thirds of Quebec's immigrants adopted the English language, he said, and if it were desired to maintain the position of the French-speaking people in Quebec, which was the only place in Canada where French had the chance to survive in a significant way, means would have to be found of convincing new migrants to adopt French. The Economic Council of Canada also saw assimilation as an issue: large-scale immigration without greater numbers of French-speakers and without increased integration of third language immigrants into the French-speaking milieu might be deeply resented by French Canadians. 'In the final analysis, the integration of immigrants into the French-speaking community will depend on the attraction exercised by the French language in Canada. This attraction is largely determined by the need to speak the language and the economic and other advantages attached to doing so.' The remark is a quotation from a noteworthy report of earlier years, that of the Royal Commission on Bilingualism and Biculturalism of 1963; to the Economic Council, this particular problem had not changed. Others' views were on different lines and served to illustrate the depth of interest which the topic aroused. Preferential treatment to one special group, the francophone people, would begin a new form of discrimination, one organisation thought; it would lead to other, similar demands, and if people and government sincerely believed in the principle of universality, there was no room for preferential treatment; certainly there was concern that the proportion of French-speaking people was dwindling, but the same could be said for the Anglo–Saxons.

A year after the committee reported, an Immigration Bill to replace the 1952 Act was tabled in the House of Commons. Unlike previous Acts, it stated explicitly the objectives of Canadian immigration law. They were family reunification, non-discrimination on grounds of race, national or ethnic origin, colour, religion or sex, concern for refugees and the promotion of the country's economic, social, cultural and demographic goals. It provided for immigration levels becoming a matter for open decision and public announcement. In the process, the Minister would consult the provinces about regional needs and labour market considerations, and he could consult other persons and organisations if he wished. The points system was retained; the sponsored class, slightly expanded, would become the family class; the nominated class would disappear.

It would be unrealistic to end any review of recent Canadian immigration without indicating the extent of emigration. Rather little is known about it, but its size is certainly important enough to influence policy-making, and its characteristics may be significant in so far as skilled persons migrate more easily than the unskilled. The only data on total emigration are figures such as those taken from part 3 of the Green Paper, followed by a note explaining that the figures for emigrants are a residual obtained by subtracting the population enumerated in the census at the end of the decade from the sum of the population at the beginning of the decade, natural increase and immigration in the intervening years. In the most recent inter-censal period, emigration apparently totalled more than half the amount of immigration. The

	Immigrants	Emigrants	Net Migration
1951–61	1543000	462000	1081000
1961–71	1429000	802000	627000

significance to immigration policy of such a loss by emigration becomes obvious when targets of population growth such as 1 per cent annually or the immigration of 100,000 persons annually, such as were mentioned to the Special Committee, are considered. At the average rate of emigration of the 1960s, it would have needed 228,000 immigrants to produce a net inflow of 100,000 persons.

Well over a century ago, the Governor-General estimated that about 60 per cent of the new arrivals in Canada moved on to the United States. Now immigration to the United States is tabulated by country of last residence, and we know that, between 1961 and 1970, some 413,000 persons immigrated from Canada. In the same period, it is likely that some 130,000 people moved from Canada to the United Kingdom.[17] Little information is available on the destinations of the other 360,000 emigrants, but certainly numbers of immigrants return to their former homes – and sometimes eventually make the further move back to Canada – and it is reasonable to suppose that as means of transport have become easier and the mobility of the individual has become greater, this trend has strengthened.

The onward movement to the United States has already lessened as a result of American restrictions dating from 1968, and as opportunities for onward migration to other countries lessen also, second (or third, or fourth) stage migration will be of less significance to Canada. The return home, on the other hand, may not lessen, unless immigrants from the new source countries show a greater propensity to remain in Canada than their predecessors did. Among persons born in the United Kingdom, for instance, emigration has been on a considerable scale. According to the 1971 census, slightly under 70 per cent of those who had immigrated from 1961 to 1971 then remained in the country, and a calculation that allows for mortality suggests that in the same decade, about 135,000 persons born in the United Kingdom (and who immigrated not only after 1961 but earlier as well) left the country – the equivalent of 43 per cent of the United Kingdom-born immigrants in the same period. Not all of them returned to the United Kingdom, of course, but it is certain that many did. There was, then, a continuous exchange of population between Canada and the United Kingdom. The old concept of permanent immigration has greatly changed in the last thirty years as the immigrants of today include sizeable proportions of persons who do not stay permanently in their new homeland, and some who probably never intended to do so.

THE SIGNIFICANCE OF THE COMMONWEALTH IN CANADIAN IMMIGRATION

Around 1960, apart from immigrants coming from Britain, there was a continuous trickle of arrivals from Australia, New Zealand and South Africa; and there were the agreements to admit trivial numbers from India, Pakistan and Ceylon as well as certain Caribbean countries – resulting, probably, from various aspects of the Commonwealth relationship such as the existence of diplomatic links and a common *lingua franca*. There was no specific reference to the Commonwealth in the new policy of 1962, when immigration was opened to the world at a fortnight's notice. The countries whose emigrants eventually benefited from it indeed included two Commonwealth members in particular, India and Hong Kong, but because the new policy applied to Commonwealth and non-Commonwealth countries equally, it is unlikely that the interests of Commonwealth countries in particular figured in its formulation.

From 1962 on there has been little evidence to suggest any further acknowledgement of Commonwealth interests in general or of concern for any one Commonwealth country in particular, whether in the White Paper of 1966, the 1967 regulations, the Green Paper or the Bill of 1976. It seems clear that in the deliberations of the two parliamentary committees the issue was without importance. Few references to specifically Commonwealth immigration have been made in Parliament itself; there seem to have been no representations from bodies with specific Commonwealth interests. In practice, the Commonwealth provides many immigrants, but the *concept* of the Commonwealth seems not to be relevant.

Here, it is useful to note again the factors that do influence immigration policy and practice. To begin with, while earlier immigrants came predominantly from the British Isles, they did so from a Britain closely bound to Canada by tradition, settlement, and personal connections, rather than from Britain as a fellow member of the Empire. More recently, as we have seen, the country's manpower needs have been the primary consideration in immigration policy, so when Britain failed to meet those needs in the 1950s, it was not for Commonwealth countries such as India and Hong Kong that the doors were opened, but for non-Commonwealth countries, where likely emigrants were numerous and education and skills happened to be such as might be recognised in Canada or easily adapted to Canadian requirements. Then, when the new era of non-preference and non-discrimination arrived in 1962, any possibly existing preference for Commonwealth countries should have disappeared as a matter of course. It is noteworthy that the subsequent attacks on the government for not abolishing discrimination or for failing to rid immigration practices of discrimination entirely were not made in support of India or some other Commonwealth country, but rather on the basis of principle. When individual countries or particular regions have been mentioned at all in recent years in the immigration discussion, it has not been in connection with the Commonwealth. For example concern was expressed in Parliament for fiancees and relatives in China and this culminated in an agreement with the Chinese Government. There was also the Minister's reassurance in 1976 to Canádians with relatives in Eastern Europe that the Government would continue its efforts to reunite their families. Certainly Canada hastened to the aid of Asians being expelled from a Commonwealth country, Uganda, in 1972, by sending a special immigration team to Kampala and waiving some of the normal requirements for immigrants, but aid on a similar scale was also extended to refugees from a non-Commonwealth country, Hungary, in 1956. The Ugandan initiative of 1972 was taken less on behalf of the Asians because they were Commonwealth citizens than because they were refugees. Refugees have always featured prominently in official and unofficial discussion on immigration, and were accorded a virtual preference in the Immigration Bill of 1976.

Probably the proximity of the United States has tended to detract from what could otherwise have developed into concern for the Commonwealth in the context of immigration. Canada's neighbour is roughly ten times Canada's size in numbers. Many of the early British stock came from the United States. Today, the continuous traffic of visitors between the two countries is great; many Canadians become familiar with the United States through attending university there, holiday-making, passing the winter months in the warmer climate, and watching American television at home every day of their lives. Conversely, many Americans have come to Canada to work in business, universities and agriculture and for holidays. The cultural community of the two countries is strong, and the knowledge that the neighbour is bigger in population and vastly more powerful helps to concentrate Canada's attention on North America rather than on more distant regions.

Canada's somewhat isolated position has probably played a part in the same process. For Britain, Canada is one of the nearer Commonwealth partners, but for the rest of the Commonwealth, except countries in the Caribbean, it is distant. Before 1939 the journey even from Britain was not undertaken lightly, and it was not until twenty years later, when air travel became not more but less expensive than travel by sea, that a journey between Canada and members of the Commonwealth other than Britain and the Caribbean became something less than a luxury. That the Commonwealth Institute in England is a long-established body, while Canada has no equivalent, is not accidental.

In practice, Commonwealth countries are important, to the extent that in 1975 almost half of all immigrants came from them – nearly double the proportion of 1960 – and three Commonwealth countries alone provided 30 per cent of them; but the Commonwealth as a political entity is hardly of significance. The less tangible ties existing between Commonwealth members such as common use of the English language and similar educational systems must have helped potential emigrants from other Commonwealth countries to think of Canada as a destination and made it easier for them to satisfy Canada's points system. On the other hand, the absence of fluency in English has not discouraged southern Europeans from coming in large numbers since the Second World War. An emigrant from India moves more easily to Canada than to, say, France, it may be thought; nevertheless, Koreans, Chileans and others with probably minimal opportunity to become conversant with English in their home countries also make the move to Canada.

There is little reason to foresee much change in this pattern in the near future. Selection standards that are non-discriminatory on grounds of race or national origin are written into the new Bill. Naturally, established flows of migration from particular Commonwealth countries are likely to grow, but so are pressures to emigrate from other, non-

Commonwealth countries. There is a trend towards widening the scope of the immigration services overseas, and non-Commonwealth countries in particular are likely to benefit from it. Selection criteria are likely to remain linked to economic and social goals within Canada as well as to the reunification of families. In all these processes, the Commonwealth is irrelevant as a principle. Would it, in practice, benefit immigrants from, say, the Philippines, if that country were a member of the Commonwealth? There is little reason to suppose so. Indeed, in the period reviewed in this chapter, two countries, South Africa and Pakistan, left the Commonwealth, with no noticeable effect on the immigration flows from them; both have in fact increased – from Pakistan as a direct consequence of the 1962 regulations, and from South Africa as a result in all probability of easier and cheaper transport and the increased mobility of professionals and the highly-skilled. It seems reasonable to foresee that in the next few years Commonwealth countries between them will continue to provide an important proportion of Canada's immigrants, but that their common membership of the Commonwealth with Canada and the concept of the Commonwealth itself will not be significant in Canada's immigration practices or the policy which lies behind them.

4 Commonwealth Migratᵢₒₙ to and from the United Kingdom

INTRODUCTION: THE PRE-WAR POSITION

Until very recently the movement of people to the migrant-receiving countries of Oceania and the Americas consisted almost entirely of Europeans; negro slaves from Africa in the seventeenth and eighteenth centuries and indentured labourers from India in the nineteenth century – moving in both cases to parts of the Americas – were the only important exceptions. Migrants from the United Kingdom and Ireland played a major part in this movement of Europeans to Oceania and the Americas, and the number of emigrants from the British Isles has been estimated to have averaged more than 150,000 annually between 1846 and 1963.[1] As Trevelyan, the historian, makes clear, there were until the end of the nineteenth century large numbers of agricultural workers in the British Isles whose major desire was to attain and farm their own land, and many of them were prepared to go overseas to do this.[2] Assisted passage schemes to Australia and New Zealand and land settlement grants in those and other countries of immigration facilitated the movement.

It was a natural result of the creation of empires that sparsely-inhabited colonies having temperate climates were peopled mainly with migrants from the respective metropolitan powers in Europe in the first instance, and that emigration from Britain in particular should have continued to be directed towards those countries with a majority British resident community. Thus of Australia's foreign-born population in 1891 83 per cent were born in the British Isles, according to census statistics of that year, and the proportion was 'fairly well maintained' until the Second World War.[3] Again, nearly 60 per cent of Canada's foreign-born population in 1901 were born in the British Isles, though the proportion had dwindled to less than 50 per cent by 1941; but Canada's ethnic population history differed from that of Australia in that the original European population of Canada was predominantly French as a result of the early French settlements; and it was not until long after the Seven Years War that the Canadian population of British origin began to exceed the French population of Lower Canada. By 1871 just over 60 per cent of Canada's population were of British origin and 31 per cent of French origin.

Throughout Queen Victoria's reign and on until the First World War the British government maintained a *laissez-faire* attitude towards emigration. After the Armistice an official Emigration Committee was established, and the Government accepted their recommendation that ex-servicemen who wished to farm or had employment offers in other parts of the Commonwealth should be granted free passages for themselves and their families. Under the free passage scheme 86,000 ex-servicemen and women, with their dependants, left the United Kingdom between 1919 and 1922 to settle elsewhere in the Empire and a much larger number of emigrants left on their own initiative. In 1922 the Empire Settlement Act became the basis for United Kingdom migration policy. This Act 'empowered the United Kingdom Government to co-operate with any oversea government or with public authorities and public or private organisations either in the United Kingdom or elsewhere in the Commonwealth in carrying out agreed schemes to provide joint assistance to suitable emigrants from the United Kingdom who intended to settle in any part of the Commonwealth'.[4] The United Kingdom government entered into schemes for assisted passages with the governments of Canada, Australia, New Zealand and Southern Rhodesia under the Act, and the work of approved voluntary organisations engaged in the promotion of settlement in overseas Commonwealth countries was assisted.

With this official view of the importance of migration from the United Kingdom to other Commonwealth countries, and the financial encouragement which accompanied it, it is not surprising that emigration in the 1920s should have been largely directed to Canada, Australia, South Africa, New Zealand and Southern Rhodesia. At least four out of every five emigrants from the United Kingdom moved to other Commonwealth countries, and the net outward movement in that decade averaged about 85,000 persons annually. The economic depression starting in 1929 reversed the flow of migration and the decade starting in 1931 brought a net migrational gain of population to the United Kingdom of some 650,000 persons, after at least six successive decades of net loss of population by migration.[5] Nevertheless, the

Empire Settlement Act of 1937 renewed the 1922 Act for a further fifteen years; the official view was that the United Kingdom should resume its encouragement of emigration to other Commonwealth countries when economic conditions once again became favourable to satisfactory settlement.

The volume of United Kingdom immigration in the 1930s consisted very largely of the return movement of former emigrants affected by the world depression. There was also a strong Irish component and a much smaller movement of political refugees, largely Jews, from Nazi Germany and elsewhere in Europe. Immigration of aliens into the United Kingdom had been controlled since 1905 under the Aliens Act. Immigration of coloured British subjects from Commonwealth countries was at a low level before the Second World War. Although all British subjects, whichever their country of origin, had the right of entry into the United Kingdom, the poverty and ignorance of most of the population of the colonial Empire combined with high unemployment in Britain resulted in the movement to Britain of only a quite small elite, and then usually for education and specialist training lasting a few years rather than for permanent settlement.

One demographic factor that helped to exacerbate the post-1945 shortage of labour in the United Kingdom was the rapid decline in family size in the inter-war years. Couples marrying in the first decade of the twentieth century had an average of 3.37 children per family, whereas couples marrying in the five-year period 1925–9 averaged only 2.2 children – the latter figure being less than half of the mid-Victorian average.[6] As a result the numbers of native British entering the labour force each year in the late 1940s and 1950s were lower than in any of the inter-war years. Doubts about whether the departure of considerable numbers of working people from the United Kingdom would be in the country's best interests once the economy had recovered from the depression were voiced in 1938 in the Report of the Oversea Settlement Board[7] but the war intervened and further public discussion of migration policy was postponed until after the battle for survival had ended.

THE EARLY POST-WAR YEARS: 1945–62

The Royal Commission on Population, which was set up in 1944 and submitted its Report in 1949, reiterated the doubts about Britain's ability to supply as many migrants as Commonwealth countries would have liked to receive in the post-war period, but considered that the political advantages to both the United Kingdom and the Commonwealth as a whole in maintaining the flow of emigrants outweighed the economic disadvantages to Britain in parting with young adult migrants when the country's native working population between the ages of 15 and 40 was certain to decline by about 1,300,000 in the period 1947–57.[8] The Commission noted that it would require an annual *net* inward balance of migration of 140,000 young adults during the ten-year period to prevent a decline of the numbers in the young age groups, but, after considering possible sources of migrants in Europe, concluded that it would be difficult to obtain immigrants on such a scale. The Commission's Report ended their consideration of problems of immigration with two paragraphs which, in the light of subsequent events, are worth quoting in full:

> 329. Even, however, if it were found practicable to secure a *net* inward balance of migration on anything like this scale, we should have to face serious problems of assimilation beyond those of training and housing. Immigration on a large scale into a fully established society like ours could only be welcomed without reserve if the immigrants were of good human stock and were not prevented by their religion or race from intermarrying with the host population and becoming merged in it. These conditions were fulfilled by intermittent large scale immigration in the past, notably by the Flemish and French Protestant refugees who settled in Great Britain at different times. There is little or no prospect that we should be able to apply these conditions to large scale immigration in the future, and every increase of our needs, e.g. by more emigration from Great Britain or by a further fall in fertility, would tend to lower the standards of selection.

> 330. All these considerations point to the conclusion that continuous large scale immigration would probably be impracticable and would certainly be undesirable, and the possibility – it can be regarded as no more than a possibility – that circumstances might compel us to consider or attempt it is among the undesirable consequences of the maintenance of family size below replacement level.

Fertility did rise in the post-war years to above replacement level, but this inevitably had no early effect on the size of the labour force. On the other hand emigration from Great Britain in the 1950s was at a rather higher level than the Commission had anticipated, although net outward migration remained below the rate of 100,000 per annum which was regarded by the Commission as the maximum which the country's economy could stand. It has been estimated that the United Kingdom provided non-European countries with a *net* total of 78,000 persons annually between 1948 and 1957 and received from the continent and Eire a net total of 46,000 persons, giving an average annual loss of 32,000 persons over the period.[9] Unfortunately the lack of adequate British official migration statistics in the post-war period, particularly up to 1964, prevents precise estimates of gross emigration and net migration being made. Nor were the statistics adequate to present even a rough picture of the effect of emigration on the economy in terms of loss of skilled manpower.

In a free democratic country such as the United Kingdom the right of the individual to emigrate is not questioned. Any figure for emigration pronounced as desirable by the Royal Commission on Population or even by the government would be unlikely to coincide with the sum total of individual and family decisions made by prospective emigrants. After the first few post-war years, however, the United Kingdom government took little practical interest in emigration to Commonwealth countries. The Conference of Commonwealth Societies passed resolutions, as for instance in 1960, that 'an increased flow of British migrants is a matter of supreme importance to the expanding Commonwealth', but such resolutions fell officially on deaf ears in Britain. The United Kingdom government, with Australian agreement, made successive reductions in their share of the cost of the Assisted Passage Scheme to Australia, and the New Zealand government operated its own assisted passage scheme without financial help from London. The majority of emigrants from the United Kingdom in the post-war period have departed because they think that Australia, Canada, New Zealand, the United States and, for a few, South Africa and Rhodesia, offer them and their children better opportunities than at home. The assisted passage schemes – in particular the scheme concluded and renewed from time to time between the Australian and British governments – have undoubtedly encouraged migration to flow strongly in particular directions, but it is doubtful whether such schemes have had a great deal of influence on the overall rate of emigration from the United Kingdom. The decisions that individual countries of immigration in the Commonwealth make from time to time to regulate the size and make-up of the immigrant flow do of course affect the emigrant flow from the United Kingdom, but these decisions are not in general ones in which the British government participates.

In the period from the end of the Second World War to 1962, Australia gradually overtook and surpassed Canada as the leading recipient country of emigrants from the United Kingdom, and Australia's position has been very easily maintained since 1962. The post-war flow of migrants from Britain to Australia only began to gain real momentum in 1948, but between 1948 and 1962 an average annual total of about 41,750 persons arrived from Britain according to the statistics maintained by the Commonwealth Bureau of Census and Statistics in Canberra. Between 1946 and 1962 an average total of just under 30,000 persons arrived to settle in Canada from England, Wales, Scotland and Northern Ireland combined, and an average of just over 31,000 persons annually from the United Kingdom and Eire combined.[10] In the last five years of the period, however, the annual average was only 18,000 persons to Canada from the United Kingdom compared with 55,000 persons to Australia.

Why did Australia take Canada's place at the top of the league table of countries receiving British immigrants? A number of seemingly valid reasons can be advanced, although it is difficult to assess their relative importance. In the first place, with its easy accessibility to Europe by air travel, Australia was no longer the remote country, from a British point of view, that it was before the Second World War. Secondly, immigration from Europe, and particularly from Britain, was strongly encouraged by the Australian government, and Britain was unable in fact to supply as many emigrants as Australia would have liked. Thirdly, Australia was and still is a country predominantly British in character, in a way in which Canada has never been in view of its minority French population, its proximity to the United States and interchange of population with that country over many decades, and its multiplicity of cultures. Fourthly, more than half of the British migrants to Australia travelled on the assisted passage scheme, making only a small contribution themselves, whereas Canada made loans only to certain eligible classes of prospective immigrants to assist in the purchase of passages. Fifthly, Canada has tended to have a higher unemployment rate than Australia, particularly during the Canadian winter. Sixthly, Australia has a kinder climate than Canada. Seventhly, Australia was a member-country of the sterling area, and Canada was not.

Although migration between countries seldom, if ever, flows at an even pace over a considerable period of years, it is a fact that the outflow of British migrants to Australia proceeded at a steadier pace than the outflow to Canada after 1948, when shipping for transporting migrants across the oceans became more readily available. The rate of immigration into Canada has been left to vary with performance of the Canadian economy, although short-term changes have also been made in the immigration regulations as a device to give some measure of control over the size of flows. In Australia, on the other hand, annual targets for immigration have been set in the light of variations in the excess demand for labour in that country.[11] Moreover, political events seem to have had a greater effect on the size of Canadian immigration than on the flow to Australia, and Canadian immigration easily reached its post-war peak in 1957 after the Suez crisis and the Russian quelling of the Hungarian rebellion, whereas the Australian intake was hardly affected by these events.

The third main receiving country for British migrants in the post-war period has been New Zealand. The pace of inflow has been fairly steady, and, between 1950 and 1962 the gross flow of British immigrants varied between a little under 10,000 per annum and a little under 15,000 persons. In relation to the population size of the receiving country, the gross flow from Britain into New Zealand has been greater than into either Australia or Canada, but New Zealand's net immigration rate from all countries combined has been fairly consistently lower than that of Australia, partly because the non-British element in New Zealand immigration has been smaller than that of Australia and partly because gross emigration as a proportion of gross immigration has been rather higher for New Zealand than for Australia.

The other two Commonwealth countries to receive considerable numbers of British migrants in the late 1940s and 1950s were South Africa[12] and Rhodesia. Emigration to South Africa from Britain fell from 30,000 in 1948 and 10,000 in 1949 to an average of a little over 5000 per annum in the 1950s – a decline which it seems reasonable to associate with the rise of Afrikaans-dominated politics in that country. Post-war migration from Britain to Rhodesia flourished for some twelve years after the Second World War, immigration policy in Rhodesia being geared to manpower requirements for skilled personnel, but was checked in the late 1950s by political events in southern Africa.

Estimates made by the Oversea Migration Board in relation to the gross totals for overseas emigration from the United Kingdom in 1957, 1958 and 1959 show that two-thirds to three-quarters of emigrants in those years were destined for Australia, Canada, New Zealand, South Africa and Rhodesia. The breakdown in those three years is given in Table 4.1.

Only a very small proportion of post-war emigrants from the United Kingdom followed in the earlier tradition of overseas migrants in

TABLE 4.1.   Destination of UK emigrants 1957–9

Destination of emigrants from the United Kingdom	Proportion of emigrants from UK in 1957	1958	1959
Australia, Canada, New Zealand, South Africa, Rhodesia	76.0	66.5	64.6
Other Commonwealth countries and colonies	11.0	17.0	18.4
Foreign countries	13.0	16.5	17.0
	100.0	100.0	100.0

Source: Oversea Migration Board Reports Fourth Report (December 1958) p. 8, Fifth Report (March 1960) p. 7; Sixth Report (December 1960) p. 7.

wishing to set themselves up in agriculture and work as independent farmers. On the other hand the very great majority of the emigrants had experience in the United Kingdom in professional, managerial, clerical and skilled or semi-skilled industrial work and were earmarked for similar occupations on reaching their countries of destination.

In the meantime, during the 1950s, a new element of magnitude entered into the United Kingdom's balance of migration, the immigration of coloured Commonwealth citizens into the United Kingdom. Gross immigration into the United Kingdom has for many decades been of sizeable proportions except in times of war, but immigrants prior to the Second World War consisted primarily of United Kingdom citizens and their dependants resuming permanent residence after periods of employment abroad, returning United Kingdom emigrants and their dependants, British subjects from the 'Old Commonwealth', Irish immigrants, and, from time to time, refugees of various nationalities. Pre-war immigrants also included a number of coloured British subjects who would now be termed coloured Commonwealth citizens,[13] but such people usually came to the United Kingdom for academic study and professional training. There were, however, some thousands of Indian and West Indian sailors and ex-sailors who settled in British ports in the inter-war years, particularly in London, Cardiff, Liverpool and Bristol. Few of these settlers were married to women from their own countries of origin, and their marriages and liaisons with white women frequently became the source of considerable racial tension and hostility. On paper there were no legislative restrictions on the entry and settlement of British subjects of any race, colour or creed in the United Kingdom, but practical considerations such as the cost of passages, the unfamiliarity of the British climate and way of life, and, above all, the difficulties of obtaining employment, ensured that coloured Commonwealth immigrants, other than sailors, were fairly few in number before the Second World War.

After the Second World War there was for a number of years nearly full employment in the United Kingdom, and the country was fortunate in obtaining as additions to the labour force in the first ten post-war years some 95,000 demobilised Polish armed forces personnel, 25,000 prisoners-of-war who decided to remain in the United Kingdom after their release and 365,000 nationals of various European countries, many of them refugees from Eastern Europe.[14] In addition there was considerable net Irish immigration into Great Britain. The shortage of labour which played a part in attracting immigrants to Britain to take up semi-skilled and unskilled work was a result of a combination of factors, including not only the indigenous demographic factors already mentioned, but also expanding employment opportunities in manufacturing and service occupations and a higher general standard of education than obtained before the war which enabled those native British who wished to do so to ignore the unskilled jobs and take advantage of more attractive occupational opportunities.[15] Newly arrived foreigners found little difficulty in finding vacancies at or near the lower end of the wage scale, and indeed aliens would not have been admitted had there not been employment of some kind for them to go to.

West Indians began to join this inflow in 1948 and Indians and Pakistanis later on. Some West Indians had joined the British armed forces and seen something of the United Kingdom in the Second World War. A few of these West Indians stayed in the UK after demobilisation and others returned later. Some commentators on the beginnings of post-war coloured immigration into the United Kingdom state, without giving sources for their information, that West Indian immigrants did not exceed 1000 in any year until 1951. Lord Mancroft, replying to a question by Lord Elton in the House of Lords in February 1956 stated that 2200 West Indians had entered the United Kingdom for settlement in 1952, 2300 in 1953, 9200 in 1954 and 25,700 in 1955. Harold Macmillan, in his memoirs, states that the coloured population of Britain was about 40,000 in 1954 compared with 7000 before the war and that in 1954 coloured immigration was four times the size of the 1953 inflow.[16] Eversley and Sukdeo quote the 1951 Census of England and Wales as giving a figure of 103,000 coloured immigrants from all Commonwealth countries, including Cyprus and Malta, which were no doubt excluded from other estimates of numbers.[17] The precise numbers are unimportant; the important points are that coloured

Commonwealth immigration began to increase rapidly in the early 1950s, that housing and social problems associated with immigration, especially in the Midlands, were brought to Parliament's attention at that time, that a few Members of Parliament, mainly Conservatives but including some Labour Members,[18] started to lobby for control of Commonwealth immigration as early as 1954, and that the influx of immigrants was the subject of Ministerial discussion late in 1954 and early in 1955.[19] There were debates on immigration policy in the House of Lords in November 1956, at the end of which Lord Mancroft underlined the United Kingdom's special position as the mother country in the Commonwealth, and in the House of Commons in April 1958 when Pat Hornsby Smith, winding up for the Government, stated that discussions were in progress with the West Indian, Indian and Pakistan Governments to discourage unsuitable immigration.[20]

If control of Commonwealth immigration had commenced in 1955 or 1956 instead of in 1962, the ugly race riots in Nottingham and Notting Hill in 1958 and later years might possibly have been avoided. Moreover, feelings would probably not have been capable of being so inflamed on the subject of New Commonwealth immigration as was in fact the case in the 1960s and 1970s, if only because numbers would have been much smaller and the housing and social problems regarded as having arisen from immigration would have been to that extent avoided or diminished. However Winston Churchill and his Conservative colleagues in the Cabinet shrank from interfering with the traditional freedom of movement between the United Kingdom and Commonwealth countries, and decided instead to concentrate on trying to persuade the main Commonwealth governments involved – those of the West Indies, India and Pakistan – to try to discourage emigration to Britain.[21] Moreover, the continuing shortage of unskilled labour in Britain was ameliorated by the large-scale immigration of coloured immigrants, and on economic grounds there was thus a case for allowing immigration to continue with at most voluntary controls arranged on an inter-governmental level. The facts that net immigration from New Commonwealth countries fell from an annual figure of over 42,000 in each of the years 1955, 1956 and 1957 to just under 30,000 in 1958, and 21,600 in 1959, and that discussion of immigration was not a feature of the 1959 election campaign, provided apparent justification for the delay in the introduction of controls. It was not until 1961 that it became clear that there had again been a very marked acceleration of immigration and the decision to legislate was taken by Macmillan's Conservative Government.

The net immigration figures for the main sending New Commonwealth countries and groups of countries for the years 1956–60 (Table 4.2) were given in a reply to a written question in the House of Commons.[22]

TABLE 4.2. Net UK immigration figures from selected New Commonwealth countries 1956–60

Year	West Indies	India	Pakistan	Cyprus	West Africa
1956	29800	5600	2100	2800	2000
1957	23000	6600	5200	1500	2200
1958	15000	6200	4700	2700	1000
1959	16400	2900	900	400	750
1960	49700	5800	2500	3200	− 550

(The minus for West Africa in 1960 indicates a net emigration).

Source: Hansard: Commons vol. 637 c 60 (questions).

Had the developing immigration remained very largely a movement from the Caribbean, it is unlikely that it would ever have reached a size which could not have been maintained on economic grounds. Peach has shown that West Indian arrivals followed a similar graphical course to the figures of employment vacancies in Great Britain until the end of 1960, and that only in 1961 and the first half of 1962 did the arrival figures cease to follow the economic indicators.[23] In view of the gradual opening of the Canadian and United States doors to more Caribbean immigrants from 1962 and 1966 respectively, it is probably fair to suggest that the United Kingdom population of West Indian origin or ethnic descent would now be little greater had there never been a Commonwealth Immigrants Act or the threat of such legislation. Indian and Pakistan migration became substantial in 1961, however, and, between the beginning of that year and the middle of 1962, when the first Commonwealth Immigrants Act came into force, net immigration from India and Pakistan combined was nearly equal to net immigration from the Commonwealth Caribbean; since 1 July 1962 net immigration from India and Pakistan has been vastly in excess of that from the Caribbean. Although immigration from India, Pakistan and Bangladesh continued to originate in particular areas of those countries, the potential size of the migrant flow from the sub-continent in the absence of control was enormous, and this factor provided the ultimate justification for legislative control of Commonwealth immigration. The need for such control was accepted by the Labour party under Harold Wilson when they came into power in 1964, despite the strong opposition to the Commonwealth Immigrants Bill by that party under Hugh Gaitskell in 1961/62.

The main moral question at stake in judging the 1962 Act is the extent of the responsibility of a declining imperial power to provide free entry to the 'Mother Country', not only for citizens of the 'White Dominions' but also for colonials and citizens of former colonies who want to improve their economic position, and for whom other migration outlets are denied. Although most of the New Commonwealth immigrants before 1962 had employment in their own countries before migration, in general they improved their earning power in the United Kingdom, though often suffering a reduction in occupational status, and the employment prospects for their sons and daughters were certainly improved in view of the very high levels of unemployment for both educated and uneducated persons in India, Pakistan and the West Indies. It was clearly impossible, however, for the United Kingdom to continue to accept indefinitely a migrant inflow of uncontrolled size from countries totalling such a large part of the world's population, and it can be argued with some justification that the early imposition of controls of flexible and as generous as possible size would have been preferable to the later imposition of more severe controls which soon degenerated into very small annual quotas of immigrant work vouchers. Fears were expressed by senior politicians on both sides of the House of Commons in the years from 1955 to 1961 that any step to end the long tradition of free entry into the United Kingdom for all citizens of the Commonwealth would inevitably weaken the bonds of Commonwealth, despite the fact that other Commonwealth countries exercised immigration control on the entry of United Kingdom citizens as well as potential migrants from elsewhere in the Commonwealth. In retrospect it may be suggested that immigration controls generously administered would have done less to weaken the bonds of Commonwealth than did the rapidly tightening controls exercised from July 1962 onwards.

When Hugh Gaitskell, as leader of the Labour opposition, argued against the Commonwealth Immigrants Bill at the committee stage, he appeared to favour differentiating between the Commonwealth West Indies for which a continuing population outlet would have been a real economic boon in view of the relatively small size of the total population of the islands, and India and Pakistan for which no emigration programme could have been large enough to alleviate their problems of employment and of the economy generally. Whether this kind of country-by-country differentiation would have been feasible in terms of Commonwealth relations is very doubtful, especially as the Old Commonwealth countries would probably have demanded favoured nation treatment in any such differentiation. The political issues were dual in nature. On the home front a growing proportion of the electorate favoured some kind of immigration control, certainly from 1960 onwards, judging by public opinion polls and election results. On the external front any move to control immigration from Commonwealth countries would have done some damage to the Commonwealth as a political institution, but it seems likely that the earlier such controls had come into force, the less damage they would have done. In 1955 Indians and Pakistanis had not started to enter the United Kingdom in sizeable numbers, and it is reasonable to suppose that, provided a limited but generously-sized entry was allowed to fill specific job offers or to meet professional shortages, the Indian and Pakistani governments would not have stood so much on their dignity to convey a feeling of damaged pride as they did in 1962. The main opposition to Commonwealth immigration control in 1955 could reasonably have been expected to come from the West Indies and from the Old Dominions; the West Indian politicians would have been vocal in their opposition, as they were in 1961/62, but as political realists would have accepted the situation once any Bill had become an Act.

On the economic side the suggestions that were made from time to time both inside and outside Parliament, more particularly the latter, that immigrants from New Commonwealth countries were a financial drain on the social security system were shown to be unfounded both by government ministers and, more particularly, by academic writers. The immigrants had little difficulty in finding employment except in relatively short periods of recession, and they had settled very largely in areas of low unemployment such as the Greater London Area and the West Midlands. Without the immigrants the excess demand for labour would have been considerably greater than in fact it was, and, as Jones and Smith argue, the economic cost of an unduly restrictive immigration policy might well have been high.[24] Immigration control with quotas related to labour shortages would not however have handicapped economic development.

Under the Commonwealth Immigrants Act 1962 work vouchers were to be issued in three categories by the Secretary of State for Employment and Productivity. Category A was for applications by employers in the United Kingdom who had a specific job to offer to a particular Commonwealth citizen. Category B was for applications by Commonwealth citizens with certain special qualifications but without a specific job offer – people such as doctors, nurses and teachers. Category C was for all other applications, and, within category C, preference was to be given to applicants who had served in the British Forces. The maximum rate at which vouchers were to be issued was for decision by the government of the day and would be subject to variation. Certain categories of dependants – the wife and children under 16 – were given by the Act the absolute right of entry to accompany voucher-holders or join them in the United Kingdom, and certain other categories of dependants were, by way of discretion, also admitted without vouchers. Bona fide students and visitors from Commonwealth countries were to be admitted without work vouchers. The first part of the Act which provided for control of immigration was to require annual renewal, but the second part providing for deportation was permanent legislation.

Migration between the Republic of Ireland and the United Kingdom was to remain free of control, despite the fact that Ireland had long since ceased to be a member state of the Commonwealth. On the other hand the White Dominions were included in the controls initiated by the Commonwealth Immigrants Act, much to the dismay and annoyance of many residents of Australia, New Zealand and Canada whose ancestors had migrated from Britain and who continued to refer to Britain as 'Home'. The exclusion of Ireland was sufficient to ensure that enemies of the Act branded it as discriminatory in terms of race and colour, for Irish immigration remained an important source of labour supply to Great Britain. Throughout the critical years when legislation on Commonwealth immigration was a matter for serious discussion the flow from Ireland to Great Britain was maintained, net immigration by air and sea from the Republic being estimated at an annual average figure of around 20,000 persons.[25] The original draft of the framework of powers to be encompassed in an Immigrants Bill included control of Irish immigration as well as immigration from all countries of the Commonwealth, on the grounds that it was politically impossible for the centre of the multi-racial Commonwealth to legislate against coloured Commonwealth immigration without also legislating against white Irish immigrants.[26] The official reason given for the final exclusion of immigrants from the Republic of Ireland from the controls incorporated in the Bill was the difficulty of establishing satisfactory migration policing on the border between the Republic and Northern Ireland, combined with Northern Ireland's understandable refusal to permit any form of passport control for travel between the Province and the rest of the United Kingdom.

It can certainly be argued that the Act was discriminatory in practical effect in terms of race and colour, even if non-discriminatory in its legal language. In fact all positive immigration policies are discriminatory, and the fundamental right of nations to determine who will be admitted as settlers has not been seriously questioned in international circles. A policy of admitting as immigrants only those with special types of skill discriminates against those without such skills; a policy of admitting only those of certain ethnic or cultural origins discriminates against those of different ethnic or cultural origins. A country of immigration must necessarily either allow free entry to all comers or adopt a selective system of admission. It does not necessarily smack of racial intolerance to believe, as many kind and tolerant people in the United Kingdom do, that immigration policy ought to be dictated by the relative ease with which different groups of people can be integrated into the native community, and the immigration policies of Australia and New Zealand and to a smaller extent Canada and the United States were, until quite recently, dictated by such a belief. The process of 'integration' depends, however, on the host community as well as the immigrants. The early West Indian immigrants came to Britain after the Second World War hoping to be welcomed by their hosts and rapidly integrated; the degree of hostility that they experienced from some of the population was not expected. On the other hand many, though not all, of the Indian and Pakistani immigrants who came to Britain intended to retain their own cultural heritage to the fullest possible extent and to create residential colonies of their own as far as possible.

In a difficult situation, when the decision to legislate had been considered and postponed for the best of motives for a number of years, the Commonwealth Immigrants Act of 1962 was as good a temporary compromise as could be expected, although it pleased neither the John Bulls who wanted all coloured immigration stopped immediately, nor the Gaitskellites and kindred spirits who believed that the legislation was unnecessary. The Instructions to Immigration Officers, made by the Home Secretary and published in accordance with the Act, were framed liberally, and the Government accepted the desirability of frequent reviews of the immigration situation – reviews which were assured by the need to include renewal of the Act in the annual Expiring Laws Continuance Act. Surprisingly enough in the light of later arguments and concern over the volume of immigration of dependants, there was relatively little discussion during the debates on the Commonwealth Immigrants Bill on the admission of dependants, although the Labour opposition did obtain a broader definition of dependants before the

Third Reading. There was no prolonged argument in Parliament on the desirability of instituting the 'guest worker' system as part of Commonwealth immigration control as an alternative to permanent entry, despite the fact that the housing situation had been one of the strong planks used by the lobby campaigning for the introduction of controls. And yet the writing was already on the wall for those able to read it. The relatively high fertility of women in the less developed countries of the Commonwealth made it fairly certain that New Commonwealth immigrant communities would form a gradually growing percentage of the British population, if the policy of family reunion in Britain was accepted, even if there were socio-economic reasons for expecting a reduction in the fertility of these women in the environment of an urban, industrial society. And the systematic forgery of passports and evasion of the Indian and Pakistani governments' own controls on emigration had already started well before the Act came into force in July 1962. This kind of evasion blossomed into an industry when dependants and pseudo-dependants in the Indian sub-continent had to start to produce documentary evidence of dependency on persons already in the United Kingdom. For better or worse, the content of the Commonwealth Immigrants Act 1962 ensured Britain's continued progress to multi-racialism.

Uncontrolled entry into the United Kingdom for people from other Commonwealth countries thus came to an end in 1962. At the 1961 census 541,000 persons born in New Commonwealth countries (including Pakistan) and 110,000 born in Australia, Canada and New Zealand were counted in Great Britain. Some of the 541,000 were, however, the white children born in New Commonwealth countries to British nationals who had worked abroad in the civil and armed services and in commerce and industry. As with migrant movements in other parts of the world, there was a heavy concentration in 1961 of migrants in the younger adult age-groups (20–45) and an abnormal sex-ratio in favour of males among the West Indian, Indian and Pakistani migrants enumerated in the United Kingdom and born in their countries of origin.[27] Even in 1961, however, the age distribution of New Commonwealth immigrants contained a higher than national average proportion of children, if children born in Britain to immigrant parents are included in the calculation.

During the four and a half years prior to the introduction of control, the balance of migration was inward. Estimates by the Registrar General of annual figures for the United Kingdom are shown in Table 4.3. The year 1957 was an exceptional year for emigration, particularly to

TABLE 4.3. Annual figures of migrational loss
and gain for the United Kingdom, 1953–64

Year	Net balance of migration
1953	− 74000
1954	− 32000
1955	− 10000
1956	− 17000
1957	− 72000
1958	+ 45000
1959	+ 44000
1960	+ 82000
1961	+ 170000
1962	+ 136000
1963	+ 10000
1964	− 17000

Source: Table 7. Oversea Migration Board Statistics
for 1964 (Cmd. 2861).

Canada, and the net balance of out-migration was high despite an extraordinary inflow of refugees from Hungary and Egypt. The years 1960, 1961 and 1962 are the peak years for immigration from New Commonwealth countries.

THE PERIOD 1962—71: IMMIGRATION

Although the Labour opposition in Parliament reserved its future position on Commonwealth immigration control at the time of the Third Reading of the Commonwealth Immigrants Bill at the end of February 1962, the party's opposition to control died with Hugh Gaitskell in January 1963. Harold Wilson took over the party leadership, and, when the renewal of the Act came up for consideration in the debate on the Expiring Laws Continuance Bill in November 1963, he stated that the need for control was not contested, although he added that he wanted negotiations with the Commonwealth governments most concerned.[28] In 1964 Labour gained power, and, in the corresponding debate on the renewal in November of that year, Frank Soskice, speaking for the Government, reaffirmed that effective immigration control was indispensable and that he was looking at the best method of dealing both with evasion of that control and at the position of marginal dependants. St John-Stevas, the new Conservative Member for

Chelmsford, described the Commonwealth Immigrants Act as a disagreeable necessity which had to be retained irrespective of Commonwealth agreement.[29] Opposition to renewal came from the left wing of the Labour party, Michael Foot, then a backbencher, hoping that the Government would consign the Act quickly to the dustbin and Tom Driberg making a vituperative speech of dissent.

Soskice told the Commons in November 1964 that there had been 162,000 arrivals passing through the controls created by the Act since July 1962. Of these 46,000 had been voucher holders, 61,000 had been dependants, and the remainder had been students and long-term visitors. He described voucher holder arrivals in the A and B categories as very valuable to the country economically; some voucher holders in the C category (that is, those without either a specific job offer or specific professional qualification) were admitted in the first two years of the Act's operation, but there were no further admissions in this category after September 1964. Of the 30,000 voucher holders admitted in 1963, nearly three-quarters came from the Indian sub-continent. That year proved to be the only year after the coming into force of the Act during which voucher holders exceeded dependants admitted in number. Between 1963 and 1967 the annual figure of voucher holders arriving descended rapidly to under 5000, as a result of a reduction in quotas, and the annual figure of dependants rose to nearly 53,000.

In 1963 and 1964 the net intake of Commonwealth citizens exceeded that of all previous post-war years except for 1961 and 1962. On 4 February 1965 the Home Secretary, answering questions from Conservatives MPs on the evasion of immigration controls, told the House of Commons that evasion was being practised on a considerable scale.[30] On 9 March the Prime Minister announced the forthcoming visit of the Mountbatten Mission to a number of Commonwealth countries to discuss the regulation of the flow of immigrants to Britain and measures to reduce evasion of immigration control. On 2 August 1965 the Lord President of the Council stated that the Government had reviewed the Commonwealth immigration programme, helped by the Mountbatten Mission Report,[31] and the Government's White Paper *Immigration from the Commonwealth*[32] stating its future policy was presented to Parliament. The main decision conveyed in the White Paper was that the rate of issue of vouchers was to be 8500 per year. From 1965 for a number of years the two main parties differed little in their broad approach to immigration policy, although there were divisions within each party on desirable administrative arrangements for testing eligibility for entry, particularly in relation to dependants, and on the way of dealing with persons holding British passports who had no residential connection, past or present, with Britain.

In retrospect the three years from the middle of 1962 to the middle of 1965 can be seen, in terms of the arrival of voucher holders, as the only years in the currency of the Commonwealth Immigrants Act in which immigration policy was in some measure related to the United Kingdom's labour force requirements. The upper annual limit of 8500 vouchers imposed by the British Government in the 1965 White Paper appears to have been determined more by political and social considerations than by the needs of the economy, although the generally upward movement in the unemployment figures during the 1960s would in itself have justified a downward trend in the issue of vouchers to immigrants. The 8500 vouchers were to include an annual allocation of 1000 vouchers to citizens of Malta 'to give effect to our special obligations' to that country, these special Maltese arrangements to be subject to review after two years; these special obligations presumably refer to the defence facilities given at that time by Malta to Britain and NATO, and to the run-down in the size of the labour force employed in serving these defence facilities.

Between July 1962 and December 1964 vouchers issued to prospective immigrants were heavily weighted with Indians and Pakistanis who were awarded 62 per cent of such vouchers as against only 12 per cent for West Indians. The remaining 26 per cent of the vouchers were split between all remaining Commonwealth countries, including Australia, Canada and New Zealand. A study of the occupational and industrial distribution of Indian and Pakistani immigrants in the labour force in 1961 and 1966 respectively suggests that the textile and metals industries must have been large-scale recruiters of Indian and Pakistani immigrant workers under category A of the system for the issue of vouchers. Indians obtained the lion's share, about 40 per cent, of the category B vouchers for those with special skills, a considerable but varying proportion of whom were doctors. Nearly three-quarters of the category C vouchers issued before their discontinuance in September 1964 went to Indian and Pakistani applications; this category, it will be remembered, related to applicants without a specific job to come to in the United Kingdom and without the special skills or qualifications required for category B.

By no means were all of the vouchers issued taken up in terms of immigrant arrivals. The 1965 White Paper records that in 1962 and the first months of 1963 a high proportion of the vouchers issued went to waste, but that later, before the issue of the White Paper, about three-quarters were being used. After 1965 the policy was that no one Commonwealth country was to receive more than 15 per cent of the vouchers issued in category A, thus eliminating any possibility of a near-monopoly of direct recruitment of Indians and Pakistanis by industry. In part at least because of this 15 per cent rule, the number of voucher holders entering the United Kingdom in the remaining years of the decade was well below the maximum issue figure of 8500, and Pakistani and West Indian voucher holder arrivals dropped by 72 per cent and 79 per cent between 1965 and 1966. There was a much more modest drop of 36 per cent in the number of Indian voucher holder arrivals owing to the preponderance of category B vouchers, which were not subject to a country quota, issued to Indian nationals.

The statistics on the control of immigration between 1 July 1962 and 31 December 1964 provide an interesting commentary on the relative movement of nationals of different Commonwealth countries into and out of the United Kingdom at a time when admission for settlement, although subject to control, was easier to obtain than in later years. When visitors and students are included in the figures, the movement of Australians and Canadians far exceed that of Commonwealth citizens from any other country. If students only are considered, Nigerians were at that time consistently at the head of the table, Indians in second place, and Malaysians consistently third. When dependants accompanying or coming to join the head of household only are considered, the West Indies collectively came first in numbers, with India second and Pakistan third; Jamaica by itself sent more dependants than Pakistan and nearly as many as India, but the movement of dependants reflected more closely the movement of heads of households two or three years earlier than the simultaneous movement of household heads. Clearly Commonwealth citizens admitted to the United Kingdom have to be classified by the purpose of their entry before any realistic analysis is possible.

Between the full census of 1961 and the sample census of 1966 the immigrant population born in New Commonwealth countries grew very rapidly. Census statistics give an annual average growth rate of 9.5 per cent, but the rate was probably more like 10 per cent in view of the officially accepted under-enumeration of New Commonwealth immigrants in the 1966 census. In comparison the growth of the Irish-born population was negligible, fresh immigration being nearly balanced by emigration. In 1966 New Commonwealth immigrants provided a third of Britain's population born abroad compared with a quarter in 1961. The British public are far from being connoisseurs of census statistics or any other official statistics, but by the mid-sixties there was a widespread uncomfortable feeling that the coloured population was growing far too rapidly. Enoch Powell's well-publicised pronouncements on the future demographic balance between white and non-white in Britain and on the dangers of racial conflict did not start to emerge until some time after the publication of the 1965 White Paper, but the statistics had a tale to tell. From 1966 until 1968 inclusive, Ministry of Labour work voucher holders entering the United Kingdom under the Commonwealth Immigrants Act did not exceed 5500 in any one year and in each of those three years dependants made up more than 80 per cent of the Commonwealth immigrants subject to control and accepted for settlement on arrival.

The 1962 Act did not apply controls to the admission into the United Kingdom of persons holding British passports who were citizens of the United Kingdom and Colonies. When the Kenyan Independence Bill was being debated in 1963, the issue of whether non-African holders of passports issued by the former Colonial government in Nairobi on behalf of the British government would be entitled to settle in the United Kingdom, if they did not in the meantime acquire Kenyan citizenship, was never specifically answered in respect of the Asian community. However the right to enter clearly existed and the immigration officers in the Home Office accepted East African Asians who held United Kingdom passports as exempt from the 1962 Act controls. When, therefore, anti-Asian feeling began to build up over and above its simmering norm in East Africa, and particularly in Kenya, in the second half of the 1960s, it was to Britain that the Asians began to look as a future home if conditions were to become too difficult for them in their countries of residence.[33] Until 1967 the number of East African Asians with British passports arriving in the United Kingdom for settlement was apparently fairly small, although, as such persons were not included in the statistics maintained under the Commonwealth Immigrants Act, 1962, the precise figures before 1968 are not ascertainable. Certainly, however, the exodus of Asians from East Africa increased greatly in volume in 1967. Steel quotes statistics indicating that in the first half of 1967 the number of Kenya Asians did not exceed 1000 in any one month, but that 1493 entered in August of that year and 2661 in September.[34] The then Home Secretary, Roy Jenkins, affirmed, shortly before his move to the Treasury in November 1967, the right of the Asians from East Africa with British passports to enter the United Kingdom, but his replacement as Home Secretary, Jim Callaghan, quickly moved to revise this policy and introduced the Bill which became the Commonwealth

Immigrants Act 1968, the principal effect of which was to bring the influx of East African Asians under immigration control. Immediately before the Cabinet took the decision to introduce legislation late in February 1968, Asian heads of household were leaving Kenya for Britain at the rate of several hundred a day. The 1968 Act introduced for the first time the concept of patriality, in that any citizen of the United Kingdom and Colonies who himself, or whose father, or whose father's father, had been born or naturalised or registered or legally adopted in the United Kingdom remained exempt from control under the new legislation. Uncontrolled entry was therefore restricted from 1968 onwards to those who in some sense already 'belonged' to Britain through ties of origin.

In attempting to judge the 1968 Act, it is necessary to contrast its effect on immigration control with the 1962 Act. The earlier Act aimed to control and regulate a potentially very large flood of immigration; the 1968 Act, on the other hand, was aimed to control the entry of a finite medium-sized number of potential migrants, many of whom were in considerable economic distress. The East African Asians were admittedly not the only persons who had retained United Kingdom citizenship after their country of residence became independent without being able to claim any previous ties with Britain through birth or ancestry; some sections of the population of Malaysia and of other former colonies were citizens of the United Kingdom and Colonies as one part of their dual citizenship, but the East African Asians were the only community likely to wish to leave their countries of residence in more than negligible numbers. The policy of Africanisation was rapidly forcing Asians out of their businesses or making them redundant when in paid employment, hence the growing economic distress among the community.

At first, entry of non-patrial United Kingdom passport holders, mostly coming from East Africa, was limited under a system of special vouchers to 1500 heads of households. Dependants, as defined in the Act, had the right to accompany or join the voucher holder for permanent settlement. The annual figure of 1500 special vouchers proved to be far lower than the demand, and over 7000 heads of households were on the waiting list for vouchers in 1970. The quota was doubled to 3000 in 1971 and an additional 1500 vouchers were made available in that year in an attempt to reduce the backlog. The demand for vouchers in East Africa increased however and the annual quota was further increased to 3500 in 1972 and to 5000 in 1975. By 1978 the queues of United Kingdom passport holders still waiting to travel to the United

Kingdom had decreased and the quota was not being fully utilised. Discussion of the government's policy towards the admission of East African Asians after 1971, and in particular on the admission of United Kingdom passport holders expelled from Uganda in 1972, appears in a later section of this chapter. Three important comments on the 1968 Commonwealth Immigrants Act, two of a political nature and one of a statistical nature, have to be made here. The first comment relates to the bitter controversy over the 1968 Bill within the United Kingdom; both Conservative and Labour parties were divided, despite the fact that most of the pressure for stricter immigration control came from the right-wing of the Conservative party. The press too was divided, but the more sober papers, headed by *The Times*, took the view that the legislation was a betrayal of the guarantees given to the East African Asians, particularly those in Kenya, earlier in the decade at the time of independence. The second comment is that the way in which the East African Asians were treated undoubtedly contributed to the souring of relations between India and the United Kingdom. The third comment is that, with or without the 1968 Act, the number of East African Asians with their families moving from East Africa to the United Kingdom from 1967 onwards, although far from huge, was of sufficient magnitude to throw off course the forecasts made by the more objective and statistically-trained observers of the future size of the coloured population of the United Kingdom. In a written answer to a House of Commons question in November 1975, the then Minister of State, Mr Lyon, stated that from March 1968 to June 1975 a total of 83,272 non-partial United Kingdom passport holders, including 57,431 dependants, had been admitted for settlement.

Reference has been made above to the fact that the 1968 Commonwealth immigrants legislation was enacted very shortly after Mr James Callaghan took over as Home Secretary from Mr Roy Jenkins. Mr Callaghan's views on immigration from the developing countries of the Commonwealth were clearly stated when he gave evidence before the Select Committee on Race Relations in May 1970.[35] He made it quite clear that it had been his policy to reduce the number of immigrants[36] and stated that part of the improvement in race relations had arisen from the fact that the British people felt that numbers were being controlled. He was content with an annual entry of about 4000 Commonwealth employment voucher holders, which, with an average of four dependants per voucher holder, implied an annual immigration figure of about 20,000 people. He thought that it was desirable 'that the Commonwealth, if it is to continue to mean something, should have special rights of access to this country, as distinct from the rights of access that are given to aliens'[37] but he considered that India and Pakistan, at any rate, were more concerned with the principle of the freedom for some of their people to come here rather than with the actual numbers coming. He admitted that the West Indies might be as much concerned about numbers as about the principle involved. For Mr Callaghan the overruling factor was the widespread concern in the United Kingdom about the large numbers of immigrants, combined with a determination to do everything possible to stop abuse of the immigration control system. The fact that the United Kingdom was not, in Mr Callaghan's view, able to absorb large numbers of British passport holders from East Africa 'in a short period of time without social tension'[38] appeared to be more important to him than the fact that many of the individuals involved were suffering from real hardship.

Further steps were taken to tighten and modify the controls on the entry of dependants. Restriction on the entry of male fiances was imposed in 1969 'because it was, in our opinion from the evidence I got from immigration officers, being abused to an extent where it was reducing the employment voucher system almost to a farce. . . . If I may give the figures, in 1965 524 fiances arrived. In 1968 3591 arrived, and there was very strong evidence that this was being used as a backdoor method for getting in if you could not get an employment voucher.'[39] This abuse of the system largely applied to fiances from India and Pakistan, but it was difficult, in Mr Callaghan's opinion, to operate on a selective basis as far as countries were concerned. Abuse of the system was also given as the reason for the raising of the minimum admission age of dependent parents from 60 to 65. Dependent children were only to be admitted if both parents were present in the United Kingdom, though in practice children under 11 years of age were allowed to join their mother if she was the only parent in the United Kingdom, a discretionary exception which was particularly important to the West Indies in view of their family structure.

Attempts to block loopholes and stop abuses of the rules governing the entry of immediate dependants had however only a marginal effect on the inflow of dependants. Eversley and Sukdeo, writing in 1968,[40] rightly stated that the disquiet about the future size of the coloured immigrant population had largely been caused by the high rate of arrival of dependants of coloured Commonwealth citizens and estimated that not more than 236,000 women and children could be expected to settle in England and Wales after the end of 1967, on the assumption that the issue of vouchers to heads of households would continue at a low level.

In 1967 the rate of arrival of dependants was at its maximum, just over 50,000 being admitted for settlement in that year, the heads of the households to which these dependants belonged having for the most part arrived several years earlier. The years 1968 to 1971 inclusive saw the admission of over 137,000 dependants of persons admitted under the 1962 and 1968 Commonwealth Immigrants Acts, and the statistics since 1971 make it clear that the estimate of 236,000 made by Eversley and Sukdeo will be considerably exceeded. Among the major immigrant groups only the number of arrivals of dependants from the West Indies has tapered off as anticipated and net immigration from that source has ceased altogether. The total of Asian dependants arriving has far exceeded the estimates and it is now accepted that estimation of further immigration of dependants is difficult, if not impossible.

Not all dependants in fact join the head of household in the United Kingdom. At the time of the 1971 census, there were twice as many male as female persons of Pakistani origin in the United Kingdom (taking into account both those born in Pakistan and those born in the UK), and for those coming from Africa the ratio was about four males to three females. This imbalance is in itself a clear indication that there is a considerable potential inflow of dependants from both Pakistan and Africa which may in fact never materialise. The number of males and females of West Indian origin were about equal in 1971, and the excess of Indian males over females was not great in relation to total numbers; however the continued tendency of Indians of both sexes to find marriage partners in India means that the Indian inflow, unlike the West Indian, is far from having been reduced to a trickle. The limitation on the immigration of fiances of women already in the United Kingdom imposed in 1969 was lifted in 1974, and the number of Indians admitted for marital reasons is far greater than from any other country.

Up to 1971 the extent of unemployment in the United Kingdom was not sufficient in itself to deter potential immigration or to encourage coloured Commonwealth immigrants to move on to other countries or return to their own countries. Coloured 'economically active' persons[41] have a higher unemployment rate than whites in the same local area, but the difference is usually narrow in times of low unemployment and widest in times of high unemployment. The sixties was a period of low unemployment though the trend was towards a higher rate. Throughout the sixties unemployment in the United Kingdom was not only far lower than in most less developed countries, but also low in relation to North America, particularly Canada.

At the time of the 1971 census 5.1 per cent of the population enumerated in England and Wales were born outside the United Kingdom. A total of 2.3 per cent of the population were born in New Commonwealth countries, including Cyprus, Malta and Gibraltar; if these three countries are excluded, 1.9 per cent of the population or just over one million people were born in what may be described as less developed countries of the Commonwealth, mainly Asian (including Pakistan), African and West Indian. A small percentage of such persons would of course have been children of British-born parents, for example the children of colonial officials. The total number of persons enumerated in Great Britain in 1971 with one or both parents born in New Commonwealth countries was over one and a half million, of whom approximately 41 per cent were born in the United Kingdom. Depending on the definition adopted for 'coloured' and allowing for the facts that persons with one or even both parents born in New Commonwealth countries are not necessarily coloured and that persons with both parents born in the United Kingdom are not necessarily white, this figure of rather over one and a half million can be accepted as a first approximation of the size of the coloured population of Great Britain in 1971. A more refined calculation of the coloured population of Great Britain at the time of the 1971 census, excluding Cypriots, Maltese and Gibraltarians, gives the number as 1,385,600 persons.[42]

It would be wrong to imagine that immigrants from New Commonwealth countries entering the United Kingdom to stay for a year or more constituted a very large majority of all immigrants after 1962. On the contrary, between 1964 and 1973, New Commonwealth immigrants made up only 36 per cent of all immigrants according to International Passenger Survey data, the Old Commonwealth countries, Australia, New Zealand and Canada, contributing 21 per cent, and foreign countries, including South Africa, 43 per cent.[43] There was, however, a considerable turn-over of migrants from Old Commonwealth countries and foreign countries, many of the immigrants from these countries entering the United Kingdom for a few years only for business or study purposes; the fact that the number of persons in the United Kingdom born in the Old Commonwealth, continental Europe, and non-Commonwealth countries in America increased by only about 125,000 between the 1961 and 1971 censuses is proof of this, for that figure represents less than two years average immigration entry. Persons born in the Irish Republic and enumerated in Britain were fewer in number in 1971 than in 1961. The only group of immigrants to increase its share of the population very considerably was the group born in New Commonwealth countries, and their numbers quadrupled between 1961 and 1971. Despite the fact that coloured immigrants have made up only just over a third of the total immigration into the United Kingdom in recent years, the permanent nature of settlement coupled with differences in skin colour and culture made it inevitable that coloured immigration should be the only type of immigration to attract much attention.

THE PERIOD 1962–71: EMIGRATION

The only reliable statistical guides to emigration from the United Kingdom for the 1960s and 1970s are the sample based International Passenger Survey organised by the British government at British airports and seaports, and the immigration statistics produced by the more statistically developed overseas countries of immigration. The pattern of emigration as indicated by this data continued in the 1960s along the same pattern as in the 1950s. In terms of gross emigration, Australia, New Zealand and Canada received just under half of all persons of whatever nationality, leaving the United Kingdom as emigrants. In terms of net migration, which gives a better picture of long-term movements, it was only the net movement of migrants into those three countries which made the United Kingdom a net exporter, rather than a net importer, of population.

According to evidence given by the General Register Office to the Select Committee on Science and Technology in May 1970,[44] gross emigration from the United Kingdom to Canada, Australia, New Zealand, and South Africa for the years 1960–9 was as shown in Table 4.4. The figures for 1960–3 were based on statistics from the receiving countries and for 1964–9 on estimates derived from the International Passenger Survey.

While the figures for all four countries inevitably vary over time with the economic conditions and, in the case of South Africa, the political conditions, of the receiving countries, it is noteworthy that total gross emigration to these four countries combined from the United Kingdom averaged nearly twice as much in the last six years of the decade, when the Labour government was in power, than in the first four years, when a Tory government was in power. It may be argued that the basis for measuring international migration changed in 1964, at about the time when the change of government took place. The same phenomenon is however observable if International Passenger Survey statistics are used to compare the period 1970–73, a period of Tory rule, with 1964–9

TABLE 4.4.   Gross emigration from the United Kingdom to Canada, Australia, New Zealand and South Africa (thousands)

Year	To Canada	To Australia	To New Zealand	To South Africa
1960	20	42	9	2
1961	12	46	12	2
1962	16	44	14	5
1963	25	62	15	10
1964	32(22)	81(65)	16(11)	15(11)
1965	42(32)	91(73)	15(9)	13(9)
1966	64(51)	84(67)	16(10)	14(7)
1967	64(50)	84(58)	15(9)	15(9)
1968	40(26)	84(55)	8(−)	17(12)
1969	34(20)	97(71)	9(3)	21(16)

The figures in brackets for the years 1964 to 1969 inclusive are for net migration.

when Labour was in power. The net migration of United Kingdom citizens as a separate group is measurable with International Passenger Survey data, and these show a very significant drop in net out-migration during the period of Tory government. The lowest figures between 1964 and 1973 for net out-migration of United Kingdom citizens were in 1971 and 1972, in the first half of the Tory period of government, before the economy really ran into trouble. The philosophy of the two parties is such that the fairly permanent latent interest in emigration on the part of a sizeable minority of the British public is perhaps more likely to be translated into action under a Labour government, when taxation tends to be higher and individual business initiative is liable to greater control.

However important or unimportant the policies of the political regime of the time may have been in providing part of the individual motivation for emigration, neither of the major political parties directly encouraged or discouraged the movement of United Kingdom citizens to overseas countries. The Commonwealth Migration Council, formed in 1946 to encourage British migration to Commonwealth countries, constantly urged the benefits to be gained from such migration, both as a means of easing population pressure in the United Kingdom and as a means of helping to maintain the ties between Britain and the Old Commonwealth. Although the Committee members have included a number of Members of Parliament, they do not as a pressure group appear to have had much influence on government policy. In their 1970 submission to the Select Committee on Science and Technology[45] the Commonwealth Migration Council complained that since 1945 the British Government had 'never done more than take a "neutral" view of migration' and had on occasion 'been positively opposed to the whole concept'. The charge of neutrality is certainly justified as far as migration to white Commonwealth countries is concerned, and the only positive encouragement given by the British government to technically well-qualified people to work in other countries of the Commonwealth has related to technical assistance programmes, and, rather indirectly, to the staffing of Commonwealth universities.

The Conservation Society are another body concerned with the stabilisation of the size of Britain's population, and recognise that a higher rate of emigration would work in the direction of such stabilisation. Unlike the Commonwealth Migration Council, however, the Conservation Society recognise the objections to a positive policy to encourage the indigenous British population to emigrate. In evidence to the Select Committee, the Society said that

A high proportion of emigrants have received higher education or possess valuable skills and hence emigration represents a substantial loss of investment in human capital. Given present economic difficulties a policy of actively encouraging emigration is unlikely to receive Government support, but future circumstances may make it possible for the Government to encourage people to emigrate, particularly if satisfactory arrangements could be made for host countries to take a higher proportion of the unskilled and economically inactive.[46]

Even without active encouragement from the government, Britons continued to emigrate to the Old Commonwealth countries overseas in the 1960s in even larger numbers than in the 1950s. Net emigration from the United Kingdom averaged 0.3 per 1000 population in the 1960s as compared with 0.2 per 1000 population in the 1950s. This was in marked contrast with the position in Western Europe, in all the major countries of which there has been a positive immigration balance since 1960 with the Federal Republic of Germany and France having by far the largest numerical net intake of migrants, but with Switzerland and Luxembourg having the largest net intake in relation to population size.

The contrast between the Western European experience and that of the United Kingdom is perhaps best exemplified by the Netherlands. Both countries in the 1950s had experienced sizeable net emigration movements to northern America and to Oceania, the emigration from the Netherlands being partly counter-balanced by immigration from the newly-independent Indonesia and the movement from the United

Kingdom by immigration from the West Indies and the Indian sub-continent. In the 1960s, however, emigration from the Netherlands to northern America and Oceania was sharply diminished in contrast to the trend of emigration from the United Kingdom which, as stated above, continued at a high level. A plausible explanation for this phenomenon lies in economic conditions. Despite short periods of economic recession, as for instance in Australia and Canada in 1961/62, the 1960s were in general a decade of rapidly expanding economies in northern America and Oceania, and the demand for suitably qualified immigrants in these regions was not easily satisfied. The decade was also a period of economic boom and high political morale in the Netherlands, one of the founder-members of the European Community. For the United Kingdom, however, the period was one of relatively low economic growth, and political malaise; the imperial role had been lost and the nation was searching for a new role in the international community and, internally, for a fairer and more egalitarian society.

For some of the British who disliked the lack of self-confidence and the series of economic crises which seemed to be such a feature of Britain in the sixties, there were real opportunities in migration to other Commonwealth countries, and the problems to be faced by immigrants in Australia, New Zealand and Canada were not as serious for the British as for other nationalities, because of the similarities in language and culture. Not all of the British who would have liked to migrate were acceptable to the prospective receiving countries, of course, but in the early 1960s Canada admitted British subjects born or naturalised in the UK provided they had the means to maintain themselves until employment had been secured or if they had relatives in the country to sponsor them, and Australia and New Zealand still had at that time built-in preferences for immigrants of British stock with the required employment qualifications. For many UK citizens who wished to emigrate, the question was not so much whether they would be accepted as immigrants elsewhere but which of a number of possible countries, both inside and outside the Commonwealth, they would go to. The UK provided the lion's share of European immigrants to both Australia and New Zealand and remained in most years the leading sending country of immigrants to Canada, despite the fact that all three countries, and most particularly Canada, accepted rapidly increasing numbers from the developing regions from the mid-sixties onwards as the result of new policies adopted by their governments towards immigrants from Asia, Africa and the West Indies.

In addition to being the leading sender of migrants to the three Old

Commonwealth countries, the UK continued to supply the Republic of South Africa with more white immigrants than any other country, even after the latter country had left the Commonwealth. Over the post-war period as a whole the UK has supplied about one-third of South Africa's white immigrants, but in more recent years the UK's share has risen to one-half and more as immigration from Western Europe, particularly the Netherlands and Germany, sunk to a low level. However immigration from the UK to South Africa, whether measured gross or net, was on average little larger than to New Zealand, a much smaller country, until 1974 when, temporarily, the movement to South Africa began to swell in volume. By 1978, however, the tide had turned once again, and the balance of migration between the United Kingdom and South Africa was northward in direction. As far as Rhodesia is concerned, net migration has been outwards in most years since the unilateral declaration of independence in 1965, the net outflow having been about 14,000 between the 1961 and 1969 censuses.

MIGRATION FLOWS AND POLICY SINCE 1971

The Immigration Act 1971, which became generally operative on 1 January 1973, provided a comprehensive basis for future immigration control and removed certain entitlements hitherto enjoyed by Commonwealth citizens but not by aliens. The Act did not, however, diminish the freedom of dependants of Commonwealth citizens settled in the United Kingdom before 1 January 1973 to enter the country, subject as before to entry clearance requirements. However, it ended the employment voucher scheme for Commonwealth citizens, under which persons with such vouchers were accepted for settlement on arrival; the work permit scheme from 1973 applied to Commonwealth citizens in the same way that it had previously applied to foreign nationals. Although the new enactment effectively eradicated the long-standing differentiation in immigration law and practice between Commonwealth citizens and foreign nationals, it had little effect on the total number of New Commonwealth and Pakistani immigrants accepted for settlement in the United Kingdom either on arrival or by revocation of initial conditions of entry. A much increased number of coloured immigrants, who entered the country initially as students, fiancees, or others with a time limit on the length of their stay, were given permission to settle from 1974 compared with earlier years to balance any diminution in the numbers accepted for settlement on arrival. The total figures of citizens

of the New Commonwealth and Pakistan accepted for settlement in the
years 1971–8 were as shown in Table 4.5.

TABLE 4.5.   Number of citizens of New Commonwealth Countries and
           Pakistan accepted for settlement in UK, 1971–8

Year	Accepted on arrival	Accepted on removal of time limit	Total
1971	35175	9086	44261
1972	59850	8669	68519
1973	25530	6717	32247
1974	25306	17225	42531
1975	34510	18755	53265
1976	36817	18196	55013
1977	· 27742	16413	44155
1978	25273	17666	42939

Sources: First Report from the Select Committee on Race Relations and Immigration.
       Session 1977–78 vol. II pp. 342–3.
       Control of Immigration Statistics 1977 (Cmnd 7160). Control of Immigration
       Statistics 1978 (Cmnd 7565).

The exceptionally large figure for 1972 followed the expulsion of
Asians from Uganda by President Amin's Government. In that year
nearly 35,000 non-British UK passport holders and their families were
admitted, mainly from East Africa. In other years since 1971 the figure
for UK passport holders accepted for settlement on arrival has not been
more than 12,000. If United Kingdom passport holders and their
families are excluded from the figures of citizens of the New
Commonwealth and Pakistan accepted for settlement on arrival the
statistics would show a declining trend in 1973 and 1974 as compared
with 1972 – under 17,000 in 1973 and a little over 14,000 in 1974
compared with 25,000 in 1972. However, the number of such immigrants accepted for settlement on arrival in 1975 and 1976 was
considerably in excess of the figures for 1973 and 1974, numbering about
22,500 in 1975 and over 26,000 in 1976, again including Pakistanis but
excluding UK passport holders and their families. Most of these were
dependants of persons already settled in the United Kingdom, and the
increase in numbers can be attributed at least in part to the instructions
given by the Home Office to speed up the process of dealing with
applications for entry clearance made by dependants in India, Pakistan
and Bangladesh of heads of families already resident in the United

Kingdom. Thus in November 1974 the *Daily Telegraph* reported that Mr Roy Jenkins planned to send seven additional immigration officers to Bangladesh to speed up the flow of dependants and double the number of entry certificates; at that time the waiting period for applicants averaged two years.[47] A month later the *Guardian* reported that delays in issuing entry certificates to Pakistani dependants averaged as much as two and a half years.[48] This 'speeding up' of the rate of entry clearance applications in the Indian sub-continent, mainly from wives and children of people already settled in the UK, certainly increased the numbers of citizens of New Commonwealth countries and Pakistan, for all years between 1974 and 1977.

From 1974 onwards, however, the figures of Commonwealth immigrants excluding patrials accepted for settlement on arrival were not much more than half the total, and the numbers accepted on removal of the time limit on their stay became numerically important. There are a number of contributory reasons for this change. Most importantly Section 7(1) of the Immigration Act 1971 states that Commonwealth citizens who were resident in the United Kingdom on 1 January 1973 (the date of coming into force of the Act) would not be liable to deportation under the Act if for five years they had been ordinarily resident in the United Kingdom; about 40 per cent of those accepted for settlement in 1975 on removal of the time limit imposed on their stay were exempted from deportation under this section of the Immigration Act. Such persons would have appeared in the overall migration statistics of earlier years, but not in the category of persons admitted for settlement on arrival; for instance they would include persons originally admitted on temporary work permits or as students.

A further important category of persons accepted for settlement on removal of the time limit imposed on their stay at the time of entry are fiances and financees. In 1975 marriage was the reason for acceptance for settlement of 9000 persons (including UK passport holders) earlier admitted for a limited period from Commonwealth countries and from Pakistan, rather over half of these being women. The immediately preceding years were not comparable because of the limitations on settlement until June 1974 of male Commonwealth citizens who entered the United Kingdom to marry. A new Immigration Rule in March 1977, under which men recently married to women already settled in the UK were no longer granted immediate settlement, led to a drop in the numbers of New Commonwealth and Pakistani citizens accepted for settlement on arrival in 1977 and 1978. As a 1977 White Paper phrased it:

No statistical presentation can indicate diversity of origin and circumstances of those from the New Commonwealth and Pakistan who can be granted settlement in the United Kingdom: e.g. the wife from Bangladesh coming to this country to join her husband, or the Jamaican boy to join his parents; the student nurse from Malaysia or West Africa who has qualified and remained here for five years; the Cypriot fiancee who marries a husband in this country; the Indian doctor who has worked here for four years.[49]

The increase in the number of coloured immigrants accepted for settlement in 1975 led to renewed anxieties, expressed both inside and outside Parliament, about the future level of immigration, and, as one manifestation of these anxieties, into the appointment by Mr Roy Jenkins, as Home Secretary, of a Parliamentary Group on the feasibility and usefulness of a Register of Dependants, from the Report of which the above quotation is taken. It was argued that, if a register of dependants was feasible, it would offer a guide to the country's statutory commitment in future years to the admission of dependants of heads of families already in the United Kingdom, and it would provide 'a factual context within which immigration policy could be discussed in a calm and rational way' without 'ill-informed, and sometimes ill-intentioned, speculation'. The Parliamentary Group, while deliberately forbearing from making recommendations, made their opinion clear that the only 'adequately useful' scheme for maintaining a register of dependants would be a compulsory register with a time limit for registration and a sanction for failure to register or withdrawal of entitlement to settle, that any such register needed to be applied only to citizens of New Commonwealth countries and of Pakistan, and that provisions would have to be made for keeping any such register up to date. Following the Group's Report, the idea of creating and maintaining a register was dropped, although it is very possible that the Conservative government elected in May 1979 will give the matter further consideration.

Early in 1976 the Home Secretary had had to admit that official 1973 Home Office statistics for net immigration of New Commonwealth citizens were incorrect owing to errors arising from the 'double counting' of departing migrants at Heathrow airport and that the net intake of New Commonwealth immigrants had been considerably larger than originally estimated. Mr Enoch Powell re-opened the controversy about immigration by stating that, in the three years from 1973 to 1975, immigration had added more than 250,000 persons to the population and by calling for the elimination of 'the admission as of right of the so-called dependants of existing residents'.[50] Only a few months later Mr Powell quoted a confidential Foreign Office report prepared by Mr Hawley, an Assistant Secretary at that Office, commenting, among other things, on the 'established industry for helping people to come to Britain' (from the Indian sub-continent) and stating that 'the pressure to come to the United Kingdom is enormous and bogus documentation to support spurious cases is all too commonplace'.

In a leading article on 29 June 1976 entitled 'Anxieties over Immigration', *The Times* discussed the widespread popular belief that there was no end to the flood of immigrants from the New Commonwealth countries and Pakistan. The article, while stressing that popular belief was to some extent based on the myths that large numbers of heads of household were still being admitted and that relatives as well as immediate dependants were admissible, agreed that the Hawley report and the increase in the number of coloured immigrants in 1975 provided some solid basis for these anxieties. There was a strong popular opinion that there was a good deal of illegal immigration, and fears of this nature were not assuaged by mere official assertions to the contrary. This article in *The Times* was quickly followed by a report in another newspaper on 'Tory Plans to Cut Immigration', in which it was suggested that the Conservative package included a register of dependants, the reduction in the number of special vouchers from 5000 to 3000 per annum, the withdrawal of the rights of foreign husbands and fiances to join British wives and fiancees, and the stricter control of illegal immigration.[51] It was in early July, shortly after this report, that the Home Secretary announced the three-member Parliamentary Group to report as soon as possible on the feasibility and usefulness of a register of dependants.

Both major political parties were split in their views on immigration policy. Most of the left-wing of the Parliamentary Labour Party, including Mr Lyon who had been Minister of State in the Home Office with responsibility for immigration in 1975, favoured a very liberal immigration policy with the benefit of doubt being given to persons claiming to be dependants in cases of uncertainty. Much of the right-wing of the Party wanted a clearly defined limit to the number of immigrants to be allowed into Britain and enhanced action against illegal immigration. Views in the Parliamentary Conservative Party ranged from those who wished to put a stop to the right of entry for dependants to those who insisted on the honourable discharge of the statutory obligation towards admission of dependants and a continued quota for the admission of East African Asians with United Kingdom passports. Immigrant organisations in Britain rather naturally tended to oppose Conservative Party immigration proposals, and indeed immigrant voting power has been generally regarded as so strongly supporting the Labour Party that it has been suggested that several marginal constituencies would not have been won by Labour in the two 1974 general elections without the immigrant vote.

Unfortunately politicians of all kinds as well as newspaper reporters and other interested observers have been quite unable to define the dimensions of the immigration problem. Some facts are known, but there is necessarily much guess-work in any attempt at an assessment. Because plans for a 1976 sample census were dropped as an economy measure, the 1971 census is the last major source of information. In the 1971 census a question was asked on the birthplace of parents as well as the respondent's own birthplace. On the basis of the answers to these questions, it is possible to make estimates of the total immigrant population, including children born to immigrant parents in the United Kingdom, and to make rather less dependable estimates of the total coloured immigrant population, including children born to coloured immigrant parents in the United Kingdom, the lesser degree of dependability being due to the lack of a direct question on colour in the census. There are of course 'white' British born in New Commonwealth countries (e.g. the children of pre-independence colonial officials) but most (though not all) of these can be excluded from the estimate for the coloured Commonwealth population by excluding persons born in New Commonwealth countries to parents neither of whom were born in such countries. It is also a matter of choice whether it is appropriate to include or exclude persons who themselves came from or whose parents came from the Mediterranean Commonwealth countries. In a discussion of migration and migration policy, it seems appropriate to include them, whereas in a discussion on race relations it would be appropriate to exclude them. Using Mrs Lomas's calculations, the number of persons enumerated in Great Britain in 1971 with one or both parents born in New Commonwealth countries and Pakistan was 1,558,000, and the number so enumerated with one or both parents born in those countries other than Cyprus, Malta and Gibraltar is estimated at 1,386,000.[52] By 1974 the official estimate of the population of New Commonwealth and Pakistan ethnic origin had risen to 1,744,000, by mid-year 1975 to 1,815,000 and in 1976 to 1,900,000. The total population had remained almost static in numbers between 1966 and 1975 and the proportion of the population of New Commonwealth and Pakistani ethnic origin had risen from 1.9 per cent to 3.3 per cent. Only fools were unable to recognise that Britain had become and would certainly remain a multi-racial society.

The advance in the proportion of coloured to total population has been so rapid that some thought about the future is not only rational, but essential. What can be said? First of all migration between the United Kingdom and the West Indies is now nearly in balance. The size of the West Indian population in the United Kingdom will now be determined by natural growth and not by migration, unless a continuing high unemployment rate in the United Kingdom causes a larger return movement to the Caribbean. The balance between the United Kingdom and the Commonwealth countries of Africa was positive in 1975 and 1976 mainly as the result of the continued net movement of East African Asian heads of households and their families holding United Kingdom passports, but movement was nearly in balance in 1977. In mid-1976 the number of United Kingdom passport holders remaining in East Africa was estimated at no more than 38,000 including dependants.[53] If that estimate were approximately correct, the flow of United Kingdom passport holders from East Africa should be diminishing rapidly by about 1980, on the assumption that the annual quota for special voucher holders is not reduced before that year. It must be pointed out that some Commonwealth African Countries outside East Africa have a number of United Kingdom passport holder residents, who have at times felt insecure about their future. In 1973 Robert Carr (later Lord Carr), then Home Secretary, talking about the mass expulsion of Asians from Uganda, stated that the United Kingdom Government would regard any further attempt to unload Asians *en masse* by an African Commonwealth country as imposing 'unacceptable strains and stresses on our society'.[54] That statement came after reports that Kenya might attempt to act in the same way as Uganda had done. Later there were reports that Malawi was considering the expulsion of that country's relatively small number of Asian United Kingdom passport holders. By early 1978 the Select Committee on Race Relations and Immigration was able to report that there were no longer any queues of United Kingdom passport holders in East Africa waiting to come to the UK and that the quotas were not being fully used. 'It appears' the Report says, 'that all those who wish to come will shortly have done so and our commitment to the United Kingdom Passport Holders in these countries will have been substantially discharged'.[55]

The statistics of Commonwealth citizens accepted for settlement either on arrival or on removal of the time limit for stay in 1975 give Cyprus, Hong Kong, Jamaica, Malaysia and Mauritius as the five New

Commonwealth countries or territories, in addition to India, Bangladesh and Kenya, which had more than 1000 of their peoples accepted. In 1974 these same five countries and Sri Lanka, in addition to India, Bangladesh and Kenya, had more than 1000 of their people accepted for settlement in the United Kingdom. Small-scale but steady Cypriot migration to the United Kingdom has been a feature for a good many years, although it has of course been controlled by immigration legislation since 1962; after the Turkish occupation of part of Cyprus in 1974 about 200,000 Greek Cypriots were made homeless and some of the refugees found their way to the UK and were admitted as short-term visitors. In 1974 and 1975 the great majority of the Cypriot acceptances for settlement were on removal of the time limit, and the fact that the specific reason for removal of the time limit in about half the cases was because of marriage tells its own story. In the case of Hong Kong, where the native-born and naturalised British subjects are issued locally with United Kingdom passports because of Hong Kong's continued colonial status, the majority of the acceptances for settlement are on arrival and in respect of spouses and dependants of persons from Hong Kong already resident in Britain. Unless and until there is an immediate prospect of a take-over of the colony by China – and there is no such prospect at present – there is unlikely to be any pressure for a major escalation of migration from Hong Kong to the United Kingdom. Jamaica is discussed in a later chapter.

Malaysian acceptances for settlement in the United Kingdom, even more than of Cypriots, are very predominantly on removal of the time limit. Malaysian students easily topped the list of student entries into the United Kingdom from Commonwealth countries in both 1974 and 1975, and it is reasonable to surmise that a considerable number of Malaysian students, particularly nurses, are given permission to settle in the United Kingdom after their studies are completed. In the year 1975, moreover, Malaysians easily topped the list of all Commonwealth countries in the annual analysis of work permits granted for a maximum period of twelve months. Outside the Commonwealth only USA, Spain and the Philippines, in that order, exceeded Malaysia in the number of work permits. Before 1969 the many Malaysian students who embarked on courses of higher education in Australia, Canada and the United States, as well as the United Kingdom, almost all returned home after completing their studies. Since the disturbing riots of 1969 in Malaysia and the increased pressures in that country to enforce the use of the Malay language in education and to favour the Malays in the employment market, young Malaysian Chinese have looked much more to countries outside Asia not only for higher education but also for permanent settlement. In Sri Lanka and Mauritius too, political and economic pressures in recent years have encouraged some sections of the population to look for emigration outlets.

The major areas of remaining uncertainty in relation to immigration commitments relate, first and foremost, to the number of non-patrial dependants of all nationalities, but particularly of India, Bangladesh and Pakistan, where the heads of households are already settled in the United Kingdom and the entitled dependants are still in their home countries; and secondly to the likely future inflow, mainly from these same three countries, of marriage partners for men and women already settled in the United Kingdom. As regards the first category forecasts of future arrivals and settlement of dependants are and always have been highly speculative and unreliable. Moreover, the lack of contemporary census data adds to the difficulties involved in forecasting. Even the suggested register of dependants would provide no certain information about the future levels of arrivals in the UK. It does seem probable that the total number of persons with the statutory right to enter the United Kingdom as dependants of immigrants will have been reduced since 1971, but not by any means by as large a figure as the statistics of those admitted for settlement on arrival as dependants would suggest. A letter to *The Times* from a Member of Parliament on 13 September 1976 went so far as to suggest that the leaked Hawley report seemed to confirm the fears of those who believed that the number of dependants waiting to enter the United Kingdom might actually be larger in 1976 than in 1971. This seems unlikely to be the case because the proportion of dependants in the total number of persons from New Commonwealth countries accepted for settlement on arrival increased from three out of every four in 1971 and 1972 (which would keep the waiting list about static on the basis of three dependants to each head of family) to nine out of every ten in 1973, 1974 and 1975, after the Immigration Act 1971 had come into force.

In 1976 much play was made of an answer by the Financial Secretary to the Treasury to a parliamentary question about child tax allowances given to wage earners in the United Kingdom for children living overseas. Mr Goodhart, the questioner, was told that 500,000 such allowances were made each year, but insufficient information was available to give similar statistics on non-resident wife allowances. A subsequent statement from the Board of Inland Revenue elicited the information that one-third of the allowances given emanated from claims by Irishmen. No specific information was given on the proportion emanating from claims by immigrants in the United Kingdom labour force whose families were in the Indian sub-continent, but the figures could be considerable. It is equally likely that the Inland Revenue inadvertently allows a considerable number of fraudulent claims for child allowances, and the statistics, however interpreted, would almost certainly provide an over-estimate of the child dependants of Commonwealth immigrants with the right to enter the United Kingdom. It must be remembered that immigrant families from both the Indian sub-continent and the Caribbean are permitted to return home and re-enter Britain, provided that the absence of the head of household is for not more than two years, and a number of the child tax allowance claims will no doubt be in respect of children who have already entered the United Kingdom at least once and are on an extended stay in their own homelands.

In addition to the tax statistics there are the figures of dependants with outstanding applications to enter the United Kingdom. These figures obviously vary from time to time. In April 1977 Mr Alex Lyon MP, former Minister of State in the Home Office, told the Select Committee on Race Relations and Immigrations that there were 33,032 dependants in the queue for entry certificates in the whole of the Indian sub-continent, and added that these 'represent most of those who want to come',[56] though the basis for that addendum is not apparent. Two months earlier he had estimated the total number of entitled dependants in the Indian sub-continent to be fewer than 80,000,[57] but here again the basis of estimation is not apparent, and his estimates appear to conflict with estimates given from time to time in reports by civil servants. If the evidence from the tax returns is regarded as putting rather too high a figure on entitled dependants, and Mr Lyon's estimate as rather too low a figure, the total number of entitled dependants as at the spring of 1977 in all New Commonwealth countries is unlikely to be fewer than 125,000 and unlikely to be more than 300,000. By no means all of these people actually want to come to Britain.

As regards the second category of marriage partners, the future flow will depend both on the rate of change of social custom in immigrant communities in the United Kingdom and on the immigration rules, which are themselves liable to be changed. In 1971 there were about 675,000 persons under the age of 20 enumerated at the census who, whether born in the United Kingdom or in the New Commonwealth or Pakistan, had one or both parents with the characteristic of birth in Pakistan or a New Commonwealth country other than Cyprus, Malta and Gibraltar. This is an average of 34,000 persons for each year of age under 20, and, of these, about half have parents one or both of whom were born in the Indian sub-continent. It is among families emanating from the sub-continent that the tradition of arranged marriage is still strong, with brides or bridegrooms often coming from the home country to join the marriage partner in the United Kingdom although customarily brides join the bridegroom's family home. In 1975 a total of just over 6500 New Commonwealth citizens were accepted for settlement in the United Kingdom after marriage, suggesting that not far short of half of Indians and Pakistanis in the United Kingdom are married to new arrivals from the sub-continent. It is reported that those whose education has been mostly or entirely in the United Kingdom prefer to marry members of their own community already settled here, and, on that assumption, the practice is likely to diminish in importance. Nevertheless nearly 4500 persons from India, and over 2200 from Pakistan were accepted for settlement on removal of the time limit by reason of marriage in 1978, so the custom is still very much alive.

The discussion in the last few pages has been in terms of numbers of potential immigrants from New Commonwealth countries and this masks the fact that each immigrant is a human being with his own talents and skills, and his own individuality. There has been too much of a tendency to lump all immigrants from New Commonwealth countries together as if they came from one mould, and policies have been framed and controversies about immigration have raged in spite of a continued dearth of sufficiently reliable factual knowledge about the immigrant communities. The statistics of the last few years indicate that the population of West Indian origin in Britain has ceased to grow through migration, and its future level will be determined by natural increase; that, whatever the precise numbers of East African Asians still unwillingly marooned in Africa, the flow of immigrants is nearly at an end; and that the major uncertainty for the future relates to migration to Britain from the Indian sub-continent, although it seems clear that the flow of migrants will continue at a fairly high level for a number of years. Quite apart from further migration, all communities of New Commonwealth and Pakistan origin are likely to form gradually increasing proportions of the United Kingdom population for the foreseeable future, if only because fertility of women in these communities, although low in comparison with their countries of origin, is high in comparison with the native British. In mid-year 1975 the population of New Commonwealth and Pakistani ethnic origins in Britain was estimated to make up 3.3 per cent of the population compared with 2.1 per cent in 1967. Taking into account all the known factors, including the lack of growth of the native British population, it seems not unreasonable to suggest that the ten-year period from 1975 to 1985 may see a further growth in this proportion to around 4.5 per cent. There are too many unknown factors to hazard any kind of a projection of the proportion of the United Kingdom population of New Commonwealth and Pakistani ethnic origin beyond 1985. It may be noted, however, that net migration and natural increase at present contribute about equally to the growth of the New Commonwealth and Pakistani population, at present running at between 4 and 5 per cent annually.

Immigrants who are citizens of Old Commonwealth countries (Australia, New Zealand and Canada) have arrived in considerable numbers over the past twelve years, although not in quite such large numbers as Commonwealth citizens from the New Commonwealth. For citizens of Old Commonwealth countries, however, immigration and emigration have been nearly in balance. This fact is illustrated by the International Passenger Survey statistics of the Office of Population Censuses and Surveys and confirmed by the very slow growth between 1961 and 1971 in the population enumerated in the United Kingdom as having been born in Old Commonwealth countries. Similarly immigration and emigration of both Irish citizens and other foreign nationals other than Pakistanis have been approximately in balance since 1965. The only two major *net* migration movements affecting the United Kingdom remain – as they have been since 1955 – an inward movement of people from New Commonwealth countries and an outward movement of United Kingdom citizens. The outward movement has been numerically larger than the inward movement, and the United Kingdom has thus retained its traditional position of being a net exporter of people.

Immigration from the United Kingdom to all the Commonwealth receiving countries has been cut since 1974 for economic reasons, and, to a smaller extent, for political reasons. Canadian immigration statistics indicate that since 1973 the United Kingdom has just about maintained its share of a falling immigration total. In Australia, however, there has been a decrease in the proportion of immigrants coming from the United Kingdom as well as Western Europe, and an increase in the proportion from Asia and the Middle East. Australia still obtains the lion's share of her highly skilled immigrants from the United Kingdom and Ireland, but the year 1975 saw an exceptionally low level of overall emigration to Australia. In that year net emigration from the United Kingdom to all Old Commonwealth countries fell by 52,900 persons, mainly as a result of large decreases in net emigration to Australia and New Zealand.[58] In compensation there were increases in net emigration to South Africa, Western Europe and the United States in 1975. The experience of the year 1976 was similar to that of 1975 except that there was an increase in emigration to Australia from the low level of 1975 and a fall in emigration to Canada; again in 1976, Western Europe and the United States were popular destinations for emigrants. In 1976 and 1977, however, the popularity of South Africa receded to such an extent that a large net outflow from the UK in the year ended mid-1976 changed to a small net inflow into the United Kingdom.

Between 1964 and 1973 emigration of United Kingdom citizens to Australia, New Zealand and Canada combined was substantially greater than to Europe, the United States and South Africa combined. It is too early to say with certainty whether the proportionately decreased emigration to Old Commonwealth countries and increase to foreign countries will be permanent, but if, as appears to be the case, highly skilled personnel are forming an increasing proportion of United Kingdom emigrants, the flow to countries that reward skills best can be expected to be maintained or increased. Equally, however, the ties of kinship and the family reunion policies adopted by the Old Commonwealth countries ensure that the flow of emigrants to these countries will revive once economic conditions improve again. Commonwealth migration seems certain to remain a dominant element in the total United Kingdom migrational pattern for many years to come.

Since this chapter was drafted, the 1979 general election has been held in the United Kingdom resulting in the return of a Conservative government. If earlier post-war history is to be accepted as a guide, emigration of UK nationals is likely to be at a low ebb in the first two or three years of the new Government's administration, particularly in view of the clear intention to restore the pay comparability of doctors, dentists, university teachers and others, which had been so badly eroded since 1974 by Labour's wage restraint policies, and the even clearer intention to reduce the levels of direct taxation. Admittedly unemployment in the UK seems certain to remain at a high level, but there are also high rates of unemployment in the traditional receiving countries. The new Government is committed in its manifesto to reduce immigration, but the methods of achieving this end have not yet been clearly spelt out.

5 Malta and the Commonwealth Connection

INTRODUCTION

The flight of the Knights of St John from Malta following its occupation by Napoleon was succeeded in 1800 by the siege of the French occupiers by the Maltese who invited Nelson to their aid. From then on the horizons of the Maltese people for new settlement have broadened. Nevertheless, during the nineteenth century most Maltese refused to look farther than the Mediterranean area for opportunities to improve their standard of living and escape from the ups and downs of the Maltese economy. Emigration was directed at the North African littoral and at certain areas in the eastern Mediterranean, but many of the migrants returned home to Malta and net migration for much of the century was only about 15 per cent of gross emigration.[1] Love of home and a desire to settle in a country near enough to home to make a return passage easy, combined with periodic but often short-lived improvements in the Maltese economy and political disturbances in North Africa and the eastern Mediterranean, were responsible for this high rate of Maltese return migration. During the nineteenth century the Empire links with the British Dominions and the linguistic and historic links between Britain and the United States failed to move many Maltese to consider migration to areas outside the Mediterranean. The official attempt to sponsor migration to Australia in the latter half of the nineteenth century was in large part a failure, although it did provide a Maltese nucleus from which later migratory movements from Malta to Australia perhaps drew some sponsorship and encouragement, for Maltese emigrants in general have drawn a great deal of comfort from being able to join a colony of their own people overseas. Official attempts were also made to start Maltese colonies in the West Indies, in Cyprus and elsewhere in the nineteenth and early twentieth centuries, without substantial success. More success attended a settlement of Maltese in Gibraltar. Where Maltese communities were established outside Malta, they were for the most part the result of unsponsored emigration and were sited on the north African coast and in Turkey. In the last years of the nineteenth century and the early years of this century, Maltese settlements outside Europe and North Africa gradually increased in size, but were still fairly small by the beginning of the First World War. Quota restrictions imposed by the Australian, United States and other governments on immigration from southern European countries, including Malta, after the First World War ensured that there was no spectacular development of stable Maltese communities in Oceania and America between the wars. Malta in fact suffered acute problems after the 1918 Armistice, because there was no industrial employment available to absorb persons discharged from naval and military establishments. The emigration authorities were apparently able to arrange the emigration of several thousand people within two years of the cessation of hostilities.[2] But from 1920 the Australian government allowed only 260 new immigrants per annum in addition to the wives and children of earlier settlers, although as the result of official representations the quota was increased in 1924 to 1200 per annum subject to the state of the economy. Entry into the United States was restricted to only 14 per annum after the 1921 introduction of quotas, although that figure was increased to 200 in 1925 and to 380 in 1929. Canada dithered on the question of allowing Maltese to share the British freedom of entry, and New Zealand classed Maltese as aliens for entry purposes despite their British subject status.[3]

In the early years after the First World War a very high proportion – 90 per cent according to Casolani – of those who registered as intending migrants were illiterate, and those who had attended school had little or no vocational training. A considerable number of Maltese continued to migrate both to the French colonies of North Africa and to France herself, but the return migration rate was high, particularly from North Africa.[4] However, gross migration to North America, Australia and the United Kingdom was somewhat higher than gross migration to France and French colonies in the first decade after the war, and net migration to the former group of countries was very substantially higher, for two-thirds of the migrants to destinations outside the Mediterranean remained in their country of settlement. The situation changed with the onset of the Great Depression. New migration to Australia, Canada and the United States was reduced to a mere trickle after 1930, and the United Kingdom assumed the role of main receiving country for

Maltese emigrants. The official annual figures for Maltese leaving their own country to settle in the United Kingdom were, however, much lower in the 1930s than in the first twelve years after the end of the Second World War. According to official figures, which should not be regarded as completely accurate, the annual numbers and destination of emigrants from 1930/1 to 1939/40 were as shown in Table 5.1. It will be noticed that the figures for countries other than Australia, Canada, the United Kingdom and the United States were a substantial proportion of the total figures throughout the decade – a sure indication that emigration to France and other Mediterranean countries had not entirely lost its appeal to the natives of Malta.

TABLE 5.1.   Number of emigrants to various destinations from Malta 1930–40

Year	Australia	Canada	UK	USA	Others	Total
1930/1	77	15	327	592	1611	2622
1931/2	63	12	187	73	926	1261
1932/3	41	6	114	76	1317	1554
1933/4	100	4	157	184	891	1336
1934/5	107	6	267	262	789	1431
1935/6	84	3	459	143	686	1375
1936/7	156	1	662	125	806	1750
1937/8	149	6	1079	259	825	2318
1938/9	305	2	672	136	446	1561
1939/40	123	—	390	156	385	1054

The absolute number of emigrants from Malta has always been small, but the population of Malta is also small, and emigration in relation to total population was high between the world wars and higher still after the Second World War. The importance of emigration to Malta arises from the fact that population density has for long been very high – it was over 1000 per square mile in 1850 and about 2000 in 1930. Moreover, natural resources are meagre. Malta had in the 1920s an official with the title 'Superintendent of Emigration', an indication of the importance attached by the Maltese government even then to the encouragement of emigration. Had economic well-being been the sole or even the main criterion for individual decisions to emigrate, there can be little doubt but that many more Maltese would have found their way to destinations outside Europe before 1914; in fact cultural factors have been equally important, and Maltese were on cultural grounds often unwilling to take advantage of the opportunities which on purely economic considerations should have been grasped.

Net migration in the inter-war years was insufficient to balance the natural increase of population. The fertility of Maltese women remained high until well after the Second World War, the crude birth rate in the late 1930s being nearer to 40 than 30 per thousand population, and the death rate around 20 per thousand. During the Second World War there was naturally no migration. By 1948 the population of Malta had risen to over 300,000 with a density of nearly 2500 persons per square mile, and natural increase was running at over 7000 per annum.

MIGRATION UNDER THE BOFFA AND OLIVIER GOVERNMENTS 1947–55

Malta received a new constitution in 1947 and the Malta Labour party under Dr (later Sir) Paul Boffa won the first general election under this constitution. The Minister for Emigration in the Boffa Government, John J. Cole, made determined efforts to promote emigration, set emigration targets and obtained financial assistance for emigration from the British government. By the time the Boffa Government took office, natural increase was running at the high level of 2.5 per cent per annum and the birth-rate 'showed no signs of falling'.[5] Because Malta has a small population, it is not unrealistic for its government to hope that international migration can go a long way in solving its population problems; nevertheless, the official target adopted of an optimum population of 250,000 or less, to be reached in ten years by the annual net emigration of 5 per cent of the population, was unrealistic. No population, unless on the run as a result of war or famine, can expect to achieve such a high rate of net migration, and, although emigration from Malta in the period 1945–57 was, in relation to total population, 'considerably higher than in any other country',[6] the target of a net migration of about 15,000 persons was not achieved in any single post-war year. Both gross and net migration exceeded 10,000 in 1954, but only in that year.

The efforts of Cole and his associates did, however, meet with considerable success and led to a quite new pattern for Maltese emigration, as the official figures in Table 5.2 indicate.

It should be explained that those who obtained financial assistance to emigrate were fairly certain to figure in the official statistics, for the funds emanated from government sources. The very great majority of those who emigrated to destinations outside Europe would fall into this category. However, the official statistics almost certainly do not include

Table 5.2.   Numbers of emigrants to various destinations from Malta
1946–55

Year	Australia	Canada	UK	USA	Others	Total
1946	86	3	870	67	252	1278
1947	366	27	1536	351	166	2446
1948	880	719	845	654	52	3150
1949	3618	258	1137	302	53	5368
1950	5563	863	1038	1022	17	8503
1951	4006	1607	1234	831	14	7692
1952	2161	680	1200	1293	11	5345
1953	1376	770	1702	683	1	4532
1954	8470	963	1690	299	25	11447
1955	6442	425	1872	266	2	9007

even the majority of those who left Malta to settle in continental Europe or the North African littoral, and the figures for migrants to the United Kingdom may be well short of completion. Official figures for net migration are not quoted, as apparently the migration authorities tended to subtract from gross migration only those who returned within two years of the outward journey to reach a net figure.

In the post-war period to 1955 some 55 per cent of registered emigrants went to Australia compared with less than 10 per cent in the 1930s. Moreover, emigration, as officially counted, was very predominantly a movement to other countries of the Commonwealth – much more so than ever before. As explained above local movements of Maltese within the Mediterranean area were to an extent unknown and not included in the official figures because the Department of Emigration was mainly concerned with migrants who qualified for passage assistance. The government scheme providing large-scale passage assistance to the country of the individual emigrant's choice was set up very shortly after the general election of November 1947 which brought in the Boffa Government, and the passage assistance was complemented by successful official overtures designed to 'obtain the goodwill and full co-operation of the receiving countries'.[7] A ministerial mission of goodwill went to Canada, the United States and Australia in September 1948 and one of the first fruits of the mission was a Passage Assistance Agreement with the government of Australia which went into operation on 1 January 1949 for five years and was subsequently renewed. Canada agreed to take a sizeable contingent of migrants from Malta, and the United States agreed to speed up facilities for the issue of visas to Maltese. And although some of the schemes ran into initial difficulties, such as the premature departure of some of the immigrants in Australia from the employment allotted to them, government-sponsored emigration proved a success for the first time in the history of Malta. Between November 1947 and March 1949, there were seven shipments of migrants to Australia, and three each to Canada and the United States, and on 31 March 1949 there were 42,000 prospective emigrants on the books of the Department of Emigration, half of whom wanted to go to Australia and the majority of the remainder to Canada. In Australia most of the Maltese ultimately settled in New South Wales and Victoria and in Canada in the Toronto area.

The cost of the emigration programme was very heavy. In the six financial years up to 1953/4, the total cost was more than 2.6 million pounds, of which the Maltese government provided 673,000 pounds and the British and Australian governments most of the remainder. Emigration did have the effect of keeping unemployment at a low level; it also, however, had the effect of depriving Malta of up to half of its skilled manpower and, between the 1948 and 1956 censuses, the proportion of the population in the 20–45 age bracket fell from 33.8 to 29.7 per cent. Moreover, there were twice as many male as female adult emigrants, causing a noticeable distortion in the sex distribution in the same age bracket of those who remained in Malta. The island colony remained economically dependent on expenditure by the Services and the level of employment consequently remained dependent on current defence policy of the British government. Diversification of the economy, which demanded skilled manpower, was badly needed. And yet, as Balogh and Seers put it, 'any development programme, which raises the hopes of the people of Malta for better living conditions and more secure jobs, would discourage emigration and therefore partly defeat its own purpose'.[8]

The Nationalist Party which took office after the 1950 election, first under the leadership of the veteran politician Mizzi, and then after his death under Dr Borg Olivier, continued to back the emigration policy whole-heartedly. Until the 1930s the Nationalist Party had been pro-Italian in outlook and had resented the changes in the educational system under which the Italian language was ousted from being the language of instruction in the schools and the university – and the language of the law courts. After the war-time attack on Malta by Mussolini's air force, any remaining pro-Italian sympathies died, and the Nationalist Party became firmly convinced that Malta's future lay within the Commonwealth and that financial support for Maltese emigration to Commonwealth countries should continue. The number of emigrants – and government expenditure on emigration – reached a peak in 1954/5, the last year of the Olivier Government before its defeat by Mintoff at the 1955 general election.

Why did the momentum of emigration rise so rapidly in the ten years after the end of the war? And why did the main migrational flow move so decisively towards the Dominions and towards Australia in particular? Before attempting to suggest answers to these questions it is necessary to examine in rather more detail than hitherto some of the post-war characteristics of the Maltese population. It has been mentioned that, after the First World War, a very high proportion of intending migrants from Malta – and indeed of the Maltese population as a whole – were illiterate. In contrast those Maltese who were of the right age to migrate after the Second World War were literate, had been to school and mostly spoke English as a second language, with Maltese itself as the first language. A higher proportion of the Maltese labour force was skilled than ever before. The Second World War had provided Malta with the opportunity to become less parochial and to develop a much greater community of interest with the United Kingdom and other Commonwealth countries. And there were already in 1945 permanent communities of Maltese origin, admittedly on a small scale, in Australia and Canada, as well as in the United Kingdom and the United States. In these circumstances it is not surprising that the energetically pursued emigration programme was a great success, backed as it was with financial assistance for migrants from the government and with both spiritual and practical assistance for migrants from the Emigrants Commission set up by the Roman Catholic Church. This Commission, which dated from 1950, arranged for the posting of priests to the new Maltese communities overseas and helped the emigrants and their relations left behind in Malta to keep in touch. The Commission supplemented the official activities of the government and itself organised charter flights between Malta at one end and Australia, Britain and North America on the other so that parents and relatives could visit emigrants overseas, and emigrants could return to visit their old homes, all at prices well below normal commercial fares.

The particular appeal of Australia for Maltese emigrants is to some extent parallel to the pull of Australia for British emigrants from the United Kingdom. Three factors need to be stressed, however. In the first place Australia, unlike Canada, stationed a Senior Migration Officer in Malta thus having on-the-spot promotion for emigration, whereas Canada's Visa Attaché visited Malta once a month from Rome. Secondly, Australia had a rapidly growing number of Maltese happily settled in that country, a point stressed in one of the Annual Reports of the Department of Labour and Emigration.[9] (One of the migrants was the same John J. Cole who was Malta's post-war Minister for Emigration!) Thirdly, and perhaps most importantly, the climate of Australia suited the Maltese much more than did that of Canada with its unaccustomed winter cold or even the milder but damp climate of the United Kingdom.

MIGRATION UNDER THE FIRST MINTOFF GOVERNMENT 1955–8

Dom Mintoff became Prime Minister of Malta in February 1955 after his Malta Labour Party had gained 23 out of the 40 seats in the country's Legislative Assembly. Malta was still a colony but with a large measure of internal self-government, though defence, civil aviation and some other subjects remained the responsibility of the Imperial Government. Mintoff, a Fabian Socialist with an Oxford education, was an advocate of 'integration' with the United Kingdom, unlike Borg Olivier and the Nationalist Party who wanted Malta to acquire some form of qualified Dominion status. For electoral support Mintoff relied considerably on the skilled and unskilled workers, including the Naval Base dock-workers, who were themselves well represented in the migrational flow overseas. Mintoff's election on a plank of integration with consequential hopes of diversification and strengthening of the Maltese economy and targets of raising wages gradually to the level of the United Kingdom were probably the most important factors in the reduction of the number of emigrants from 9007 in 1955 to 4492 in 1956 and only a little over 3000 in 1957 and 1958. The official line taken by the Mintoff Government was that 'emigration must carry on but at a rate to be determined by the tempo of the economic development of Malta. Within this limitation emigrants will continue to receive financial and other help. . . . The annual rate of emigration . . . should be of an average not exceeding 5000 persons.'[10] Clearly the Mintoff Government placed much less importance on emigration than did earlier post-war governments. Not only were fewer Maltese disposed to emigrate in this period, but there were an abnormally large number of former migrants who returned to Malta, attracted doubtless by the government's policy of full employment and improvements in social welfare. Net emigration, which had been running at 80 or 90 per cent of gross emigration in the 1946–54 period, had fallen to less than 50 per cent of gross emigration in 1957.

Australia remained the leading recipient country for Maltese emigrants, but she lost some ground to the United Kingdom and Canada. Emigration to destinations other than these three countries remained at a very low level. In 1957 over 1000 migrants returned to Malta from Australia and the Minister thought that emigrants 'were being misled about the local situation in Malta, and appealed to all with relatives in Australia, England and Canada not to paint too rosy a picture of conditions in Malta'. But the influx of returned migrants continued.[11] Obviously too high a rate of return flow of former migrants was regarded as just as disastrous as too high a rate of outward flow of skilled new emigrants.

In the meantime, although three-quarters of those who voted in the 1956 Integration Referendum expressed themselves as in favour of integration with the United Kingdom, a very sizeable proportion of the electorate abstained from voting, and it became clear that the Maltese Roman Catholic Church and the political parties in opposition to the Maltese Labour Party were opposed to integration. A further reason for the failure of the integration talks between the Maltese and British Governments was the fear entertained by the Maltese about the future of the dockyard and naval base. The collapse of the talks, although clearly having serious implications for the Maltese economy, did not lead to an immediate return to the scale of emigration seen in 1954 and 1955. The constitution was suspended in 1958 and Mintoff ceased to be Prime Minister, but emigration from Malta did not rise again until 1963, by which time Malta was on the verge of independence.

EMIGRATION FROM MALTA AFTER 1958

Official statistics indicate that Maltese emigrants opted for Commonwealth host countries to a greater extent after 1958 than ever before. Between the wars only one-third of emigrants went to Commonwealth countries; between 1945 and 1959 some 90 per cent went to Commonwealth countries; in the fifteen years after that to 1974 the proportion was nearly 95 per cent. In the first post-war period just over 55 per cent of all emigrants went to Australia and in the fifteen years to 1974 that proportion increased to 60 per cent. Post-war Maltese migration to Australia has been a classical case of chain migration. The only other important host countries in recent years have been the United Kingdom and Canada in that order. The volume of Maltese emigration to the United Kingdom remained remarkably steady in the fifteen years to 1974 considering the fluctuation in the UK economy in that period and the progressive diminution in the originally very generous quota of immigrant vouchers allotted to Malta under the Commonwealth Immigrants Act. The official statistics of Maltese emigrants for the years 1959 to 1974 inclusive by principal countries of destination are as shown in Table 5.3. Within this period there was direct rule until 1962, the

TABLE 5.3. Numbers of emigrants to various destinations from Malta 1959–74

Year	Australia	Canada	UK	USA	Others	Total
1959	1875	472	744	174	—	3265
1960	2304	509	878	142	8	3841
1961	2140	213	1112	108	7	3580
1962	2051	371	1129	76	7	3634
1963	4152	905	1332	92	98	6579
1964	5923	1181	1597	87	199	8987
1965	5349	1113	1444	84	100	8090
1966	2258	648	1092	282	60	4340
1967	2081	752	856	261	21	3971
1968	1564	478	638	258	54	2992
1969	1229	394	683	299	43	2648
1970	1469	332	640	219	36	2696
1971	1762	308	527	178	23	2798
1972	1853	467	597	213	33	3163
1973	2416	768	603	253	19	4059
1974	2595	755	581	252	6	4189
Total, 1959–74	41021	9666	14453	2978	714	68832

National Party under Dr Borg Olivier was in power from 1962 until 1971, with Maltese independence coming in 1964 under his leadership, and Dom Mintoff has been Prime Minister since 1971. For both main political parties it remained conventional wisdom that relatively large-scale emigration was essential to Malta's economic well-being, but attempts have been made from time to time by one party or the other to make political capital on matters relating to the scale of emigration and the political affiliations of the emigrants. The *Malta News* of 29 April 1966, which supported Mintoff, stated in criticising the Nationalist's budget proposals that the Government preferred to ameliorate the problems of the economy and of employment by intensifying the emigration drive rather than by generating new forms of industrial activity within Malta, and the paper affirmed that the Nationalists were aiming at an emigration target of 10,000 people, although actual emigration in 1966 and thereafter fell very markedly from the 1965 level. Probably the employment opportunities resulting from the construction boom and the growth of industry and tourism was largely responsible for the decline in emigration after 1965. Both parties tended to accuse the other of encouraging and assisting the emigration of their opponents; in fact well-known politicians on each side of the political fence were among the emigrants, and, once it was clear that a party supporter was determined to emigrate, no one was likely to attempt to stand in his way.

When the Malta Labour party under Mintoff returned to power in 1971, the position did not change overnight and in fact gross emigration was on a rather larger scale in 1972, 1973 and 1974 than in the last four years of Olivier's Government. In the 1973 seven-year plan, provision was made for continuing emigration, though at a diminishing rate. Until 1974 net emigration remained at well over 85 per cent of gross emigration, if official figures are to be accepted. By 1976, however, net emigration had fallen below zero; in other words more former migrants were returning to Malta than new migrants leaving the country. In that year the number of returning migrants was 4670 and the number of new emigrants only 1107. The election in 1976 which renewed Mintoff's mandate was accompanied by exaggerated promises on the part of some Labour party spokesmen about the availability of work in Malta's expanding and diversifying economy. However, the basis for presentation of net migration statistics changed in the mid-1970s, the figures of returning migrants including for the first time those who returned to Malta after more than two years overseas and did not therefore forfeit the passage assistance given to them on the outward journey. Net migration after 1974 is thus not comparable with earlier official figures. The Malta Labour party hailed this reversal of the migratory stream as a success for its policies, and certainly the tremendous drive made by the Mintoff Government to create jobs for everyone and to welcome home former emigrants who chose to spend their retirement in Malta was a major contributory factor.

The euphoria was however short-lived. By the middle of 1977 the Maltese Government was telling earlier emigrants to stay in the countries to which they had moved and not to return to Malta for the time being. Mintoff had to try to create 12,000 new jobs before 31 March 1979 to fill the void created by the ending on that date of the agreement on the lease of military facilities, and he could not contemplate a further addition to the problem by allowing further returned migrants to register for work in the Employment Offices.[12] The Government shifted its position from being ostensibly pleased at the return of emigrants to requiring that former emigrants returning after 1 May 1977 would not be permitted to register for employment for a two-year period. Apparently some two-thirds of the 3000 emigrants who returned between May 1975 and May 1976 registered as unemployed, implying that many had been misled about the employment prospects. By no means all return migrants were intent on spending merely a pleasant retirement in Malta.

Clearly there was a difference in attitude towards emigration between the Olivier Government from 1962 to 1971 and the subsequent Mintoff Government. The Olivier Government was conservative and middle-class and the Labour Party accusation that emigration was seen by the Nationalist Party as the answer to unemployment had an element of truth. Nevertheless, it was the Nationalists who started the road to industrial development and who gave Malta a name in the tourist industry. The Mintoff Government of the 1970s made and continues to make tremendous efforts to create an economically viable Malta without any dependence on military bases. In the period 1971–6 a state airline, a state shipping company and a small trawler fleet were established with help from various countries. Substantial progress was made, with assistance from the Chinese government, towards building a new dock to accommodate the largest oil tankers. Chinese assistance also led to the opening of a carpet factory, a spinning mill, a decorative glass factory and a chocolate factory and further ventures were started with technical and capital investment from other countries; by no means all these ventures have been successful. Some of the Labour party spokesmen were, however, undoubtedly over-optimistic about the rate at which new jobs could be created, and their exuberance created the false impression among Maltese communities in Australia and elsewhere that not only a peaceful retirement for older people but also assured employment for younger people was available in Malta for Maltese nationals.

One reason for the big increase in return migration was the transferability of pensions from the host country to Malta for a former emigrant who had settled back home on retirement. Those who returned were following the classic economic response of a reasonably successful emigrant who has worked in countries where both cost of living and wage levels are much higher than in his country of origin. In Malta food prices have been kept down by subsidy, by government bulk buying and by efficient price controls although there was a change of policy in 1977, cash assistance being substituted for subsidy. Income tax concessions are available to Maltese who resettle after twenty or more years abroad, and this makes the island an attractive place for the old emigrant who is homesick. Bearing in mind the large stream of emigrants in the 1950s, it must be expected that the return flow of former emigrants reaching pensionable age will continue.

Demographically the position in the 1970s was totally different from that in the late 1940s and early 1950s. In 1970 the rate of natural increase of population was only about one-third of the rate twenty years previously, mainly as a result of a very substantial fall in the crude birth-rate over the twenty-year period, and particularly during the 1960s. From 1963 until 1974 net emigration of Maltese nationals exceeded natural increase in every year. By 1972 the local population (that is, excluding British servicemen and their families) was once again below 300,000, and the demographic explosion had been averted, partly through emigration of nearly 130,000 between 1946 and 1972 and partly through the reduction in the rate of natural increase from 2.5 per cent to about 0.7 per cent per year.

Commonwealth membership was vital to Malta in the execution of the emigration programme, for the very great majority of post-war emigrants went to Commonwealth countries. The current population of Maltese extraction in Australia, including those born in Australia to Maltese parents, is certainly a six-figure number and some estimates put the figure as high as 400,000. There are also now substantial Maltese colonies in other countries, especially the United Kingdom and Canada. The reduction in the rate of emigration from Malta and the net immigration in 1975 and 1976 has not of course been due solely to the pull of Malta's expanding economy. Changes in migration policy in Australia and the United Kingdom together with the recession which has affected those and other migrant receiving countries have restricted the scope of new migration in the last two or three years.

After the Commonwealth Immigrants Act of 1962 came into force in the United Kingdom, Malta received generous treatment and in the British White Paper of August 1965[13] Malta was, as a temporary measure, allocated 1000 out of the total of 8500 vouchers to be issued annually, 'to give effect to our [British] special obligations to Malta'. Allowing for dependants this quota naturally implied an annual maximum inflow of Maltese emigrants substantially in excess of 1000. As the number of Maltese emigrants to Britain was 1092 in 1966 and less than 1000 in every subsequent year, it is clear that the quota of 1000 vouchers was never filled despite the fact that some British firms organised recruitment campaigns in Malta.[14] By 1972 Malta's annual quota of work vouchers had been progressively reduced to 500, but even then the quota was not filled as many Maltese to whom employment vouchers were issued did not ultimately arrive in the United Kingdom. The United Kingdom figures of vouchers issued and admissions of voucher holders from 1965 to 1971 are shown in Table 5.4.

TABLE 5.4.   Vouchers issued to Maltese passport holders 1965–71 in UK

Year	UK Ministry of Labour employment vouchers issued	Admissions of voucher holders in UK
1965	1071	716
1966	806	651
1967	762	537
1968	746	539
1969	770	468
1970	846	478
1971	634	331

Source: Commonwealth Immigrants Acts 1962 and 1968. Statistics. Annual Reports

After 1 January 1973 the admission of Maltese, as with both other Commonwealth citizens and the nationals of non-Commonwealth countries, was governed by the immigration controls provided under the Immigration Act 1971 and the numbers admitted with work permits for twelve months (the nearest equivalent to the employment vouchers issued under the Commonwealth Immigrants Act) continued to decline slowly. Maltese, however, figured prominently among those admitted with work permits for less than twelve months, that is for seasonal work. In general, however, the employment situation in the United Kingdom made it increasingly difficult for non-EEC nationals to obtain work permits for entry into Britiain between 1974 and 1978.

The decrease of Maltese emigration to Australia was largely a result of new immigration restrictions introduced by the Australian Government under Prime Minister Whitlam in the second half of 1974. In the financial year 1 April 1975 to 31 March 1976, gross emigration to Australia fell to 637 persons, according to Maltese statistics, compared with 2076 in the previous year; the figure of 637 was the lowest since 1947. The severe immigration restrictions remained in force until the Whitlam Government was defeated at the polls, and in practice the high level of unemployment and the faltering Australian economy under the

Gorton Government continued to make migration to Australia from Malta a doubtful proposition. Nevertheless, according to the Emigrants Commission, there were 3000 persons waiting to emigrate to Australia in July 1976, and the current low level of migration between the two countries is probably temporary. Indeed, bearing in mind the family reunion aspect, which has always been stressed in post-war Australian immigration policy, and the fact that the Maltese community in Australia is the largest outside Malta itself, it would be very surprising indeed if population interchange between Australia and Malta did not continue, although possibly at fairly low levels of net migration in view of the attractions of Malta for retirement.

Maltese emigration to the United States and to Canada has not been as numerous as emigration to Australia, nor is it likely to be in the foreseeable future. Maltese emigration to the United States was adversely affected by the US Immigration and Nationality Act of 1952 and was restricted by quota until the Immigration Act of 1965 which led to the abandonment of the national origins scheme and the admission of immigrants in order of application for visas. Despite that all-important amendment to US immigration legislation and the introduction in 1966 for the first time of passage assistance for Maltese migrants to the United States, the number of such migrants never exceeded 300 up to 1974; no substantial Maltese communities have been established in the United States, apart from one in Detroit.

Maltese emigration to Canada fluctuated considerably, as post-war United Kingdom emigration to Canada has done, with the employment situation in the latter country. The 1962 Canadian immigration legislation which emphasised education, training and skills, rather than ethnic preferences, was followed by an upsurge of emigration to Canada for three or four years, though it is likely that conditions in Malta at that time were almost as important as the Canadian legislative changes in that rise in emigrant numbers. The points system introduced into the Canadian immigration system in 1967 resulted, whether directly or by chance, in a downturn in the number of Maltese immigrants, and the more stringent controls introduced in the winter of 1974 made it still more difficult for Maltese prospective emigrants to gain admission to Canada. Although the Maltese community in the Toronto area is well established, efforts to secure the foundation of a new Maltese settlement in Manitoba in 1967 and 1968 were not successful.

Maltese emigrants to Canada, as well as those going to Australia, have had all but a few pounds of their passages paid from official sources. The great majority of those going to Australia have received passages under the successive-agreements made between the Australian and Maltese governments, in most cases at Australian expense. The passage money for Maltese migrants to other receiving countries has been found by the Maltese government, with some assistance from the Colonial Development and Welfare Fund in the earlier post-war years. From 1970 assistance with passage money has been given for emigration to any country, those destined for Australia, New Zealand, Canada and the United States receiving the full fare less £10 each if aged between 19 and 60, less £5 each if aged between 14 and 18, the full fare without deduction if under 14. For other destinations the emigrant receives three-quarters of the fare in assistance. In addition there are special grants made to emigrants in certain circumstances, for instance if he or she had been unemployed for three or more months before departure or on social assistance for six weeks before departure. If the emigrant fails to remain in his adopted country for a minimum of two years, the passage money and allowances granted must be returned.

The aid given to emigrants has not been purely financial. Mention has already been made of the Emigrants Commission, set up by the Roman Catholic Church in 1950. A Maltese newspaper article in 1976 written by a member of the Commission[15] reviewed its work over twenty-five years. Courses are arranged for intending emigrants dealing with matters such as the employment position, the educational system, house renting and purchasing, social services and religious practices in the countries of destination. Courses are run for Maltese girls intending to marry foreigners. The number of visits to Malta each year by former migrants is put as high as 10,000 and some of these visitors return to look for a wife; the Commission has set up a 'Valentine Scheme' whereby young people could meet during visits of migrants from overseas. The sex imbalance among migrants and among the population of parts of Malta means that the scheme will tend to encourage marriages in which both partners are Maltese.

The Commission also deals with a considerable diversity of problems arising, for instance, from mixed marriages, divorce, illegitimate children, imprisonment and death overseas. Often the family remaining in Malta would be affected by such events, and the Commission can arrange, for instance, for relatives in Malta to look after the children of marriages which are running into difficulties. The Commission pays particular attention to the problems that might arise when single girls emigrate either permanently or on seasonal employment. For instance there is now a flourishing Maltese colony in Spalding in the United Kingdom, which the Commission has been able to keep under its wing;

Maltese women go to Britain for seasonal work in canning factories in Spalding and elsewhere, and some of these seasonal workers have found husbands in Britain.

Clearly emigration from Malta is as highly organised as, for instance, immigration into Australia, and the existence of such organisation is a further indication that, from a Maltese point of view, the current recession in the emigrant flow is regarded as a temporary aberration from normality. Although the crude birth-rate has fallen, the age group now reaching the popular age for emigration as young adults are the product of the very high birth rate of the immediate post-war years, and, if the receiving countries of the Commonwealth, and particularly Australia, set their immigration targets at a rather higher level once again, there will be no lack of Maltese wishing to make the move.

MALTA AS A COUNTRY OF IMMIGRATION

Paradoxically, bearing in mind Malta's high population density, a certain kind of immigrant has been welcome in Malta. These immigrants are not permitted to take employment in Malta and have to satisfy certain income or capital ownership requirements. The scheme began in 1964, when the Maltese Government hit on the idea of trying to attract for settlement retired people with adequate means in order to fill the gap left by the outgoing Services families created by the run-down of British military and naval expenditure. Persons settling in Malta under this scheme became known as 'sixpenny settlers' in view of the fact that income after all personal reliefs was subjected to tax at only $2\frac{1}{2}$ per cent or 'sixpence in the pound', as it then was under the old pounds, shillings and pence currency.

The original income requirements were pitched at a level suitable to attract people of about the same income level as the Services families who were to be replaced. There was a modest increase in 1968 to a minimum of £1400 per annum for a single person and £1600 for a married couple. The policy proved to be extremely successful, for the new settlers not only brought in spending power and a modest tax yield, but also provided a much-needed stimulus to the building industry, as a result of their demands for new housing, and to the tourist industry by encouraging visits by friends and relatives on holiday. In addition the new residents, being mainly in the older age-groups, provided a substantial yield of death duties!

In 1971, with the accession of a Labour government in Malta, the income conditions for new applicants for settlement were revised, although the requirements for existing settlers were left unchanged. The new requirements were that the newcomer must bring income of at least £4000 per annum into Malta and have capital of at least £35,000; alternatively he must have at least £100,000 capital and pay not less than £1000 annually in income tax. All settlers were in future to pay income tax on a scale starting at 10 per cent with a maximum rate of 25 per cent, this change being made in full consultation with existing settlers. The Prime Minister made no secret of his preference that overseas Maltese should make Malta their retirement home rather than that Malta should continue to attract large numbers of foreign settlers. This was in marked contrast to the expressed policy of the opposition Nationalist Party, which announced in 1976 that when in power they would endeavour to increase the number of foreign settlers to 10,000, representing 3 per cent of the population.

Apart from those who formally applied for and obtained a permit for permanent residence, a number of persons have become *de facto* resident in Malta by applying for permission to reside temporarily on permits which have to be renewed every six months. This type of permit differs from the ordinary tourist permit in that it carries an obligation to spend not less than six pounds per head daily during the sojourn in Malta. Many of these temporary permit-holders can meet the *per diem* requirement without being able to satisfy the capital ownership criterion for permanent residence.

A minor, and ultimately self-balancing migration exercise took place in 1972/3, when Uganda expelled those of its citizens who were of Indian ethnic origin. Malta was one of the countries that volunteered to take care of some of the refugees while they sought fresh homes, whilst being unable to accept any for permanent settlement. The expenses for caring for these refugees were paid by the United Nations, and the exercise was expected to be complete in about six months, though the time span was in fact a little longer because of the difficulty of finding permanent host countries for some of the refugees. Eventually the 500 Ugandan citizens succoured by Malta were found places overseas, mainly in Australia and Canada, and all had left by the middle of 1973.

6 Emigration from Jamaica

INTRODUCTION

International migration has played a more important part in the demographic history of the Caribbean than in most developed countries outside the Americas and Australasia, and Jamaica is no exception to this rule. For the last 100 years emigration has been a feature of Jamaican society, with the exception of the period 1921–43, when the net movement was inwards due to the decline of employment opportunities abroad. Until 1921 emigration from Jamaica was largely to nearby territories in the Americas, including Panama and Latin America, and, later, Cuba and the United States. Volume was however small, net emigration being 2480 in the decade 1881–91, 2200 in the twenty-year period 1891–1911, and 7710 in the decade 1911–21. These figures are small even compared with most of the annual net emigration totals for the years since 1950, as Table 6.1 shows.

The renewed outflow from Jamaica in the early 1950s was largely to the United Kingdom. This was a more distant destination for Jamaican emigrants than in earlier years, but war-time service in the armed forces had given some thousands of Jamaicans experience of living and working in Britain. In the immediate post-war period the United Kingdom was the only major industrial country to which Jamaicans could travel without immigration control at destination, and a growing number of them took advantage of this. In the 1930s and during the Second World War unemployment in Jamaica had been at distressingly high levels, whereas there was not only full employment but an actual shortage of certain types of labour in the United Kingdom. The United States was, however, all but closed to Jamaican immigration as the result first of the Immigration Act of 1924 and then the Immigration Act of 1952, more commonly known as the McCarran–Walter Act; the latter provided that any immigrant born in a colony or dependancy – and Jamaica at that time was a British colony – was counted against the immigration quota of the governing country, but in addition no colony or dependancy was allowed more than 100 persons, excluding non-

150

TABLE 6.1. Jamaica: net migration
1881-1973

Period/year	Net balance
1881-91	-2480
1891-1911	-2200
1911-21	-7710
1921-43	+1200
1950	-1710
1951	-4450
1952	-3880
1953	-4300
1954	-8400
1955	-18900
1956	-17400
1957	-15200
1958	-8200
1959	-13100
1960	-30300
1961	-38500
1962	-28700
1963	-7300
1964	-13500
1965	-6500
1966	-8900
1967	-24000
1968	-26000
1969	-29000
1970	-23000
1971	-31000
1972	-26000
1973	-26000

A negative figure indicates net emigration,
a positive figure net immigration.
Sources: G. Roberts and D. Mills, *Study of
External Migration Affecting
Jamaica, 1953-1955* (UCWI,
1958) p. 60.
G. Roberts et al., *Recent
Population Movements in
Jamaica* (Kingston: 1974) p. 6.
G. E. Ebanks, 'Jamaica' in A.
Segal (ed.), *Population Policies in
the Caribbean* (Lexington: 1975).
Economic Survey of Jamaica, va-
rious years.

quota immigrants such as spouses and child dependants. Jamaican migration to Canada was even more difficult in the immediate post-war years, as black persons were held to be inadmissable unless they fell into certain preferred classes such as agricultural labourers and domestic servants. It was not until after the relaxation of immigration controls in both the United States and Canada in the 1960s, combined with the imposition of controls on the entry of Commonwealth citizens into the United Kingdom in 1962, that the two North American countries began to provide the main outlets for Jamaican emigration. The United Kingdom, Canada and the United States, have been the only countries to which Jamaicans have emigrated in any numbers in the last twenty-five years; unlike other Commonwealth Caribbean territories, Jamaica was left almost entirely out of the intra-federation movements,[1] and, more recently, Jamaica has been virtually unrepresented in the movements to Trinidad and the US Virgin Islands.[2]

Before discussing emigration from Jamaica and Jamaican views on the immigration policies of the three main receiving countries in more detail, it is necessary to say a few words about information on external migration to and from Jamaica. Although it is generally acknowledged that the overall quality of demographic data in Jamaica is relatively good, migrational data are the weakest link in the chain. The difficulties of recording adequately the significant outflow of Jamaicans, the permanent and temporary re-entry of nationals, and the massive influx of tourists are acknowledged; nevertheless, the amount of information that is available from Jamaican sources on external migration is minimal. Other than total numbers, destination and sex, the data available on emigration in official Jamaican publications such as the yearly· *Economic Survey* have been obtained from the countries of destination. This procedure, as the *Economic Survey* of 1970 acknowledges, involves a delay of twelve months before the sex, age, and occupation information on migrants for any one year is available. Such data has in any case only been provided for Canada and the USA; the British (Home Office) statistics do not classify migrants by occupation, or by age, except to identify children as being those less than 16 years old. Perhaps a more basic limitation of the data available on Jamaican external migration, but one that is by no means peculiar to that country, is the discrepancy in the total numbers of migrants, as recorded by the Jamaican authorities, and by the authorities of the receiving countries. Although the variation is generally not of too great an order, a factor that should be taken into account in deciding which figure can be taken to be most reliable is that the recorded totals of Jamaican emigration are widely believed to be considerably underestimated, in that a certain (unknown) proportion of permanent emigration is not recorded as such.[3] Furthermore, the extent of illegal immigration, particularly into the United States, by Jamaicans is thought to have been quite extensive in recent years.[4] Nevertheless, although it is necessary to bear in mind the above caveats concerning the Jamaican figures, it is possible to identify clearly the trends and volumes of emigration from that country, and further, in conjunction with several small-scale studies, to examine the characteristics and the type of migration.

JAMAICAN EMIGRATION FROM THE SECOND WORLD WAR TO 1962

As has been mentioned, there was no restriction on the entry of Jamaicans into the United Kingdom until 1962. One estimate is that 85 per cent of the people leaving Jamaica during the period 1953 to 1964 were heading for Britain.[5] The first real sign of movement was the arrival of 492 West Indians on the 'Empire Windrush' in 1948, and further boatloads of West Indians arrived in the next few years. The movement did not however gain any major dimension until after the McCarran–Walter Act became law in the United States in 1952. The numbers of Jamaicans moving to and from Britain in each of the years 1953 to 1962 are shown in Table 6.2 and the division of the gross migration to Britain, subdivided into men, women and children is shown in Table 6.3.

Before examining the figures in Tables 6.2 and 6.3 in detail a few words must be said about Jamaican reaction to the passage of the McCarran–Walter Act. In the late 1940s some 1000 Jamaicans were migrating to the United States each year,[6] and the new legislation had the effect of reducing drastically this annual intake. Protests were made both in the United States and in Jamaica. The Jamaica Progressive League, an American group composed mainly of American citizens of West Indian birth, was reported as stating that it was quite obvious that the new legislation was inspired by considerations of race and that the real purpose of the Act was to discriminate against coloured West Indians.[7] In Jamaica itself, although there was relatively little comment, a resolution in the House of Representatives in July 1952 claimed that the Act discriminated directly against people of the West Indies. Later in the year a Jamaican newspaper expressed hopes that modifications would ultimately be brought about which would make immigration control less oppressive to 'friends of America'.[8] These modifications were ultimately made, but not until 1965.

T_ABLE_ 6.2. Jamaican migration to Britain 1953–62 (gross and net)

Year	To Britain	From Britain*	Net
1953	2210	133†	2077
1954	8149	182†	7967
1955	18564	99†	18465
1956	17302	757	16545
1957	13087	1376	11711
1958	9993	1992	8001
1959	12796	2318	10478
1960	32060	1791	30269
1961	39203	1558	37645
1962	22779	2868	19911
Total	176143	13074	163069

* With respect to returning migrants, the *Economic Survey* of 1963 notes that it is impossible to say how many of those returning to Jamaica from Britain intended to stay permanently.
Source: † Roberts and Mills, *Study of External Migration Affecting Jamaica, 1953–1955* (UCWI, 1978) p. 103. Figures for emigrants who had left Jamaica for Britain in search of permanent employment, 1953–55.
All other figures from *Economic Survey of Jamaica*, various years.

T_ABLE_ 6.3. Jamaican migration to Britain 1953–62 (number of men, women and children)

Year	Men	Women	Children	Total
1953	1284	875	51	2210
1954	5178	2861	110	8149
1955	11515	6718	331	18564
1956	9144	7577	581	17302
1957	6257	6097	733	13087
1958	4425	4509	1059	9993
1959	6410	4955	1431	12796
1960	18372	11258	2430	32060
1961	19181	16276	3746	39203
1962	8434	10207	4138	22779
Total	90200	71333	14610	176143

Source: *Economic Survey of Jamaica*, various years.

In order to place the Jamaican migration to Britain in context, it is necessary to indicate the rates of emigration. Peach calculates that emigrants during 1953–61 constituted 9.2 per cent of the 1960 census population.[9] Discussion of the possible reasons for the large-scale emigration from Jamaica during the 1950s have tended to focus on the economic aspects rather than the social. Furthermore, the conventional approach to migratory movements has generally been taken, in that the 'push' and 'pull' factors behind the movement to Britain have received the most attention. In the first systematic study of Jamaican emigration, Roberts and Mills place the high level of unemployment and underemployment as the most significant factor tending to stimulate emigration in the early 1950s.[10] Although recognising that there had been some improvement in the economic situation in the post-war period, the authors believed that unemployment had provided the major element in the 'push' inducing emigration from the island.[11] Although at the time of their study, migration from Jamaica to the United Kingdom had been in operation for only three years, a period too short to permit the study of the interrelationship between the volume of emigration and economic conditions in the United Kingdom, Roberts and Mills also stress the importance of the 'pull' provided by the economic situation in Britain.

In a later detailed analysis of emigration rates and demographic and economic indices, Peach argues that although factors of population pressure and unemployment in the British West Indies must be taken into account as factors allowing emigration to take place, it was the demand for labour in Britain which directly stimulated it.[12] With respect to Jamaica in particular, Peach shows that emigration occurred against a background of economic improvement. In the 1930s, when unemployment was at its worst, there had been no net emigration, even though entry to the United States was not yet restricted; between 1953 and 1962 Jamaica had one of the world's highest rates of economic growth, and it was during this period that emigration was at its highest.[13] The external factor determining the rise and fall in emigration rates was the fluctuating demand for labour in Britain. Only in 1961 did this relationship break down, for in that year fear of forthcoming British control of immigration precipitated an unprecedented outflow from Jamaica.

The interrelationship between Jamaican migration rates and the demand for labour in Britain is, of course, only one aspect of the movement. The informal communication links that were gradually established, starting with the Jamaican ex-servicemen who remained in Britain, enabled the knowledge of job opportunities to be percolated, mainly through kinship networks, to the hitherto uninformed working population. A further necessary condition for emigration was the ability of the individual to finance the move. The proceeds of land sales to bauxite companies apparently represented one source of finance for early migrants[14] and, as the number of emigrants increased, remittances were forwarded from Britain to pay the fares of dependants and to provide loans to friends and relatives. In a sample of 364 Jamaican emigrants in 1961, Davison found that over half of the women's passage money was paid for by gifts from the UK, and one-third of the men's by gift or loan from the UK.[15] As to the availability of transportation, the expansion of travel agencies and transporting companies kept pace with increasing demand.

The majority of migrants went to England to seek employment. However, the emigrants by no means represented only the unemployed of Jamaica. Whilst the emigration of the genuinely unemployed may be more easily understood, the motivations of the previously employed are obviously more complex, and in addition, are of importance as a reflection of socio-economic conditions and opportunities in Jamaica as perceived by the individual. It seems clear that many skilled and semi-skilled workers in the West Indies failed to obtain satisfaction from working conditions in their home environment and this led to the desire to emigrate, but no systematic study has been made of individuals' motives for emigration.

The Jamaican emigration data shown in Table 6.3 provides information as to the sex of adult migrants and the numbers of children. For further information about the characteristics of the emigrants in the 1950s it is necessary to rely on a few contemporary studies carried out on a small scale in Jamaica. Such studies indicate, as expected, that the vast majority of the migrants were aged between 15 and 40. Less than one-third of the migrants questioned in the surveys were legally married; however, in view of the particular patterns of marriage in Jamaica, this statistic has little meaning. Whether the unions were legal or not, it appears that family migration was rare, and the vast majority of the migrants were not accompanied by children on leaving Jamaica. In the early stages of Jamaican emigration, residents of Kingston, the capital, were apparently more prone to emigration than people from the rest of the island. As the decade progressed, the migrant stream included a growing proportion of residents of rural districts of Jamaica. The shift in area of origin of Jamaican migrants reflected the growing proportion of migrants who were unskilled workers and of lower educational achievement towards the end of the decade, although persons with middle skills – the upper ranks of the 'lower' classes – continued to figure prominently in the outflow. The migrants contained proportions with both elementary school education and higher education which were above the national average. Classification of the migrants by occupation and employment status has been attempted but without much success. It does, however, appear to be fairly well established that emigrants included artisans, sugar factory workers, land-owning peasants and, particularly from the Kingston area, members of labour unions.

Although emigration from Jamaica to the United Kingdom before 1962 was essentially a spontaneous and individual movement and there was no government sponsorship (as there was in, for instance, Barbados), the Jamaican government did implicitly encourage the outflow. As early as 1953, the Premier of Jamaica stated his belief that the country had gained from migration, particularly in the relief of population pressure and unemployment. Emigration from Jamaica to all destinations during the period from 1943 to 1960 has been calculated to have resulted in a net loss of 195,000 persons to the island, equivalent to one-third of natural increase during this period.[16] Although natural increase was running at about 23 per 1000 population per annum, the actual growth experienced was about 15 per 1000. Table 6.4 shows the annual figures for natural and net increase for the years 1950–62.

TABLE 6.4. Jamaica: population statistics 1950–62

Year	Births	Deaths	Natural increase	Net emigration	Net increase
1950	46400	16600	29800	1700	28100
1951	48400	17300	31100	4450	26650
1952	48500	16800	31700	3880	27820
1953	51200	15500	35700	4300	31400
1954	53600	16200	37400	8400	29000
1955	55900	15300	40600	18900	21700
1956	58300	14900	43400	17400	26000
1957	60400	14000	46400	15200	31200
1958	62100	14300	47800	8200	39600
1959	64800	16700	48100	13100	35000
1960	68400	14300	54100	30300	23800
1961	66100	14200	51900	38500	13400
1962	66900	14800	52100	28700	23400
Total	—	—	550100 (100.0%)	193030 (35.1%)	357070 (64.9%)

Source: Economic Survey of Jamaica, various years.
    Digest of Statistics, Jamaica, various years.

As far as the employment and economic effects of emigration from Jamaica in the 1950s are concerned, there seems to be general agreement that the country gained rather than lost from the movement. Jefferson has estimated that, in the absence of emigration, the unemployment rate in 1960, instead of being 13.5 per cent, would have been not much lower than the 1943 rate of 25.1 per cent.[17] The migration of skilled workers may have resulted in some loss of total production, but per capita production appears nevertheless to have been greater in 1962 than at the end of the war. Migration certainly brought substantial earnings of foreign exchange to Jamaica through migrants' remittances. The social effects of emigration were, however, in part detrimental, in that the majority of emigrants left their children with relatives and friends in Jamaica, temporarily and sometimes permanently, leading to a breakdown of family life and a probably higher incidence of social work cases among children with parents abroad.[18] It should, however, be borne in mind that the fostering of children is a longstanding and prevalent feature of Jamaican family organisation.

In more general terms, the social implications may be seen in context of aspirations to a higher standard of living. The prestige attributed to an individual who has emigrated to the United Kingdom has frequently been noted, as also the exploitation of achievement in the UK to validate the individual's prestige on his return. As Kuper comments, whereas for some poorer Jamaicans migration has obviously reduced the distance between themselves and both the bourgeois of Jamaica and the white communities, there may be a tendency for others, particularly the intelligentsia, to return embittered by metropolitan racialism.[19]

The perceived importance of Jamaican emigration to both the country and the individual was to be clearly demonstrated in the reactions in Jamaica to the discussions which led up to the United Kingdom Commonwealth Immigrants Act of 1962. As pressures grew in Britain to enact legislation to control Commonwealth immigration, Norman Manley, the Jamaican Prime Minister at the time, stressed repeatedly his belief that the central issue involved was that of colour, and not economics. In a speech in Birmingham in June 1961,[20] he noted that Britain's unemployment was less than 5 per cent, that the housing problem had existed before migration began, and that if any control was imposed on immigration the move would be interpreted world-wide as one based solely on colour prejudice. In October of the same year, following reports of the Conservative Party conference where the Home Secretary had spoken, if only implicitly, of impending immigration controls, Manley cabled London to protest against 'this departure from traditional policy . . .'.[21] A cable sent to Prime Minister Macmillan on the same day by Alexander Bustamante, Leader of the Opposition, demonstrated his support for Manley's stand.

During the second half of 1961, Manley was the only Jamaican leader who was reported to have spoken out repeatedly against British control of migration, and although his attitude changed from one of remonstration to one of resignation, he consistently maintained that the proposed legislation was based on considerations of colour alone. Coloured immigrants in the United Kingdom, he maintained, were making a substantial contribution to the easing of labour shortages, and housing problems were not caused by the migrants. The British Government had yielded to popular clamour, in his opinion, and were failing to take the strong and decisive stand which should inspire a multiracial Commonwealth. Manley received full support from the Jamaican press in his criticisms of British proposals to introduce control of Commonwealth immigration.

Protests and rhetoric gradually gave way, however, to a resigned acceptance of the inevitability of immigration control, whatever the implications for Jamaica and the Commonwealth, and the argument gradually shifted to the need for Jamaican (and other West Indian) leaders to tackle the problem of rapid population growth and to plan for new job creation. As a last fling, Manley proposed that there should be a Commonwealth Conference on the whole issue of migration control, but this proposal was turned down by the British Prime Minister. It became clear in the early months of 1962, however, that the British legislation was not to be as harsh as had originally been feared, and, at about the same time, came the announcement that Canada was to relax her immigration laws. The proposed change in Canada's policy was received in Jamaica with a considerable amount of reserve and does not appear to have diverted attention away from Britain. The *Daily Gleaner* believed that it would still be necessary to look to Britain and the United States for the solution to Jamaica's unemployment problems,[22] and Norman Manley, in London for Jamaican independence talks, stated that he did not see much prospect of substantial migration to Canada.[23]

Before Jamaica attained independence on 2 August 1962, there was a general election and a change of government in the country. The Jamaican Labour Party won the election and Alexander Bustamante became Premier. In his first formal statement as Premier, Bustamante stated that his Government would welcome the return of trained Jamaicans from abroad to help in the task of building a new nation. A further plank in the new Government's policy was to seek alternative outlets for emigrants. In addition, although a population control programme as such was not at that time thought necessary, the *Five Year Independence Plan 1963–8* stated that the Government would seek to bring about a greater awareness of the implications of population growth and population pressure in the island, and of the national problems arising therefrom. In the 1950s emigration from Jamaica to the United Kingdom had been not only a demographic and economic 'safety valve' but a social and political one too. Something had to be found to take its place.

JAMAICAN EMIGRATION FROM 1962

In the first four years after 1962, net emigration from Jamaica to all destinations fell from the very high levels of 1960, 1961 and the first half of 1962 to the more modest levels experienced in the middle 1950s. Hopes were expressed in Jamaica that, after the attainment of independence, the United States would grant non-quota entry to Jamaicans and the natives of other newly independent West Indian countries. The American farm labour programme had provided seasonal employment for a limited number of Jamaican agricultural workers from as far back as 1934, one clause of the standard contract providing for the deduction and remittance to Jamaica of a percentage of the workers' wages. The number recruited under this programme increased gradually from 2674 in 1955 to 5898 in 1960 and 9721 in 1962.[24] The proposals made by Manley in June 1962 in the Jamaican House of Representatives were, however, not for an extension of this programme, but for the provision by the United States of an important alternative outlet for permanent migration. Several government representations were made to the United States government on the subject in the course of the following three years, and, when a new Immigration Bill was under consideration in Congress in 1965, the possible changes in the overall immigration policy of the United States received considerable attention. It was, however, recognised that immigration into the United States would never be without some control, and could not therefore take the place of the pre-1962 movement to Britain.[25] Nevertheless, as Table 6.5 shows, the number of Jamaicans admitted as immigrants to the United States nearly quadrupled in 1967 as compared with 1966 and there was a further major increase in 1968. After an initial delay in taking advantage of the new opportunities, Jamaica started to take a high proportion, in relation to her population, of the total of 120,000 immigrants a year allowed to western hemisphere countries, and by the early 1970s the United States Embassy was reported as being one of the busiest in the world from the point of view of granting visas for residence in America.

TABLE 6.5. Jamaican migration to the United
States of America 1962–72

Year	Numbers
1962	1573
1963	1880
1964	1762
1965	1837
1966	2743
1967	10483
1968	17470
1969	16947
1970	15033
1971	14571
1972	13427
Total	97726

The figures are for Jamaican *citizens* admitted as
immigrants to the USA and therefore will include
those coming from countries other than Jamaica,
including a few hundred each year from the UK.
Source: *United States Immigration & Naturalisation
Reports.*

Despite the affirmation in the Canadian Government's White Paper
in 1966 that Canadian immigration policies must involve no discrimination by reason of race, colour or religion and the translation of this
principle in 1967 into the creation of the points system, emigration from
Jamaica to Canada has not approached the volume of the movement to
the United States in recent years. The figures for immigrants to Canada
whose country of last permanent residence was Jamaica did rise,
according to Canadian statistics, from 1407 in 1966 to 3459 in 1967 and
2886 in 1968, but in practice the points system and the generally rather
specific requirements of Canada's immigration provisions meant that it
was the skilled and professional workers, rather than those with lower
grades of occupational skill, who had the chance to enter Canada, and
such persons appeared to prefer to enter the United States if they could.

The progressive removal of longstanding discriminatory clauses in
Canadian immigration policy did not in fact receive as favourable a
reception in Jamaica as might have been expected. The general feeling in
the latter country, two years after the first moves had been made, was
that the immigration policy was still unfair, in that only those people
with skills needed in Canada were to be admitted. A *Daily Gleaner*
editorial expressed the view that a fair immigration policy was one that

admitted any people of any race or nation who wanted to help themselves; it was suggested that countries such as Canada, Australia and the United States had a duty to help to solve the problems that stemmed from increasing poverty in countries that had a larger population than their economies could handle.[26]

That a relaxation of Canada's immigration policy would be of great economic significance to Jamaica was to be emphasised frequently during the Canadian–Caribbean Conference held in Ottawa in July 1966. In June Donald Sangster, the Acting Prime Minister, had stressed the strong ties which had long existed between Canada and the West Indies, and the need to strengthen those links. The importance of an extension of trade agreements was also stressed, as was the opportunity for Canada to provide the leadership of Commonwealth countries in the region in view of the abandonment of that role by Britain. At the conference, Sangster called for easier entry into Canada for West Indians; he referred to the thousands of Europeans admitted to Canada over the years and the fact that there still remained an admitted need for labour and stated that he saw no reason why West Indians should not be admitted. He suggested that seasonal labour and assisted passage schemes might be possible, and reminded the conference that West Indian workers in Britain and the USA had always been well spoken of. Stressing the fact that the Caribbean countries were examining possible internal solutions to population pressure, Sangster stated that these could only be long-term projects; meanwhile, he said, the present unemployment situation was threatening the political and social stability of the area.[27]

Canada's announcement at the end of the conference that discrimination in the assisted passage scheme would be ended, and the domestic workers annual quota increased, was greeted by the *Gleaner* as merely 'icing to cover the same cake'; the promise to extend the farm labour scheme, if it proved to be successful, was regarded as being more significant.[28] The increase in the categories of semi-skilled workers and sponsored migrants that would be allowed to seek admission, however, were seen by the Jamaican Prime Minister to be 'positive gains'.

In the meantime the United Kingdom Commonwealth Immigrants Act of 1962 had brought the migration of male adult Jamaican workers to Britain nearly to a halt. As can be seen from Table 6.6 Jamaican migration to Britain after 1 July 1962 was largely a movement of women and children, and children made up more than 80 per cent of the flow from 1966 onwards. As has been mentioned above, the majority of earlier migrants had left children in Jamaica, and many of these were brought to England to join their parents. It should be noted that the figures published in the Jamaican Economic Surveys are generally somewhat lower than those presented in Table 6.6; apart from the

TABLE 6.6. Jamaican migration to Britain 1962–72

Year	Men	Women	Children	Total
1962 July–December	656	2110	1737	4503
1963	984	2937	3609	7530
1964	1011	2983	5980	9974
1965	964	2029	6167	9160
1966	257	830	5990	7077
1967	314	725	7381	8420
1968	210	410	4168	4788
1969	153	292	2350	2795
1970	104	267	2094	2465
1971	79	237	1443	1759
1972	64	178	1378	1620

These figures are for Jamaican *citizens* admitted to the UK, and include employment voucher holders, dependants and others admitted for settlement; long-term visitors and students are excluded from these tables.
Source: Commonwealth Immigrants Act 1962/Acts 1962 and 1968, *Statistics*, yearly (London: HMSO); Cmnd 2379, 2658, 2979, 3258, 3594, 4029, 4327, 4620, 4951, 5285.

likelihood of recording discrepancies, the difference may be explained in part by the fact that British Home Office statistics record immigrants by citizenship and not by country of last permanent residence. British International Passenger Survey statistics show that the country of last residence for a small proportion of Jamaican citizens was either the United States or Canada. A higher proportion of Jamaicans leaving the United Kingdom were destined for Canada and the United States than Jamaica, and one study found that many Jamaicans migrated to Britain solely for the purpose of obtaining visas for the United States.[29]

The White Paper on immigration from the Commonwealth, published in London in August 1965,[30] effectively closed a door that, for Jamaicans, was already nearly shut. Although the ceiling on the issue of immigrant work vouchers was much reduced following the publication of the White Paper, the numerical effect was much harder on Asians than West Indians. Nevertheless the Jamaican Government, whilst acknowledging Britain's right to restrict immigration, expressed itself as 'very disturbed and disappointed at the announcement', and Sangster, the Acting Prime Minister, added that it was 'more than apparent that the new restrictions are based on colour and not on economic considerations. This is most unfortunate in a multi-racial Commonwealth'.[31] Emphasising that there was a continuing need for Jamaican emigration and that the Government would persist in making 'the strongest representations' to the British Government, he stated that his own Government would 'maintain the stand that Britain owes to it her colleagues in the Commonwealth to give them preference in immigration for employment purposes'. Other speakers of both main parties in the House of Representatives expressed disillusionment with Britain as Head of the Commonwealth, and there was a growing feeling of disillusion among the Jamaican population in Britain with their host country as the 'mother country'.[32] There was, however, no question of Jamaican secession from the Commonwealth either on the issue of migration or on the question of Rhodesia, an issue on which Jamaica had differed strongly with the United Kingdom. Despite the disappointments of the previous twelve months, Donald Sangster, as Acting Prime Minister, was able to say in September 1966:

> I don't think anybody would want to break up the Commonwealth, it has done an outstanding job in its field and has the capacity and the opportunity, particularly in the multi-racial field, of welding peoples together.[33]

The year 1967 marks a turning point in Jamaican emigration. From that year onwards, the numbers of immigrants admitted to the United States, whose country of last permanent residence was Jamaica (and the great majority of whom were undoubtedly Jamaicans) exceeded by a considerable number in each year the number of Jamaican citizens admitted to the United Kingdom. Even the Canadian figures of immigrants admitted whose country of last residence was Jamaica began to exceed the United Kingdom figures of Jamaican citizens as the figures in Table 6.7 show.

Clearly the Commonwealth connection has ceased to be of such importance to Jamaica from the point of view of outlets for migration, and, when in 1968 the British Government hastily pushed through the second Commonwealth Immigrants Act, there was little comment in the island. Although the new measure was seen by the *Daily Gleaner* as a clear breach of faith, it was recognised that it was designed to control the inflow of East African Asians, and not West Indians, into the United Kingdom.[34]

Although Britain's credibility as Head of the Commonwealth continued to be questioned on grounds of racial prejudice, it is significant

TABLE 6.7. Admissions of Jamaicans to United States, Canada and United
Kingdom 1967–72

Year	Admitted from Jamaica as last residence United States	Canada	Admission of Jamaican citizens United Kingdom
1967	10483	3459	8420
1968	17470	2886	4788
1969	16947	3889	2795
1970	15033	4659	2465
1971	14571	3903	1759
1972	13427	3092	1620

that at the end of 1968, the Jamaican Government, supported by the local press, was asserting its belief in Commonwealth trade and the importance of the preferences afforded by the United Kingdom.[35] On that account Jamaica's Commonwealth association was still valued. When in January 1969 Jamaica attended the Commonwealth Prime Ministers' Conference in London, there was in the Jamaican press continued extensive analysis of the meaning of the Commonwealth. In a significant editorial on 16 January the *Gleaner* stated that Jamaica's Commonwealth policy had been one of rejecting merely sentimental views while refusing to jettison useful traditions, and a week later the same paper commented that, although politically the Commonwealth had little meaning left, there were economic benefits to be gained by membership, particularly for the less developed countries.[36] Although the general climate at that time was that of a willing acceptance of Commonwealth membership, Jamaica's simultaneous move to join the Organisation of American States (OAS) in view of the perceived economic benefits must be seen as a significant indication of an awareness of the importance of regional economic co-operation and allegiance. Membership of the OAS was seen to be essential to Jamaica's financial future and Hugh Shearer, the New Prime Minister, defended entry on the grounds that the Commonwealth provided no defence agreements for the area.

Although still concerned to encourage employment overseas of unskilled and semi-skilled Jamaicans, one of the Government's primary concerns at that time was the increasing exodus of skilled and professional Jamaicans, particularly to North America, and also the general failure of appeals to Jamaicans abroad to return home. Unlike the earlier migration to Britain, which was essentially unselective, the movement to North America has been, and continues to be, a drain on the reservoir of skilled and professional workers in Jamaica. The occupational distribution and the total number of workers and of dependants migrating to the United States in the period 1965 to 1972 are shown in Table 6.8. The relatively high figures for unskilled workers in 1967, 1968 and 1969 are made up largely of female domestic workers. For other years Table 6.8 shows the high rate of acceptance of skilled and professional workers in relation to the total migrant stream. The occupational distribution of workers migrating to the United States is quite unrepresentative of the occupational distribution of the Jamaican labour force as a whole. The distribution of Jamaican migrants to Canada by occupation is equally unrepresentative of the occupations of the Jamaican labour force, only about a quarter of the working immigrants being semi-skilled or unskilled. The proportion of clerical workers is rather higher and the proportion of professional, technical and administrative workers rather lower in the Canadian intake as compared with the United States intake.

Despite the growing volume of net outward migration since the early 1960s, mainly directed to North America, the unemployment rate in Jamaica has simultaneously been on a rising trend. The principal reasons for this are, firstly, that a significantly high proportion of the emigrants were not workers, but wives, children and other dependants and secondly, that the less skilled workers, the majority of the growing Jamaican labour force, found it increasingly difficult to obtain employment outside Jamaica. A contradictory situation thus developed within the country. Despite a continuing surplus of manpower, there remained a serious lack of needed skilled and professional workers, necessitating the employment of non-Jamaicans. However, the *Second Five Year Plan* of the Jamaican Government viewed the 'dynamic imbalance' in supply and demand for Jamaican skilled manpower as only partly attributable to the 'brain-drain': other factors are seen to be firstly, the 'recent rapid transformation and expansion from a predominantly traditional-agrarian towards a modern industrial structure . . . ' and, secondly, the 'lagging skill development facilities and opportunities' and the bias in education against technical and vocational subjects.[37].

Not, perhaps, surprisingly, the appeal to skilled and professional

TABLE 6.8. Jamaican migrants to the USA 1965–72: occupational groups

Occupation	1965	1966	1967	1968	1969	1970	1971	1972
Professional/technical/related	176	346	1357	1777	1704	1056	1078	810
Administrative/executive/managerial	13	45	110	150	176	222	183	194
Clerical	167	205	686	1347	1360	1061	783	797
Sales	15	29	83	146	161	128	121	105
Craftsmen	168	212	501	1117	1610	1798	1411	1150
Other skilled	223	374	1145	2017	1880	1803	1508	1403
Semi-skilled	2	83	13	18	49	68	50	6
Unskilled	118	141	3754	6952	4868	1899	2120	1846
Total workers	882	1435	7649	13524	11808	8035	7524	6311
Per cent total migrants	48.01	52.31	72.97	77.41	69.70	53.45	49.78	47.00
Dependants	955	1308	2834	3946	5139	6998	7317	7116
Total migrants	1837	2743	10483	17470	16947	15033	14571	13427

Source: *Second Five Year Plan 1970–1975*, vol. II, part 4, p. 15.
Economic Survey of Jamaica, various years.

Jamaican emigrants to return to contribute to the development of their own country did not meet with a major response. Some of the earliest such calls were made to Jamaican nurses, for during the 1960s Jamaica appeared to be training nurses largely for export. As early as 1964 the first of many calls to nurses was made by the Matron of Kingston Public Hospital who urged trained nurses to give the island a few years of their services before they emigrated. A stronger appeal to nurses was made a year later by the Acting Prime Minister who urged nurses to resist the temptation to leave their own people in Jamaica to do without nursing care while they themselves went to better paid jobs in Canada and the United States.[38] Such appeals to Jamaicans, whether in nursing or in other professions, to consider their country's needs before their own were to be reiterated by Jamaican politicians and in the press in the following years. However, it did appear that, whilst there was serious concern about the effect of the brain-drain on the economic development of Jamaica, the inability of the country to provide sufficient inducement, financial or otherwise, for her citizens to return, or to stay, was acknowledged. Notwithstanding the implications of the emigration of skilled manpower for the nation's economy, the Jamaican government has not been prepared to impose any curb on travel abroad and on emigration.

In general the demographic effect of the outflow from Jamaica since 1960 has been undoubtedly beneficial. Although fertility continued at a high level after 1960 and the rate of natural increase exceeded 3 per cent a year, the emigration outflow was sufficient to ensure that the actual rate of population growth was only about 1.5 per cent a year. In the years from 1967 to 1971 net emigration exceeded net increase, as Table 6.9 shows. Remittances from emigrants have been of considerable economic significance: in both 1971 and 1972, over 2 million Jamaican dollars were remitted from the United States to the home country.

In conclusion it must be admitted that, although Jamaica still seeks outlets for surplus unskilled labour, the United States is now seen as the country providing many of the opportunities offered for Jamaican migrants by the United Kingdom until 1962. Canada is the only one of Jamaica's Commonwealth partners to offer scope for migration in any way comparable with the United States. Even Trinidad refuses to allow unrestricted entry to nationals of other Commonwealth Caribbean countries, but this stand is· readily accepted in Jamaica in that unemployment and social pressures have long been serious problems in Trinidad, whose immigration policy is therefore regarded as realistic. Australia is seen as being closed to Jamaicans, and the African states of

TABLE 6.9. Jamaica: population statistics 1963–71

Year	Births	Deaths	Natural increase	Net emigration	Net increase
1963	66800	15300	51500	7300	44200
1964	69300	13500	55800	13500	42300
1965	69800	14100	55700	6500	49200
1966	71400	14300	57100	8900	48200
1967	67400	13300	54100	24000	30100
1968	65400	14600	50800	26000	24800
1969	64668	14094	50574	29000	21574
1970	64375	14352	50523	23000	27523
1971	66277	14078	52199	31500	20699
Total	—	—	478296 (100.0 %)	169700 (35.48 %)	308596 (64.52 %)

Source: Registrar General, Jamaica, cited in Ebanks, 'Jamaica' in Segal (ed.), *Population Policies in the Caribbean* (Lexington: 1975) p. 52, Table 3–4.

the Commonwealth require only a few specific skills. From time to time Guyana has been suggested as an effective safety valve and is a possible recipient for some of Jamaica's surplus unskilled labour, but that country seems to be more intent on attracting back her own emigrants than on undertaking any serious programme to attract immigrants from other Commonwealth countries. For Jamaica regional co-operation with its big neighbour, the United States, both in respect of migration and economic ties generally, seems to be becoming more important than co-operation with her Commonwealth colleagues.

7 Migration between Commonwealth Countries of Africa

by William Gould and R. Mansell Prothero

INTRODUCTION

Twelve states in Africa are currently members of the Commonwealth. They comprise its largest intra-continental group in area though not in population. Each of the twelve has a relatively similar experience within the last century of having been a dependent colony, protectorate or mandated/trusteeship territory under administrative and economic control from Britain. Each has become independent within the last twenty years, beginning with Ghana in 1957 and ending with Swaziland in 1967. Each has a similar experience of international migration. The emphasis has been very much on migration within Africa between one country and another, though examples of long-distance, inter-continental, migration may be cited to and from each state. In this important respect, therefore, the African experience is quite different from that of the Commonwealth countries in the Indian sub-continent and in the Caribbean from where there has been major inter-continental emigration, particularly to Britain.

The importance of relatively short-distance, intra-continental, movement immediately raises for consideration the significance of the colonial connection and Commonwealth membership in creating past and contemporary patterns of international migration. To what extent have patterns developed as a result of agreements and co-operation between countries with these similar experiences? Would similar patterns have developed as a result of spontaneous interaction regardless of political, economic or other affiliations? Many contemporary flows clearly pre-date in their origin the establishment of colonial rule with its designation of territorial boundaries and certainly cannot be attributed either to it or to subsequent political development. For example Hausa and Yoruba traders from present-day Nigeria extended their traditional activities not only into present-day Ghana but much further afield, and indeed are to be found not only in former British territories but throughout large parts of western and equatorial Africa, having been involved in trade in these areas for several centuries.[1] Other flows originated in the colonial period, notably the migration of wage labourers, as for example from western Kenya to the sugar estates in southern Uganda, though in this case the largest group of non-Ugandan workers came from the Belgian Trusteeship Territory of Ruanda–Urundi.[2] While there was certainly free mobility of labour within colonial blocks there was also free mobility between them. Other international migrations have originated since independence, notably the growth of large refugee populations which include refugees from one Commonwealth country to another; for example Jehovah's Witnesses who fled into Zambia from religious persecution in Malawi and refugees from political and tribal persecution in Uganda since 1971 who have gone to Kenya and Tanzania.[3] Such flows of course manifest the antithesis of Commonwealth co-operation.

In many respects 'the British connection' and Commonwealth membership appear not to have been important factors influencing movement. Yet in some instances the direction and size of specific flows have come about as a result of past and current co-operation between sending and receiving areas, where both are Commonwealth members. Where co-operation exists it was undoubtedly at its greatest during the colonial period when there was some co-ordination of economic and social policies; for example encouraging the mobility of labour through inter-territorial organisations such as the East African High Commission (Kenya, Uganda and Tanzania) and the West African Currency Board covering the British colonies in that part of Africa. Since independence the flows have been reduced as each country has developed its own policies. These policies have been largely influenced by economic as well as political nationalism and have had the effect, directly and indirectly, of raising barriers to impede or to prevent movement.[4] Foreign-born populations who had entered during free movement in the colonial period remain as legacies of such past conditions, but they are now seen as foreign nationals rather than simply migrant workers from another territory. As a result there is considerable restriction on their being allowed to work in some sectors of economies where previously they were active. Economic policies discriminate against foreigners regardless of their origins. Nigerians in Ghana found

themselves in no more favourable a position than Voltaics during the
expulsion of aliens from the country in 1969 and many were treated
more severely.[5] In no case during the colonial period were there overall
agreements on migration between British territories though in some
instances preference could be given to those employed in specific jobs or
to nationals of particular countries deriving from more general agreements. The East African Community, for example, prohibited the
expulsion of the nationals of its members.

The past colonial and the present Commonwealth connection has
been most important in inter-continental migration into Africa. Settlers
from Britain came to the plateau and mountain areas of East, south-
central and southern Africa as farmers and miners, and in particular
went in large numbers to Rhodesia and to South Africa. While the latter
states are no longer members of the Commonwealth, associations with it
remain through previous links and it would be unrealistic to attempt to
discuss international migration within southern Africa without including them.[6] The development of the whole migration system for Africans
in the southern part of the continent has been dependent on the
economic wealth of these two states and consequent demands which
attracted labour from a wide area, including countries that continue to
be part of the Commonwealth. Although a vast political gulf exists
between the Republic of South Africa and Rhodesia on the one hand
and the rest of the continent on the other, migrant labour from adjacent
countries continues to move to them to work on their farms and in their
mines and towns.

Migrants from Asia came to eastern and southern Africa as a result of
direct British colonial policy. Indian traders had operated along the East
African coast throughout the nineteenth century, but with the establishment of colonial rule at the end of the century they were able to extend
their activities inland. More important, however, was the importation of
indentured labourers from the Indian sub-continent to build the railway
inland from Mombasa and through to Uganda in the early years of the
present century. Many of them stayed and, with further immigrants
from the sub-continent, provided the main element in the middle and
lower sectors of commerce in Kenya, Tanzania and Uganda. Asians
functioned similarly, though to a lesser extent, in Zambia, Malawi and
Rhodesia. In South Africa Indians were brought in as indentured
labourers to the sugar estates of Natal and the majority of their
descendants continue to live there though they are no longer employed
mainly on the sugar plantations. This migration parallels that of
workers of the Indian sub-continent to estates in the West Indies,

Malaysia and elsewhere, and could have taken place only in a colonial situation.[7] Migrations out of Africa were numerically greatest before colonial times through the slave trade from West Africa to colonies in the Americas. In part this trade was an inter-colonial movement, although there were no formal British colonies in Africa at the time. At the present time migrations of Africans from the continent are of minor importance to both sending and receiving countries. The brain drain from Africa has not yet reached anything like the scale that it has from the Indian sub-continent. Educated and highly skilled Africans can in general still find sufficient opportunities with an acceptably high standard of living in their own countries or in other African countries. Those who leave Africa for further specialist education, often on Commonwealth-sponsored schemes, usually return even though there may be no formal requirement for them to do so.[8] Available data on Africans in Britain are derived principally from censuses, but the interpretation of 'the place-of-birth' returns allows considerable speculation. Altogether 169,205 persons were recorded in the 1971 UK census as having been born in 'the New Commonwealth' countries of Africa, about 15 per cent of the total born in 'the New Commonwealth' (Table 7.1). The majority

TABLE 7.1. Persons born in New Commonwealth African countries recorded in the UK Census 1971

Country of birth	Total
Ghana	11215
Kenya	59500
Malawi	2545
Nigeria	28565
Rhodesia	7905
Sierra Leone	3175
Tanzania	14375
Uganda	12590
Zambia	5740
Other New Commonwealth countries	18590
Total	164200

Source: Population census, 1971, Country of Birth Tables, Table 3.

of these were undoubtedly Asians (from Kenya, Uganda, Tanzania, and smaller numbers from Malawi and Zambia) or Europeans (from Kenya and Rhodesia). It may be that there were only about 50–60,000 black

Africans of whom the largest number from any one country were from Nigeria. These small numbers are in striking contrast to the large inflows from India, Pakistan, Bangladesh and the West Indies into Britain. They contrast also to large inflows into France from former French African territories, particularly Algeria, Morocco, Tunisia and Senegal.

This introduction has sought to highlight some of the principal features of Commonwealth international migration inside and to and from Africa as it has developed in the present century. The details of the roles of colonialism and the Commonwealth connection in these migrations are obscure, though it would seem that any direct influences are less at the present time than they were during the colonial period. Inter-Commonwealth migrations are less important for African countries than for Commonwealth countries in other continents. The following discussion seeks to elucidate further these roles and to identify the extent to which migration can be viewed as a Commonwealth concern.

The variety of conditions in Africa is such that further investigation requires the consideration of regional groupings of countries. The first of these includes the four Commonwealth countries of West Africa which are spatially separate from one another. In East Africa the three Commonwealth countries are contiguous. To the five Commonwealth countries of southern Africa must be added, for the purposes of this discussion, the Republic of South Africa and Rhodesia. Though they are not members of the Commonwealth they continue to play a major role in migrations from Commonwealth states.

WEST AFRICA

In contrast to other groupings of Commonwealth countries in Africa the four countries in West Africa are distinctive in being geographically separate from one another. Nigeria, Ghana, Sierra Leone and Gambia are each separated by at least two non-Commonwealth countries.

British commercial interests in West Africa began with the development of the slave trade, and after its abolition in the early nineteenth century continued with the growth of the legitimate trade which succeeded it.[9] These trading activities required the establishment of no more than points of contact along the coast to effect the exchange of foreign goods for indigenous products. Thus the British established themselves at the mouth of the River Gambia, at several places along the Gold Coast where they built forts (or took over those set up by earlier

European trading groups), at Lagos and, more tenuously, on the coast of the Bight of Benin and in the creeks of the delta of the River Niger which provided a main trading artery into the interior. The earliest British colony in West Africa was set up at Freetown and associated with the settlement there of freed slaves from the Americas at the end of the eighteenth century.[10]

From these points of initial contact trading activities were extended inland in the nineteenth century and the commercial spheres of influence which were developed formed the basis of the British territories of the Gambia, Sierra Leone, the Gold Coast and Nigeria. Over these colonial rule was extended in the European scramble for Africa at the end of the nineteenth century and the beginning of the present century. British administration was further extended after the First World War by the acquisition of parts of German Togoland and of German Cameroons under mandate from the League of Nations, continued after the Second World War under trusteeship for the United Nations. Political independence was extended to all the British West African territories in the late 1950s and early 1960s. In 1957 the Gold Coast became Ghana (into which British Togoland was incorporated); Nigeria became independent in 1960, Sierra Leone in 1963 and the Gambia in 1966. After a plebiscite the northern part of the British Cameroon joined Nigeria while the southern part joined with the French Cameroon to become the Republic of Cameroon, the only anglophone/francophone country in Africa. The Gambia, Sierra Leone, Ghana and Nigeria maintain their anglophone connection through membership of the Commonwealth.

The geographical separation of the anglophone countries has inevitably inhibited the movements of population between them on any large and organised scale. Reference has been made earlier in this chapter to the long-established spread of Yoruba and Hausa traders from present-day Nigeria, which pre-dated the extension of British influence let alone British administration. These movements and those of other peoples associated with particular socio-economic activities (e.g. pastoralism) occurred without reference to a *Pax Britannica*, though they may have been reinforced after it was established.

The Gambian enclave sandwiched within Senegal has been the focus of movements from adjacent territories and from francophone countries farther afield (Mali and Guinea), but because of its relatively isolated location in the west its contacts with other anglophone countries have been few.[11] Sierra Leone, more particularly Freetown by reason of the early establishment of a British colony there, provided small numbers of people who moved to other areas of anglophone interest and subsequent administration in West Africa in the nineteenth and early twentieth centuries.[12] The establishment in Freetown of an elitist Creole population, with which was associated the development of relatively advanced missionary-based educational facilities, led to the formation of three migrant groups. Professional people, educated initially in Freetown particularly in Fourah Bay College (associated with the University of Durham until the setting up of the University of Sierra Leone) and then outside West Africa, provided some of the doctors, lawyers and teachers for the Gold Coast and Nigeria. There was a larger group of educated though not professionally qualified people from Freetown who made important contributions in the lower and middle echelons of administration and commerce as these were developed in the Gold Coast and Nigeria. There were thirdly those from Sierra Leone who were recruited into the army and served in the other British territories in West Africa. Many from each of these groups elected to settle in the countries in which they were employed either during or on completion of their service. Though the numbers involved in each group were small their importance was considerable, particularly in the professions and in the middle and lower levels of administration. The establishment of western-type education (again initially by the missions) in the Gold Coast, at a later period than in Sierra Leone, also provided people who moved to serve abroad. They were important particularly with the establishment by 1900 of a British administration over the whole of the vast territory of Nigeria because of the shortage of suitably qualified indigenous persons there to work as clerks, interpreters and in similar jobs.

The full establishment of colonial rule in West Africa by the first decade of the twentieth century brought the clear demarcation of boundaries between territories and the firm establishment of the Gambia, Sierra Leone, the Gold Coast and Nigeria embedded within the vaster areas of predominantly francophone West Africa. The British colonial administration for each of these territories was distinct and separate and throughout the first half of the twentieth century only a few British West African institutions were established. They involved only small numbers of people and thus contributed little to migration between the territories. While there was a common currency its contribution to facilitate inter-territorial movement was inhibited by distance and intervening non-British territories. For example, of the total population of foreign-born enumerated in the 1960 census in Ghana less than 25 per cent was Nigerian while a greater proportion came from Upper Volta and more than a third of the total was from

Togo. Throughout West Africa during this period there were relatively free movements of people occurring between British, French and other colonial territories. In some areas more precocious economic development associated with the cultivation of cash crops and the exploitation of minerals for export produced demands for labour and consequently movements of people to satisfy these from areas less well endowed and economically developed.[13] The major labour demands were in the southern areas of West Africa and the major sources of supply in the north. There were seasonal migrants from parts of northern Nigeria who moved to the south of the Gold Coast, but in this case the movements were associated essentially with economic need and demand and not with the fact that both these territories were under British colonial administration.[14] Migrant streams were for the most part composed of adult males who moved from their home areas in the dry season to seek work and who then returned to them to farm at the onset of the next wet season. The numbers who were involved are known only in the vaguest terms for the movements were for the most part not controlled and went largely unrecorded. They were not the product of inter-territorial colonial administrative or commercial planning, though they were influenced less directly by administrative decisions (e.g. to levy taxes) and commercial developments.[15] They were essentially West African, for the most part temporary rather than permanent, involving those who were contributing strength rather than skill to economic development.[16]

The colonial era in British West Africa brought non-Africans, mainly from the UK, to fill the higher-level administrative, professional and commercial positions. They were essentially transient migrants who might spend much if not all of their careers in one territory. They were moved about within that territory on tours of duty extending from eighteen to twenty-four months interspersed with periods of leave outside West Africa of from four to six months.[17] They were small in number relative to the indigenous population among whom they were working but were out of proportion to this in their importance in administrative, social and economic development.

Unlike other parts of Africa controlled by the British the West African territories experienced no development of a permanent European settler population based on land alienation and the development of associated services. Except in very limited respects land alienation to non-Africans was expressly forbidden and the large farms and plantations of parts of East and southern Africa and the growth of sizeable European urban populations were unknown in the Gambia,

Sierra Leone, Gold Coast and Nigeria. Asians from the Indian sub-continent came to West Africa only in small numbers, largely to participate in commerce. There was no indentured labour as on the eastern side of the continent. Asians were not permitted to own land and their part in retail trade and other commercial activities has been on a small scale.

With a few notable exceptions political independence for the former British territories in West Africa has brought little change in movements between them, or to and from other Commonwealth countries elsewhere in Africa. Exchanges of very small numbers of professional specialists have occurred, for example, in legal and educational fields.[18] Understandably anxious to promote national self-interests, the intention of the West African governments has been to limit inter-territorial movements of population to a lower level than during colonial times.[19] Stricter controls have been imposed on movements across international boundaries. Periodic restrictions on the immigration of foreign African nationals have been imposed, usually involving small numbers only. The major exception was the Aliens Compliance Order in Ghana in the latter part of 1969 which was enacted after considerable political, economic and social discontent within the country which became focussed on the large numbers of resident non-Ghanaian Africans. The Order required all aliens without residence permits to obtain them within two weeks or to leave the country. Those who would not or could not comply with these requirements were expelled and it is likely that approximately 200,000 aliens left within six months.[20] Though the largest proportion in this category were Voltaics, considerable numbers of Nigerians were involved and no consideration was given to them in respect of their anglophone and Commonwealth connections. In 1960 Nigerians were the third largest foreign migrant group in Ghana, 23 per cent of all foreign migrants. By 1970 they represented only 10 per cent and had decreased more than any other group.

Refugee movements in West Africa have not involved the transfer of any large numbers of people between Commonwealth countries, though small numbers of those who have become politically *persona non grata* have been involved. However, the most important of these – ex-President Nkrumah of Ghana, and General Ojukwu, former leader of the breakaway state of Biafra in Nigeria – found political asylum in the francophone Ivory Coast and not in a Commonwealth country. Undoubtedly in each case it would have been politically embarrassing if refuge had been sought in one of the latter.

Overall the fragmentary data that can be put together indicate the relatively small numbers officially identified as having moved from one Commonwealth country to another in West Africa (Table 7.2). The largest group by far is of Nigerians who are still in Ghana notwithstanding the measures taken against them in 1969–70. For groups in Nigeria there are no data available since census reports for the 1960s and 1970s have not been published. However, caution is required in respect of any of the figures given. It is possible to be enumerated in a census and not to declare that one is a foreign national, and it may be expedient to do so. Figures are therefore most likely to be underestimates.

TABLE 7.2. West African Commonwealth nationals by country of nationality and country of enumeration, about 1975

Country of nationality	Country of enumeration		
	Gambia	Sierra Leone	Ghana
Gambia	—	3400	100
Sierra Leone	400	—	3000
Ghana	*	4600	—
Nigeria	*	7300	55500

* Number is insignificant.

Source: Based on recent censuses and surveys.

The number of British as a proportion of non-African expatriates in the Gambia, Sierra Leone, Ghana and Nigeria has fallen since political independence but the number of expatriates from all non-African Commonwealth countries has increased. They work in various social and economic activities financed by the countries themselves and through bilateral and multilateral aid agreements. Nigeria, for example, with its revenues from oil for investment in social infrastructure has recruited substantial numbers from the Indian sub-continent into the medical and educational professions. But recruitment is not restricted to Commonwealth countries and extends to Eastern Europe and to North America. Most recently Nigeria has been recruiting professional people from Ghana where economic depression has resulted in limited employment opportunities and low salaries. Almost all of these professional employees are on contracts for limited periods of time, many are not accompanied by dependants, and when this does occur the numbers involved are small. The reverse movement from West African Commonwealth countries to other parts of the Commonwealth outside

Africa is not large but its importance is out of proportion to the actual numbers involved. The major component is of students seeking higher education. While the majority of these have continued to come to the United Kingdom there are now more who go to other Commonwealth countries, particularly Canada and Australia, than was the case in the past.

Overall there is little that can be identified as specifically 'Commonwealth' in the character of migration between countries within West Africa and between them and other parts of the Commonwealth. English as a common *lingua franca* facilitates such movements when they do occur, though within West Africa it is probable that an indigenous *lingua franca* such as Hausa is even more important for large numbers who move. The absence of contiguity and the linear, ethnic and social distance which separates Commonwealth countries in West Africa, have been factors of greater importance inhibiting movement. These factors, together with strong nationalist tendencies which tend to restrict the movements of non-nationals unless they have specialist contributions to make, are likely to remain dominant in the future.

EAST AFRICA

Kenya, Tanzania and Uganda comprise a large, continuous block in East Africa. They constitute an area of extremely uneven population distribution with a very wide spectrum of economic circumstances, ranging from traditional, relatively closed subsistence economies to wholly market-oriented cash crop and plantation systems and urban-based manufacturing. This range of economic conditions occurs in each of the three countries, though the extent to which any one type predominates varies from one country to another. Their formal political structures, which have in their turn had influence on the nature of their economic structures, appeared to differ in the colonial period. Uganda was a British Protectorate, Kenya largely a Crown Colony (its coastal strip throughout most of the colonial period being a Protectorate of the Sultan of Zanzibar) and Tanganyika (formerly German) a British Mandated Territory of the League of Nations, and subsequently a Trusteeship Territory of the United Nations. However, these formal differences weighed much less than the fact that overall they were under British control, such that for half a century East Africa was a relatively cohesive economic and political whole. Since independence (Tanganyika 1961, Uganda 1962, Kenya 1964, Zanzibar 1964), there has been the unification of Zanzibar and Tanganyika as Tanzania in 1965, but overall there has been the disintegration of the colonial entity into three fiercely nationalistic and even antagonistic economic and political units.

Migration in this region has been a recurring feature of each society and economy. Before the colonial period there was some long distance mobility of salt and ivory traders, but from the 1850s the integration of the region began to develop through the penetration of European explorers, missionaries, traders and eventually colonial government officials, inland from the east coast. By 1914 the ports of Mombasa and Dar-es-Salaam were linked by rail to Lake Victoria and Lake Tanganyika respectively.[21] Distance, the main barrier to movement, was effectively reduced, peaceful conditions were established and the volume of mobility could increase. A normal pattern of interaction between neighbouring countries would be expected, but in the colonial period the barriers to migration between the countries were much lower than might have been the case. With free trade, common currency, taxation and postal services, and a *lingua franca* (Swahili), movement was made much easier.

With the railways came the introduction of export crops and the development of a cash economy. In German Tanganyika, especially round Tanga, sisal estates were developed. In Uganda, especially in the Kingdom of Buganda along the northern shores of Lake Victoria, there were early developments in cotton production. Cash cropping created a demand for labour, satisfied at first in Uganda from immediate family sources, but then with paid labour, which was initially available locally and then increasingly from distant areas where there was no cash crop production. Most of these sources of labour were in the same country as the areas to which the labourers went to work, but in some instances labour was attracted across the newly-created political boundaries. For Uganda, for example, there were three major foreign sources. First and most important was German and subsequently Belgian Ruanda–Urundi, poor, with high density of population, effectively an extension of the major source area of labour in western Uganda; southern Sudan, at the time part of an Anglo–Egyptian Condominium, provided labour, particularly for the military; and the high density Luo and Abaluya areas of western Kenya were a third foreign labour source.[22] There were labour-surplus and labour-deficient areas and the political relationships of one to another did not matter as much as the economic relationships because labour was available from a variety of sources. These movements were 'inter-territorial' rather than truly 'international', free of much restriction whether they were from within or from beyond the three countries of East Africa.[23]

From the beginning of the twentieth century part of the process of colonial development was the arrival of immigrants from the metropolitan country and from other colonies. Land was made available in the Kenya Highlands for extensive farming, and Kenya was seen as a 'White Man's country',[24] a view that was strengthened after 1923 with the declaration of the Devonshire Commission that the Highlands ought to be reserved for European farming.[25] There was some land alienation in Tanganyika largely made during the German period,[26] but relatively little in Uganda,[27] and the European populations of these countries remained much smaller than in Kenya. Many Europeans, in all three countries, were senior colonial officials or in key positions in the private business sector. In these activities they were supported by immigrants from the Indian sub-continent, who came originally as indentured railway workers and petty traders. They became increasingly middle-ranking civil servants and skilled artisans as the colonial authorities saw the need for a larger group of middle-level workers than they felt the local population could provide, at least in the short-term.[28] Nonetheless, skilled workers did come increasingly from African sources as education and experience of economic development advanced. Most skilled Africans worked within their own country, but some became international migrants, particularly specialist groups such as railway workers or builders from Kenya whose skills were in demand throughout East Africa.[29]

During the colonial period there were few barriers, economic or political, to continuous movement between the three countries. However, though there were few barriers to *flows*, there were institutional and social constraints on the extent of the *stocks* of migrants in the major destination areas. Housing was a problem, and in some areas, notably Uganda, land tenure laws prevented immigrants, whether African or non-African, from buying land.[30] Immigrant Africans thus developed the familiar pattern of circulation with non-permanent urban residence, so that while at any one time there would be a foreign population, the individuals comprising that population would be constantly changing. In this respect international migrants were no different from internal migrants.[31] Although there was some sponsored inter-territorial resettlement from overcrowded areas of Kenya into Busoga and Bunyoro in Uganda, East Africa in terms of migration overall was not an integrated unit.[32] As many migrant labourers came from outside the three countries as moved between them.[33]

At independence there was optimism that the process of integration of the three states would continue. Indeed, Tanganyika was prepared to delay the date of its independence for one year if it were to mean that all three countries could achieve independence simultaneously, and then move forward into closer economic and political co-operation.[34] The infrastructure of the East African High Commission of colonial times was strengthened particularly through the East African Common Services Organisation which operated a common currency and common postal services, railways, ports and airlines and various research organisations. The creation in 1967 of the East African Community was the culmination of the processes of integration. However, economic nationalism gradually began to undermine this unity and separate currency, taxation, and immigration and customs organisations were established.[35] The separation was exacerbated by political difficulties until eventually in 1977 the East African Community collapsed, having fought a rearguard action over the previous decade to maintain and to further unity. Barriers to international migration are now higher than at any time since 1875, with unconvertible currencies, severe immigration controls, much political and some military hostility and regular border closures between each country and both its neighbours. Movements of people that continue are often of those who are involved in illegal activities, as in the alleged smuggling of Uganda coffee into Kenya at the height of the coffee price boom in early 1977, and of refugees from Uganda into Kenya and Tanzania. From November 1977 until well into 1979 there were no direct airflights between Kenya and Tanzania, and the border between the two countries was closed.[36]

This disruption of the colonial pattern of free movement has also affected stocks of foreigners within as well as flows of migrants between the three countries. Table 7.3 gives the foreign population from other African countries in Kenya, Tanzania and Uganda in 1969, 1967 and 1969 respectively, as enumerated in the most recent census in each country. The foreign population was enumerated separately in each by country of birth and by country of citizenship, so that some indication of the relationship between stocks and flows is suggested. However, any such interpretation is affected by the difficulty of separately identifying 'citizenship' and 'place of birth' in a part of the world where citizenship may be an ascribed or perceived category rather than a legal one. If there were pressures for international migrants to identify themselves with the local people the numbers identifying themselves as 'citizens' would rise.[37] Until about the time of the censuses in the late 1960s the need was not great to identify by citizenship in this kind of situation, but with

TABLE 7.3.   Foreign residents in Commonwealth East African countries

| | Kenya 1969[1] | | Tanzania 1967[2] | | Uganda 1969[3] | |
Country of origin	by place of birth	by citizenship	by country of birth	by citizenship	by country of birth	by citizenship
Kenya	—	—	97069	39675	154096	117633
Tanzania	39249	26360	—	—	51876	33618
Uganda	33472	17232	13868	5468	—	—
Rwanda	514	4855	35270	26012	253154	161953
Burundi	536	227	75520	29063	78723	40024
Zaire	479	412	17286	2772	155392	63998
Sudan	313	1944	354	194	56156	65204
Somalia	1617	3519	1977	1510	nes	nes
Mozambique	nes	nes	130324	60915	nes	nes
Malawi	nes	nes	17807	9174	nes	nes
Zambia	nes	nes	11370	5749	nes	nes

Country of residence

nes: not enumerated separately.

[1] Includes total population.
[2] Includes total population.
[3] Includes Africans only.

pressures that have since built up against foreign workers the numbers shown in the censuses will have been affected.

Over 5 per cent of the 1969 census population of Uganda were recorded as 'non-citizen', but over 8 per cent of the population had been born outside the country.[38] The largest group of foreigners was from Rwanda, Burundi and Zaire, the majority of whom were unskilled rural labourers in the coffee areas of Buganda, but others were refugees in settlements scattered throughout the north and west of Uganda. Over 1 per cent of the population of Uganda was identified as citizens of Kenya, with 1.6 per cent having been born in Kenya; these proportions were approximately three times those for Tanzanians. Mozambique was the major source of foreigners in Tanzania but many of those enumerated in 1967 were refugees and they have since returned to their country of origin. Apart from this special case Kenya was the largest source of immigrants in Tanzania which overall had a much lower proportion of foreign migrants than Uganda, and had a net loss of migrants to Uganda. Less than 1 per cent of the population of Kenya were foreign migrants, and she had a net migration loss to her Commonwealth neighbours.

The situation expressed in these data for the late 1960s has since altered considerably. Though no census data are available to provide any comparative quantitative indices of the extent of change, some of the events and processes described have had the effect of altering the numbers of foreign migrants in each of the three countries. Uganda has been more affected than either of her neighbours. Up to 1971 and the coup which brought General Amin to power, there were considerable pressures for Ugandanisation of the country's economy. This pressure was felt particularly by the Asian community, but also by Kenyans many of whom occupied skilled or semi-skilled jobs in the private sector and in the East African Community.[39] Many Kenyans left Uganda, but the general process was much accelerated after 1972 and was associated with the expulsion of the Asians as part of an abrupt attempt to Ugandanise the economy. Kenyans suffered for economic reasons; Tanzanians suffered for political reasons – as alleged 'spies' from the country where ex-President Obote of Uganda was given asylum.[40] General Amin also threatened Rwandans with expulsion, but no action was taken.[41] In 1972 and 1973 after the Addis Ababa agreement which ended the civil war in Southern Sudan, many Sudanese refugees returned home. The net effect of this return flow was reduced somewhat by the recruitment of an unknown number of Sudanese into Amin's army.[42] Overall, therefore, there has been a general exodus of foreigners, and Uganda has rapidly changed, under conditions of political and economic chaos, from a country of net immigration to one of net emigration. Not only have the stocks of foreigners been reduced, but there has been an emigration of Ugandans as refugees. These are often skilled and educated officials who have fled as individuals or with their families to seek jobs in Nairobi and elsewhere, but there are also Ugandan refugees in settlements sponsored by the UN High Commission for Refugees in Kenya and in central Tanzania.[43]

Development policies in Tanzania since the late 1960s emphasise the need for self-sufficiency and the values of family labour. Thus the opportunities for labour migrants, and particularly foreign labour immigrants, are less than they were a decade ago. There have been inflows of refugees (largely from Burundi) since the census, but with the return of refugees to Mozambique the net inflow has been lessened. Kenya has remained least affected of the three countries by changes over the last ten years. Despite it having the highest rates of economic growth in. the region, labour has not been attracted from neighbouring countries, largely because Kenyan labour has been taking up the relatively few jobs that are available, and local unemployment is a major problem. Kenyans returning from Uganda, and to a lesser extent from Tanzania, have added to the labour market.

The non-African populations have also continued to change in number and character since the late 1960s, but the change from colonial patterns began earlier in that decade. Table 7.4 compares the number of Asians and Europeans in the three countries at the common census of 1959 and the censuses of the 1960s. In 1959, five years before Kenya's independence, the White Highlands were still reserved for European farmers. By 1969 this was no longer the case and farmers had been bought out as part of the independence agreement. Some European farmers remain in Kenya, but many left for Britain, South Africa or Rhodesia. In total the European population in Kenya fell by some 40 per cent in ten years and, perhaps more importantly, it has changed in character. Permanent residents have been replaced to some extent by temporary residents; skilled individuals have been hired by government or private industry from a wider range of European and North American countries than was the case in the colonial period, but still with a high proportion from Britain.[44] As in Nigeria skilled personnel are required to further economic development in Kenya, and are predominantly urban-based and on short-term contracts. Their continuing presence has been supported by the government, in the face of strong opposition from local job seekers, as necessary in the short-term

TABLE 7.4. Racial minorities in East Africa

Race	Country of residence						
	Kenya		Tanzania			Uganda	
	1959	1969	1959	1967	1959	1969	
Europeans	66400	40593 (3889 citizens)	20534	16884	10866	9533	
Asians	169600	139037 (60994 citizens)	71660	75015	69103	74308 (25657 citizens)	

to maintain economic growth. Economic considerations have had priority over Kenyanisation.[45]

This priority has been explicitly rejected in Uganda, and to a lesser extent in Tanzania. The number of Europeans in both countries has fallen much more rapidly than it has in Kenya. The exodus of Europeans from Uganda arises from the general economic deterioration referred to previously. In Tanzania, where there has been structural change rather than decline, much attention is given to self-reliance; Europeans who are in the country tend to be very highly specialised, in general committed to the political situation in which they find themselves. The distribution of origins of these skilled Europeans is also rather different with an increased proportion of Scandinavians.

In the 1960s the recorded Asian population of Tanzania and Uganda rose slightly, but in Kenya it fell significantly. At the time of independence in all three countries there were specific agreements about the Asian populations allowing them to choose between citizenship of their country of origin, or of their country of birth, or of Britain.[46] In the 1960s the numbers obtaining local citizenship was considerable (Table 7.3), but the pressure began to be exerted on the Asians to relinquish some if not all of their economic power to local people. This first took the form of restricting trading licences for non-citizens to urban areas only, so that the distribution of the Asian population became even more predominantly urban than formerly. In Kenya, by the mid-1960s restrictions on trading extended into the urban areas. Small retail shopkeepers were being squeezed out, and many left the country. This process has continued steadily, and at present in Kenya only citizens may be involved in retail trading. Estimates of the numbers of Asians in Kenya vary widely from 50,000 to 100,000.[47]

A similar gradual process of pressure on Asians might have been expected in Uganda, were it not for the overtly racist policies of the Amin Government which resulted in the mass revoking of formal citizenship rights, and the expulsion in 1972 of all Asians but for an estimated 1000.[48] The human suffering and political implications of this move had a world-wide impact because of the severe and arbitrary character with which it was implemented. However it must be seen as an extreme example of the general process that has been evident throughout Africa of identifying foreign traders, African or non-African, as economic scapegoats for much greater internal problems. The Ugandan case came to the world's attention partly because of General Amin's behaviour, but also because Britain was involved in a legal sense as the former colonial power which had legal responsibility for those Asians who held British passports.[49] The responsibility for those Asians of indeterminate citizenship was eventually shared by other Commonwealth and non-Commonwealth countries, notably Canada, which offered them asylum.[50]

East Africa has produced major changes in the last decade, and certainly these changes have had a much greater effect on the stocks and flows of international migrants than was evident in the years immediately following independence. Reduction of both stocks within and flows between three Commonwealth countries has occurred without any direct recourse to the idea and the function of the Commonwealth as an institution for co-operation. Indeed in the recent events Commonwealth membership has seemed largely not to have mattered.

SOUTHERN AFRICA

For a number of reasons Commonwealth migrations in southern Africa have been distinct from those in other parts of the continent. A far greater number of countries is involved in political circumstances which vary not only between these countries but also between them and elsewhere in Africa. Permanently settled white populations are involved in the largest numbers, and besides this most important expatriate group there are sizeable numbers of Asian peoples who are also permanently settled. Economically southern Africa has experienced greater development in agriculture, mining and industry than any other part of the continent. In entrepreneurship this development has been associated with the white population and continues to be controlled by them for the most part to the present day. However, labour requirements for these developments have been met mainly by the recruitment of Africans, involving their movements both within and across international boundaries, from areas of low economic development and potential to those of more precocious economic development. These distinctive features in southern Africa are complexly interrelated.

Political developments in the past and present-day political circumstances which affect movements are linked very closely with the establishment of white settled populations and the economic developments in which they have been involved.[51] White settlers came to the Cape region of southern Africa before the end of the seventeenth century, growing in numbers in the succeeding centuries with continuing inflows from Europe. Most recently these inflows from Europe have been supplemented by the immigration of whites from countries in tropical Africa after these had achieved political independence. Reference has been made previously to white settlers who left Kenya in the decade 1955–65 for Rhodesia and South Africa. More than any other states in southern Africa, Rhodesia and South Africa have developed as 'white men's countries'. Their physical environments, being largely extra-tropical, were inviting for permanent settlement and their vast potential for a range of economic developments was readily appreciated, especially from the latter part of the nineteenth century onwards. While whites of Dutch and British origin settled in the most southerly parts in the eighteenth and the first half of the nineteenth century, providing the bases for the present day Afrikaans- and English-speaking populations of South Africa, major penetration inland and northwards with permanent settlement did not occur until the end of the nineteenth century and the early decades of the present century. Not until the present century were the countries of Northern Rhodesia (now Zambia), Southern Rhodesia (now Rhodesia/Zimbabwe), Nyasaland (now Malawi) and the Union of South Africa and the High Commission Territories of Bechuanaland (now Botswana), Basutoland (now Lesotho) and Swaziland designated. To these were added after the First World War the former German West Africa (now Namibia) under League of Nations mandate and subsequently UN trusteeship. Among the majority, but not all, of these a variety of colonial relationships were established with Britain and among all wider relationships within the Commonwealth were developed. Political circumstances have changed markedly over time and with them these relationships have changed also. The Union of South Africa broke its Commonwealth ties and became the Republic of South Africa in 1961. Southern Rhodesia made its illegal unilateral declaration of independence in 1965 and thereby severed its legal Commonwealth connections. Zambia and Malawi became independent African states in the early and middle 1960s and were followed in independence shortly afterwards by Botswana and Lesotho, and more recently Swaziland. All of these countries remain within the Commonwealth.

Although the Commonwealth relationships of South Africa and Rhodesia/Zimbabwe are broken it is necessary to include them for any meaningful consideration of movements of population into, out of and within southern Africa. They are the two countries to which the largest numbers of whites were attracted in the past and where they are still to be found. South Africa has developed for whites on a much greater scale than Rhodesia both in terms of the numbers involved and in terms of political, social and economic structures combined in *apartheid* which makes whites pre-eminent. For the most part Rhodesia has been a pale reflection of South Africa. Between 1955 and 1975 the total net inflow of 53,000 whites to Rhodesia was less than the net immigration of whites into South Africa in any two years between 1963 and 1972.[52]

With the rising tide of African nationalism in the southern parts of Africa, which has come to the full in most countries, with the development of African Homelands (Bantustans) within South Africa and the increasing power of African nationalism in Rhodesia, white migration to South Africa and to Rhodesia has declined in overall terms within the present decade.[53] Rhodesia's white population grew rapidly after the Second World War, declined a little in the early 1960s and then grew again in the second half of the decade, immigrants coming mainly from the United Kingdom and from South Africa. With the coming of black majority rule in 1979 a movement of whites from Rhodesia to South Africa began, and this flow could become a flood if the situation in Rhodesia were to become chaotic with an even greater breakdown of law and order. By the end of 1978 it is estimated that the white population in Rhodesia, which was 263,000 at the end of 1977, had fallen to between 230,000 and 240,000.

The population of four million whites in South Africa remains relatively stable in numbers. In the fifty years from 1924 to 1974 there was a net gain of half a million white immigrants. More recent annual net gains were 30,958 in 1975 and 40,029 in 1976, but in 1977 for the first time in many years there was a net loss of 1178. In that year gross immigration of whites was 24,822, of whom an average of 600 a month came from Rhodesia while others came from the UK, Mozambique, Zambia and West Germany.[54]

In the remaining truly Commonwealth countries of southern Africa the number of whites is small in relative and absolute terms. The number in Zambia rose to a peak of about 75,000 in 1961 then fell to under 50,000 in the years immediately after independence. Those who remain are very largely persons (with dependents) on contract and therefore, as in East Africa, they are not permanently settled. They are to be found for the most part in the major urban centres. Of the European population by country of citizenship in 1969, 51.2 per cent were from the UK and 20.5 per cent from non-European countries outside Africa; this indicates the new links with the USA as well as with Canada, Australia and New Zealand.[55]

Populations of Asian origin are only large in the Republic of South Africa (approximately 500,000) and they represent the descendants of those who were brought as indentured labour, mainly from the Indian subcontinent, in the last part of the nineteenth and early years of the present century.[56] Under *apartheid* Asians have experienced political disadvantages, while socially and economically their position has been somewhere between that of black and white. Movement into South Africa from Asia has been very strictly controlled and therefore any growth in this population has come largely from natural increase. The very small Asian populations in Zambia and Malawi have had some economic discrimination shown against them but not so great as to warrant any major emigration as in East Africa.

Africans are preponderant in numbers in the two white-dominated states of South Africa and Rhodesia and in the independent southern African states that continue the Commonwealth connection. Their international movements have been and continue to be largely between countries in southern Africa. Strict control is exercised on the movement of South African blacks within and out of the country, but there have been major movements of Africans as labourers into South Africa from adjacent countries. Indeed the major movements that have occurred between all countries in southern Africa are associated with labour demand and supply. Southern African countries have been criss-crossed by flows of African labourers with South Africa as the major but not the only focus of the movements.[57]

Early agricultural developments by Europeans were dependent upon African labour for the unskilled work required and demands increased with the agricultural expansion in South Africa, in Southern Rhodesia and along the line of the railway in Northern Rhodesia (Zambia). More recently demands for agricultural labour have contracted with changing technology and political developments though they are still considerable. Now they are largely met from within each country involved, but there is also the illicit movement of agricultural labourers into South Africa, as for example from Swaziland, undoubtedly encouraged by employers because of the low wages that can be paid. For such movements no accurate data are available.

Far and away the most important labour movements have been to mining developments – on the Zambian 'Copperbelt', on the Rhodesian High Veldt, and to various parts of South Africa but particularly to the gold mines of the Witwatersrand and the Orange Free State. Migrant labour has been encouraged by employers for both political and economic reasons. Labour is for the most part transient, employed for limited periods of time under contract. Labourers circulate between home and work areas, maintaining their roots in the former and not being permitted to establish roots in the latter. In this way labour has been unable to develop as a political force while its economic organisation (i.e. in trade unions) has been limited. Economic developments from European initiative and under European control have been possible because of this large reservoir of cheap labour being available. For example, during colonial times in Northern Rhodesia Africans were required for work in urban areas, but towns were not intended as a permanent place of residence for Africans on any large scale.[58] This situation has of course changed with political independence in Zambia, but Rhodesia has continued rigorous control of movements. In South Africa influx control is exercised over the internal movements of the whole of the African population, while official in and out movements of African labour from other countries come under one of the strictest systems of control in the world.[59]

The patterns of migrant labour movement, in respect of areas of origin and areas of destination, have always been clearly defined, though the former in particular have changed both relatively and absolutely over time. Destination areas that have been referred to have remained relatively the same, expansion occurring as in South Africa with the development of the goldfields in the Orange Free State, or reduction with curtailed production as in the Copperbelt in Zambia during periods of economic depression. In economic depression there is a marked tendency to employ labour from within a country before that originating from other countries. Low levels of economic returns and of economic potential, associated with a limited environment and the demands of increasing population, were the important factors in designating the major areas of origin of migrant labourers. Political and other factors have influenced them over the course of time. Among countries with Commonwealth connections Malawi and Lesotho have been outstanding sources of labour for South Africa. Other important source countries have been Botswana and Swaziland with Zambia and Rhodesia of lesser importance (Table 7.5).[60]

Some movements have been free and spontaneous, others have been subject to official controls which were not always effective, while in the case of South Africa controls have been very strictly enforced. At the time of the earliest developments of European agriculture and mining in Northern and Southern Rhodesia, demands for labour were not easily satisfied and incentives and pressure were instituted to produce the numbers required. Foremost among these was the imposition of an annual tax which had to be paid in cash thus requiring Africans to turn from the traditional largely subsistence economy either to cultivate cash crops or to go off for periods of time to labour on European farms or in

TABLE 7.5. Black workers employed on mines affiliated to the South African Chamber of Mines, by area of origin (thousands)

Year	Area of origin						
	South Africa	Lesotho	Botswana	Swaziland	Mozambique	Tropical*	Total
1970	96.9	71.1	16.3	5.4	113.3	98.2	401.2
1971	86.5	68.7	16.0	4.8	102.4	107.8	386.2
1972	87.2	78.5	17.5	4.3	97.7	129.2	414.3
1973	86.2	87.2	16.8	4.5	99.4	128.0	422.2
1974	90.1	78.3	14.7	5.5	101.8	73.1	363.5
1975	121.8	85.5	16.6	7.2	118.0	15.5	364.7

* Areas north of latitude 22° S.

Source: F. Wilson, *International Migration Reivew, 10,* part 4 (1976) Table 3.

the mines. Recruiting systems were set up, though in Northern and Southern Rhodesia the proportion of labour recruited was small.[61]

In Northern Rhodesia following the economic depression of the early 1930s the demand for labour was met entirely from a free flow. In Southern Rhodesia it was necessary to stimulate supplies of labour and a Free Migrant Labour Transport Service was established in 1934 to bring migrants from surrounding countries to a number of dispersal points within Rhodesia. This service continued to operate until the 1950s with a peak in 1953 when it transported 71,549 migrants into and 43,434 out of the country, after which its importance seems to have decreased. The demands on the expanding economy in Southern Rhodesia led in 1946 to the setting up of a Rhodesian Labour Supply Commission which sought to recruit labour mainly in Nyasaland (Malawi) and also in some districts of Mozambique. During the period of the Federation of Rhodesia (North and South) and Nyasaland, when the three countries were closely linked, labour immigration was controlled by a variety of measures operative within and between them. For example, the Foreign Migratory Labour Act in 1958 declared it illegal for labour from countries outside the Federation to be employed in urban areas of Southern Rhodesia, except for Umtali. In the years following this piece of legislation 42,700 adult males moved from Nyasaland (Malawi) and 8600 from Northern Rhodesia (Zambia) into Southern Rhodesia. By 1969 the respective flows had dropped to 9400 and 1400, and in 1974 were recorded as 3900 and 500.[62]

In respect of foreign migrant labour for South Africa recruiting/contract systems have controlled movements since before the end of the nineteenth century.[63] The two major organisations have been the National Recruiting Corporation (NRC) set up in 1912 which recruits in Lesotho and Swaziland, and the Employment Bureau of Africa (before 1977 the Mines Labour Organisation) with its recruiting arm the Witwatersrand Native Labour Association (Wenela). The Mines Labour Organisation was established in 1900 and through agreements which the South African government entered into with governments in southern and south-central Africa it recruited specified numbers of labourers. Recruitment has involved adult males only on contracts for specified periods of time (usually ten to twelve months), with arrangements for transporting them to and from the mines and for remitting a proportion of wages back to their home areas during the period of employment. While until the 1960s the range of recruiting was little affected by political circumstances, it was influenced by other factors, as for example the restriction of recruiting to areas outside the tropics between 1913 and 1926 because of the high rates of infection, particularly from pneumonia, among labourers from tropical areas. This problem was overcome with the development of protective vaccination and at their most extensive the activities of Wenela ranged from Botswana, Malawi, Rhodesia, and western Zambia into the southern part of Tanganyika which were then all under British control, as well as in Portuguese-controlled territories, mainly Mozambique.[64] This range has been progressively attenuated by the coming of political independence to Tanzania (1961) and Zambia (1964) and the action of their new governments in ending agreements with the politically-unacceptable, white-dominated government of South Africa. In contrast Malawi, where recruiting began in 1903, for long-established economic reasons permitted it to continue even after independence in 1966. Despite these economic reasons the Malawi Government unilaterally brought recruitment to an end in 1974 following a plane crash in which Malawian labourers returning from South Africa were killed. Since 1977 it has again been permitted, with a target of 20,000 labourers which was probably not reached. Rhodesia in 1974 entered into an agreement with South Africa for an annual recruitment of 20,000 Rhodesian labourers. This was temporarily limited in 1976 when for the first time there was more black labour for South Africa than was required.

Botswana (40,000 recruited in 1976), Swaziland (21,000 recruited in 1976) and Lesotho continue to supply labour through Wenela and the NRC. The economies of the first two of these countries rely relatively, though not absolutely, upon remittances from migrant labour. Lesotho which is geographically isolated within South Africa had 200,000 labourers working in South Africa in the mid-1970s and is dependent absolutely upon their remittances. These three countries are in other respects economically closely bound to South Africa, with whom they are in a customs union.[65] Plans for developing their respective economies provide scope for further disengagement by Swaziland and Botswana from their migrant labour ties with South Africa, but the prospect of disengagement for Lesotho irrespective of its geographical position is very limited.[66] It is felt by many outside South Africa that the recruitment of migrant labour should end even at the cost of these countries increasing their dependence on South Africa in terms of investment and trade. Developments towards this are likely to be reinforced by moves within South Africa to rely more upon internal sources of black labour for mining and for other economic activities.[67] These moves are the result of some lessening of the pressures of *apartheid*, but probably much more importantly are related to a wish by South Africa for less dependence upon countries that are deemed politically to be increasingly less reliable. Overall there has been a reduction in movements of labour between countries in southern Africa with a Commonwealth connection. Large but now decreasing numbers continue to move only to South Africa. Within individual countries there are substantial minorities of Africans who originate from adjacent countries. In Zambia in 1969 out of a total African population of nearly four million just over 200,000 came from adjacent Commonwealth countries (24 per cent from Malawi, 29 per cent from Rhodesia and 11 per cent from Tanzania) compared with 290,000 in the census of 1963.[68] Immigrant Africans in Zambia in the early 1960s were shown to contribute proportionately more than indigenous Zambians to the labour force in mining, quarrying, manufacture and construction. Since independence the Zambian government has promoted the indigenisation as well as the Africanisation of jobs which would account for some of the fall in the numbers of the immigrant Africans in the country. In 1978 it was reported that 500 Tanzanians had been expelled from the Copperbelt and that a further 3000 might leave to escape harassment.[69] Furthermore in countries from which these immigrants come, which are also recently independent, there have been increasing demands for those with skills to facilitate new social and economic developments. There are thus incentives as well as pressures for such people to leave Zambia.

While political events and attitudes in southern Africa – particularly the opposition of the independent African states to the continuing white-dominated regimes in South Africa and Rhodesia and economic nationalism in recent difficult economic circumstances – have brought about the attenuation of international labour migration, they have at the same time promoted other forms of movement. Reference was made in the introduction to the persecution of political and religious groups which has forced their adherents to seek refuge in other countries. Political dissidents have been forced, or have elected, to leave South Africa and Rhodesia and have become refugees in neighbouring countries. For the most part they have until recently been from elitist groups and are to be found in the capital cities of Botswana, Zambia and Mozambique. Dar es Salaam in Tanzania has become a major focus for dissidents and the headquarters of several political groups that they have formed. These elite are few in number but their importance is out of proportion to their size in organising the movements against continuing white rule.

   Greater numbers of ordinary Africans have moved out of Rhodesia as
refugees into Zambia, Mozambique and Botswana, under pressure from
guerilla fighters, with some of them being recruited into these forces.
Numbers in the various categories of refugees are difficult to come by,
generally they are not known and it may in any case be politically
imprudent to reveal them. Earlier in this decade estimated totals of
refugees for specified countries in southern Africa were for the most part
small, and by far the largest numbers originated in non-Commonwealth
countries (Table 7.6).[70] These figures were issued by the United Nations

TABLE 7.6.   Refugees in southern Africa 1972

	Country of reception			
Origin	Botswana	Kenya	Tanzania	Zambia
Angola	4300			17200
Mozambique			58000	6400
Namibia	50		50	900
South Africa	100	100	100	300

Source: UN High Commission for Refugees.

High Commission for Refugees and in that respect are 'official', though
they were almost certainly underestimates. In 1976 there were reported
to be 36,000 refugees in Zambia from Angola, Mozambique and South
Africa, and in Botswana there were 1000 from Rhodesia and 500 from
South Africa. A more recent figure of 12,000 refugees from Rhodesia in
Botswana has been reported. The numbers of black refugees in southern
Africa is likely to increase, and there is likely to be an increased flow of
whites from Rhodesia to South Africa, while the number of labour
migrants moving between countries in southern Africa has diminished
and is likely to decrease further for political and economic reasons.

CONCLUSION

Each group of African Commonwealth countries dealt with in this
chapter exhibits particular characteristics in the movements of population which are dependent on geographical, political and economic
factors. The four countries in West Africa are geographically separate
from each other and in the past and at the present time experience little

direct movement of people between one another. Movements to them from non-African parts of the Commonwealth have been unimportant. In East Africa the geographical contiguity of the three countries predisposes to movements between them and such movements have been facilitated by administrative and economic infrastructures which were established in colonial times and continued into the 1970s. Political factors have now operated to bring these infrastructures down and inter-country movements of Africans within East Africa are now largely composed of refugees. Immigrant non-African groups from Asia and the United Kingdom came to East Africa in colonial times but have been considerably reduced in numbers with political and economic developments since independence. In South Africa a large white minority originating from past migration remains in control, but uncertainties about the future militate against the further immigration of whites on any large scale from the UK or from other parts of the white Commonwealth. In present circumstances the migration of non-whites from outside Africa is virtually prohibited. In Rhodesia the dominant position of the small white minority is being rapidly eroded. The consequent uncertain political and economic future is resulting in net outflows of whites, which at the present time are small in scale but could increase in volume very rapidly.

Political and economic factors have combined to curtail the movements of migrant labour from Commonwealth countries in southern Africa to both South Africa and Rhodesia. South Africa, which has been the principal employer of this labour, is now taking steps to reduce dependence on this resource. The effects of all these measures on socio-economic conditions in countries which in the past were the main suppliers of international labour migrants are difficult to calculate.

While the colonial connection with Britain has undoubtedly played some part in developing and facilitating international movements in Africa, these also occur as freely between countries with a Commonwealth connection and others without it. While the majority of former British colonial territories in Africa have continued as members of the Commonwealth after their independence, this membership is of little significance in respect of movements between them. Political and economic nationalism limits almost all movements, and the inter-national boundaries of all African states have become more important and meaningful than they were in the colonial era. Discrimination is made within African countries against Africans from other parts of the continent, as well as against non-Africans. The latter are received where they are required to assist in economic and social development, and in anglophone African countries those who are from countries where English is commonly spoken have some advantage. However, African countries at the present time draw very widely in the world for their skilled personnel, and contemporary rather than past political links together with cost factors are likely to be as important in determining the engagements of non-African personnel as any past connection or current Commonwealth membership.

In their relations with one another Commonwealth countries in Africa are likely to be more influenced by their membership of the Organisation of African Unity or of regional organisations in Africa than they are by Commonwealth membership. Independent Commonwealth African governments in southern Africa see their position as 'front-line states' in the struggle against South Africa and Rhodesia as being of the greatest importance. West African countries see their future lying most importantly as members of the Economic Community of West African States, which includes anglophone, francophone and lusophone (Portuguese-speaking) countries and which is proposing, among other things, the free movement of population between member states. When the latter comes about it will be easier to move between Nigeria and any other West African country, as it is easier to move between the UK and other EEC countries, than it is to move between Commonwealth countries in Africa and non-African countries of the Commonwealth. Within Africa in general 'Commonwealth migrations' in any real sense do not now exist.

8 The Prospects for Migration between Commonwealth Countries

Most observers of trends in international migration appear to feel that voluntary migration in the 1980s and probably for the rest of the century will not be on the scale witnessed in the twenty years from the early 1950s to the early 1970s. On the other hand political factors leading to refugee migration are impossible to predict, and it may well prove to be the case that such migration from South East Asia and the Middle East will increase in volume in the 1980s.

The ending of the availability of cheap and abundant oil, on which Western economies had become dangerously dependent, was confirmed in the first half of 1979 after the initial warning in 1973/74. The rapid economic growth and full employment of the 1950s and 1960s in most of the industrialised countries was built on a basis of cheap energy, and the disintegration of this base seems certain to ensure high levels of unemployment for the next decade or two. Where there is persistent unemployment, important sections of public opinion are likely to be hostile to immigration. In the United States, for instance, recent studies have indicated much greater public support for reducing the level of immigration in 1975 than in 1970 among all religious and educational standard groups.

Nevertheless a few governments may see further immigration as desirable despite unemployment. At the time of writing in summer 1979 the Australian government looks to an increase in the net intake of migrants from the present level of 50,000 persons a year to a total of 70,000 a year or so, a considerable proportion of whom are certain to be Asians. And the Canadian government has certainly not shut the doors of its country to further immigration, although admission will continue to be highly selective.

The intake of immigrants by Australia and Canada seems certain to become increasingly non-European in the decade of the 1980s if refugee migration as well as economic migration is taken into account. If this proves to be the case, Commonwealth migration will be a smaller part of the total migrational flow into those two countries, for refugee migration is likely to be largely non-Commonwealth in origin. On the other hand, there seems to be every reason to suppose that migration to the two countries from elsewhere in the Commonwealth will maintain its share of non-refugee migration, because of the linguistic and other advantages and established migration links which help with relatively rapid integration of United Kingdom and other Commonwealth citizens.

If the significance of the Commonwealth in the flow of migrants into Commonwealth countries was determined entirely by current immigration legislation, the only possible conclusion could be that there was now no special relation of any kind between Commonwealth countries which had an influence on the content of the migrant flows. The absence of preferences enshrined in laws is not, however, the most important factor. Much more vital are the personal relationships and the cultural characteristics held in common between the populations of the United Kingdom and certain other Commonwealth countries. A very large number of people in the United Kingdom have a close relative living in Australia, Canada or New Zealand. In 1971 there were over 2,200,000 persons born in the United Kingdom and living in these three countries, over one million of these in Australia alone. Almost all of the Asian population living in all four countries just mentioned have relatives in their old home areas, mostly in Asian Commonwealth countries, and contact with their people back home is usually maintained by occasional home visits. Whatever the official policies may be, many people in the United Kingdom, Australia, Canada, New Zealand, Malta, Mauritius, Fiji, Jamaica, Barbados and other Commonwealth Caribbean countries, as well as Hong Kong and parts of India and Bangladesh, have a vested interest for family reasons in the maintenance of Commonwealth migrational links. They will certainly want to try to ensure that family reunion programmes, to which Commonwealth countries of immigration are committed in principle, continue even if in a modified form.

Some Commonwealth developing countries, particularly those in the Caribbean, are looking increasingly to the United States for migrational outlets. This was described in respect of Jamaica in Chapter 6. There is in fact a growing tendency generally for migrants to move within their own broad geographic region, as, for instance, Southeast Asians do in respect of Australia, Pacific Islanders in respect of New Zealand, and Maltese and Cypriots in respect of Europe and the United Kingdom.

Those Commonwealth countries that have not already developed and maintained a tradition of emigration to or immigration from other Commonwealth countries are unlikely to do so on any sort of large scale in the future. Commonwealth migrational links make a kind of club within the totality of Commonwealth countries, consisting of all the more developed and a few of the less developed members, the latter largely those with well-developed educational systems and with economies that do not provide the occupational opportunities to match the education. Commonwealth countries in Africa are not, as has been seen in Chapter 7, interested in Commonwealth migration, and they are not, and are not likely to become, members of this inner club. It would perhaps be not too fanciful to suggest that those member countries that are most interested in the maintenance of the Commonwealth as a political institution are almost coincidental with those which have an active interest in Commonwealth migration.

Notes

Chapter 1

1. The author is indebted to Mr Brian Lythe of the University of Auckland for providing documentation relating to New Zealand's immigration policy.

Chapter 2

1. These, and subsequent settler figures quoted in the text, (and in tables as SAg) differ from the published statistics of settler arrivals (SAs) because they include not only an estimate of visitors who later decided to stay permanently (VAc) but also an estimate of 'second-timers', i.e. former settlers departing permanently who later changed their minds after some time back in their country of origin and decided to come to Australia for a second time. VAc are included in settler arrivals (SAg) while second-timers are excluded. Likewise settler loss figures in the text and tables (SLg) do not correspond to published figures of former settlers departing permanently (SDs): SLg includes both SDs and former settlers who left as residents going on short trips abroad but who never came back, and also former settlers whose stay in Australia was so short that on leaving they were counted as visitors departing.

Chapter 3

1. The Green Paper on immigration appeared in 1974 in four parts: part 1 – 'Immigration Policy Perspectives'; part 2 – 'The Immigration Programme'; part 3 – 'Immigration and Population Statistics'; part 4 – 'Three Years in Canada'.
2. *Ottawa Citizen*, 20 January 1962.
3. J. G. Diefenbaker, *One Canada*, vol. II, pp. 208, 213, 219.
4. *Green Paper*, part 1, pp. 29–31.
5. Ibid., p. 23.
6. *Green Paper*, part 2, p. 80.
7. G. D. McQuade, 'Trends in Canadian Immigration', *International Migration*, vol. II, no. 3 (1964).
8. *Green Paper*, part 3, pp. 40–3.
9. Ibid., p. 73.
10. *Green Paper*, part 1, p. 33.
11. J. Henripin, *Immigration and Language Imbalance* (Ottawa: 1974) p. 37.
12. *Montreal Star*, 4 February 1975.
13. *Globe and Mail*, 5 February 1975.

14. *The Sun*, 4 February 1975.
15. *Victoria Times*, 5 February 1975.
16. *Minutes of Proceedings and Evidence* of the Special Joint Committee of the Senate and of the House of Commons on Immigration Policy, Issue no. 53.
17. Based on data from the United Kingdom's International Passenger Survey.

Chapter 4

1. United Nations, *The Determinants and Consequences of Population Trends*, vol. I (New York: 1973) p. 226.
2. G. M. Trevelyan, *History of England*, 3rd edn. (London: 1945) p. 659.
3. R. T. Appleyard, *British Emigration to Australia* (Canberra: 1964) pp. 28–9.
4. *First Annual Report of the Oversea Migration Board* (July 1954) Cmd 9261, pp. 5–6.
5. *Royal Commission on Population. Report* (HMSO, 1949) Cmd 7695, p. 15, Table VII.
6. Ibid., p. 25.
7. *Oversea Settlement Board Report*, Cmd 5766 of 1938.
8. *Royal Commission on Population Report*, pp. 122–30.
9. Appleyard, op. cit., p. 22.
10. *Canadian Immigration and Population Study. Immigration and Population Statistics* (Ottawa: 1974) Table 3.2.
11. See Appleyard, op. cit., pp. 43–5.
12. Still at that time a Commonwealth country.
13. At that time such persons would have been either British subjects or British protected persons.
14. ILO, *International Migration 1945–57*, pp. 139–40.
15. Ibid., p. 234.
16. Harold Macmillan, *At the End of the Day* (Macmillan, 1973) p. 73.
17. David Everseley and Fred Sukdeo, *The Dependants of the Coloured Commonwealth Population of England and Wales* (London: Institute of Race Relations, 1969).
18. Labour Members who in 1954 wanted the early introduction of control of Commonwealth immigration included Reid (Member for Swindon) and Hynd (a Member for Sheffield).
19. Macmillan, op. cit., pp. 73–4.
20. *Hansard*: Lords vol. 200 col. 391 etc.; Commons vol. 585 col. 1415 ff.
21. Macmillan, op. cit., p. 74.
22. *Hansard*: Commons vol. 637 col. 60 (questions).
23. G. C. K. Peach, *West Indian Migration to Britain* (Oxford University Press, 1968).
24. K. Jones and A. D. Smith, *The Economic Impact of Commonwealth Immigration* (Cambridge University Press, 1970) p. 162.
25. The Central Statistical Office's *Monthly Digest of Statistics* (June 1966) gives net immigration for the period 1958–64 at about 137,000.
26. *Round Table* no. 203 (June 1961) pp. 282–3 and no. 205 (December 1961) pp. 64–6.
27. The age and sex distribution and other socio-economic characteristics of the immigrant population in 1961 are analysed in Jones and Smith, op. cit.

28. *Hansard*: Commons vol. 685 col. 365.
29. *Hansard*: Commons vol. 702 col. 275–91.
30. *Hansard*: Commons vol. 705 col. 1284–8.
31. *Hansard*: Commons vol. 717 col. 1057.
32. Cmd 2739.
33. The clearest statement of views on this subject from a British politician is contained in David Steel's *No Entry* (London: 1969). Steel was very strongly opposed to the 1968 Commonwealth Immigrants Act.
34. Ibid., pp. 132–3.
35. Select Committee on Race Relations and Immigration. Session 1969–70. *Control of Commonwealth Immigration* vol. II pp. 786–808.
36. Ibid., p. 790.
37. Ibid., p. 787.
38. Ibid., p. 801.
39. Ibid., p. 793.
40. Everseley and Sukdeo, op. cit.
41. The term 'economically active' is used in the internationally accepted census definition, and of course includes those looking for work, even if only part-time work.
42. G. B. Gillian Lomas, *Census 1971. The Coloured Population of Great Britain* (London: Centre for Environmental Studies, 1973) pp. 98–104.
43. *Population Trends* no 1 (Autumn 1975) (HMSO) p. 3, fig. 2.
44. First Report from the Select Committee on Science and Technology, Session 1970–71 *Population of the United Kingdom*. Appendix II.
45. Ibid., pp. 283–7.
46. Ibid., p. 295.
47. *The Daily Telegraph*, 11 and 12 November 1974.
48. *Guardian*, 9 December 1974.
49. Home Office. *A Register of Dependants*. Cmnd 6698, p. 7.
50. *The Times*, 6 January 1976.
51. *The Daily Telegraph*, 1 July 1976.
52. Lomas, op. cit.
53. Home Office, op. cit.
54. *The Times*, 26 January 1973.
55. First Report from the Select Committee on Race Relations and Immigration, Session 1977–78, para 116.
56. *The Times*, 21 April 1977.
57. *The Times*, 14 February 1977.
58. Office of Population Censuses and Surveys Monitor MN76/2 issued May 1976.

Chapter 5

1. C. A. Price, *Malta and the Maltese* (Melbourne: 1954) p. 223.
2. H. Casolani, *Awake Malta or the Hard Lesson of Emigration* (Government Printing Office, Malta, 1930) p. 15.
3. Ibid., pp. 52–64.
4. Ibid., p. 72.
5. C. A. Price, 'Migration as a Means of Achieving Population Targets', a

paper presented to the *CICRED Seminar on Demographic Research in Relation to Population Growth Targets*, 1973.

6. ILO, *International Migration 1945–57*, p. 187.
7. *Report* of the Department of Emigration, Malta, 1948–49, p. 2.
8. Thomas Balogh and Dudley Seers, *The Economic Problems of Malta. An Interim Report* (Government Printing Office, Malta, 1955) p. vi.
9. *Report* of the Department of Labour and Emigration, Malta, 1967, p. 24.
10. *Report* of the Department of Labour, Social Welfare and Emigration, Malta, 1956, p. 12.
11. *Report* of the Department of Labour, Social Welfare and Emigration, Malta, 1957, p. 10.
12. Joe Scicluna '"Don't come home", Mintoff tells emigrants' in *Commonwealth*, August–September 1977, p. 9.
13. *Immigration from the Commonwealth*, Cmnd 2739.
14. *Report* of the Department of Labour and Emigration, Malta, 1965, p. 14.
15. *Sunday Times of Malta*, 28 November 1976.

Chapter 6

1. E. P. Reubens, *Migration and Development in the West Indies*, (Kingston: Institute of Social and Economic Research, 1961) chapter V, A.
2. A. Segal, 'Population Policies and Caribbean Crisis' in A. Segal (ed.), *Population Policies in the Caribbean* (Lexington: 1975) pp. 9–10; Social Educational Research and Development Inc: *Aliens in the U.S.V.I.* (Silver Spring: 1968); See also report in *Daily Gleaner*, 5 March 1971.
3. G. Roberts and D. Mills, *Study of External Migration Affecting Jamaica, 1953–1955* (Institute of Social and Economic Research, UCWI, 1958) pp. 108–12; *Second Five Year Plan, 1970–1975* (Kingston: Central Planning Unit) p. 1.
4. Segal (ed.), op. cit. Notes to tables A8–9, p. 229. A. de Roulet, US Ambassador to Jamaica: text of speech published in *Daily Gleaner*, 18 June 1972.
5. O. Jefferson, *The Post-War Economic Development of Jamaica* (Kingston: Institute of Social and Economic Research, 1972).
6. *Daily Gleaner*, 23 May 1952.
7. *Daily Gleaner*, 10 June 1952.
8. *Daily Gleaner*, 31 December 1952.
9. C. Peach, *West Indian Migration to Britain, A Social Geography* (Institute of Race Relations, Oxford University Press, 1968).
10. Roberts and Mills, op. cit., pp. 2–4.
11. Roberts and Mills give the overall unemployment rate of 1943 as 29 per cent (although stressing the problem of definition); but present no further figures to illustrate the improving economic conditions. Such data can be found in various economic studies of Jamaica, e.g. Jefferson, op. cit., p. 28, where it is shown that unemployment declined from 139,000 in 1943 to 111,000 in 1953, that is from 25 per cent of the labour force to 17.5 per cent. In 1960, 88,500 were unemployed, 13.5 per cent of the labour force. During this period the GDP in Jamaica showed a rate of growth of 10.0 per cent per annum (Jefferson, op. cit., chapter 2).

12. Peach, op. cit., p. 3.
13. Ibid., pp. 24–7.
14. Jefferson, op. cit., p. 23.
15. R. B. Davison, 'West Indian Migration to Britain 1955–1961', *West Indian Economist, 4,* 1–4 (1961).
16. G. Roberts et al., *Recent Population Movements in Jamaica,* CICRED Series (Kingston: 1974) p. 9.
17. Jefferson, op. cit., p. 30.
18. A. Kuper, *Changing Jamaica* (London: 1976) p. 11.
19. Ibid., pp. 107–8. This latter point may be more relevant to the emigrants from independent Jamaica, i.e. in more recent years, and will be discussed further in a later section.
20. *Daily Gleaner,* 13 June 1961.
21. *Daily Gleaner,* 13 October 1961.
22. *Daily Gleaner,* 23 January 1962.
23. *Daily Gleaner,* 3 February 1962.
24. *Annual Abstract of Statistics 1968* (Department of Statistics, Jamaica).
25. See, for instance, statement of L. Newland, Jamaican Minister of Labour, quoted in the *Daily Gleaner* 28 August 1965.
26. *Daily Gleaner,* 5 June 1964.
27. *Daily Gleaner,* 9 July 1966.
28. *Daily Gleaner,* 11 July 1966.
29. O. Patterson, 'West Indian Migrants Returning Home', *Race, 10,* no. 1 (1968).
30. *Immigration from the Commonwealth,* Cmnd 2739 (HMSO, August 1965).
31. Jamaican Hansard, *Proceedings of the House of Representatives*: Session 1965/66, 31 March 1965–5 August 1965, pp. 428–53.
32. Cf. an article, 'The Jamaican migrant who no longer trusts the British', *Daily Gleaner,* 15 August 1965. During a visit to Britain later in the year, Norman Manley was also to comment on this development.
33. *Daily Gleaner,* 5 September 1966.
34. *Daily Gleaner,* 1 March 1968.
35. R. C. Lightbourne, Minister of Trade and Industry, *Daily Gleaner,* 14 September 1968.
36. *Daily Gleaner,* 22 January 1969.
37. *Second Five Year Plan 1970–1975* vol. II, part 4 (Central Planning Unit, Kingston).
38. *Daily Gleaner,* 6 October 1965.

Chapter 7

1. A. L. Mabogunje, *Regional Mobility and Resource Development in West Africa* (Montreal and London: McGill and Queens University Press, 1972) pp. 58–65; Z. Dobosiewiz, 'Traditional Trade and Population Migration as Integration Factors in West Africa', *African Bulletin, 14,* pp. 145–59; J. S. Eades, 'The Growth of a Migrant Community: the Yoruba in Northern Ghana' in J. Goody (ed.), *Changing Social Structure in Ghana* (London: 1975) pp. 37–57; M. Sudarkasa, 'Commercial Migration in West Africa, with

Special Reference to the Yoruba in Ghana', *African Urban Notes, 131* (1974) pp. 61–103.

2. P. G. Powesland, *Economic Policy and Labour: a Study in Uganda's Economic History*, East African Studies no. 10 (Kampala: East African Institute of Social Research, 1957).

3. W. T. S. Gould, 'Refugees in Tropical Africa', *International Migration Review, 8*, part 3 (1974) pp. 347–65.

4. For a general review see the Special Issue of the *International Migration Review, 8*, part 3 (1974) on 'International Migration in Tropical Africa'.

5. M. Peil, 'The Expulsion of West African Aliens', *Journal of Modern African Studies, 9*, part 2 (1971) pp. 205–9.

6. South Africa left the Commonwealth in 1961. Rhodesia is still a member *de jure*, but since the illegal Unilateral Declaration of Independence in 1965 its membership may be regarded as suspended. It remains to be seen if and when independent Zimbabwe will resume participation in the Commonwealth.

7. For a general overview of the history of migration from the Indian subcontinent to Africa see J. S. Mangat, *A History of the Asians in East Africa* (Oxford University Press, 1969); M. Palmer, *History of the Indians in Natal*, Natal Regional Studies no. 10 (1957); F. Dotson and L. O. Dotson, *The Indian Minority of Zambia, Rhodesia and Malawi* (New Haven: Yale University Press, 1968).

8. P. Visaria, 'The Determinants of the Brain Drain' in G. Tapinos (ed.), *International Migration. Proceedings of a Seminar on Demographic Research on International Migration*, (Paris: CICRED, 1974) pp. 102–4.

9. A. G. Hopkins, *An Economic History of West Africa* (London: Longman, 1975); R. Oliver and J. D. Fage, *A Short History of Africa* (London: Penguin, 1975).

10. C. H. Fyfe, *A History of Sierra Leone* (London: 1962).

11. K. Swindell, 'Family Farms and Migrant Labour: the Strange Farmers of the Gambia', *Canadian Journal of African Studies, 12*, part 1 (1978) pp. 3–17, and 'Strange Farmers, Navetanes and Tillibunkas: the Development of Migrant Groundnut Farming in the Gambia', *Journal of African History* (1979, forthcoming).

12. Fyfe, op. cit.

13. R. M. Prothero, 'Migrant Labour in West Africa', *Journal of Local Administration Overseas, 1* (1962) pp. 149–55; J. Rouch, 'Migrations au Ghana', *Journal de la Societé des Africanistes, 26* (1957) pp. 33–196.

14. R. M. Prothero, 'Migratory Labour from North-western Nigeria', *Africa, 27*, part 3 (1957) pp. 251–61.

15. S. Amin, 'Introduction' in S. Amin (ed.), *Modern Migrations in West Africa* (London: Oxford University Press for International African Institute, 1974).

16. E. Berg, 'The Economics of the Migrant Labour System' in H. Kuper (ed.), *Urbanization and Migration in West Africa* (University of California Press, 1965) pp. 160–81.

17. See e. g. R. Heussler, *The British in Northern Nigeria* (London: Oxford University Press, 1968).

18. E. A. Yoloye, 'Educational Exchange Between West African Countries',

West African Journal of Education, 14, part 3 (1970).
19. K. Ahooja-Patel, 'Regulations Governing the Employment of Non-Nationals in West Africa' in Amin (ed.), op. cit.
20. Peil, op. cit. and *International Migration Review,* op. cit.; N. O. Addo, 'Foreign African Workers in Ghana', *International Labour Review, 109* part 1, (1973) pp. 47–68; K. de Graft Johnson, 'International and Internal Migration in Ghana' in OECD, *The Demographic Transition in Africa* (Paris: OECD, Development Centre, 1971) pp. 81–9.
21. For a general discussion of the colonial penetration into East Africa see L. H. Gann and P. Duignan, *Colonialism in Africa 1870–1960* vol. 1. *History and Politics of Colonialism 1870–1914* (London: Cambridge University Press, 1969).
22. A. I. Richards (ed.), *Economic Development and Tribal Change* (Cambridge: Heffer for East African Institute of Social Research, 1954); C. C. Wrigley, *Crops and Wealth in Uganda,* East African Studies no 12 (Kampala: East African Institute of Social Research, 1959).
23. A. W. Southall, 'Population Movements in East Africa', in K. M. Barbour and R. M. Prothero (eds.), *Essays on African Population* (London: Routledge and Kegan Paul, 1961).
24. Associated particularly with Lord Delamere. See his biography: E. Huxley, *White Man's Country* (London: Chatto and Windus, 1935).
25. R. S. Odingo, *The Kenya Highlands: Land Use and Agricultural Development* (Nairobi: East Africa Publishing House, 1971).
26. L. H. Gann 'Economic Development in Germany's African Empire', in L. H. Gann and P. Duignan (eds.), *Colonialism in Africa 1870–1960* vol. 4, *The Economics of Colonialism* (Cambridge University Press, 1975).
27. Wrigley, op. cit., pp. 26–7.
28. Chanan Singh, 'The Historical Background' in D. P. Ghai (ed.), *Portrait of a Minority: Asians in East Africa* (London: Oxford University Press 1965) pp. 1–3.
29. R. D. Grillo, *African Railwaymen: Solidarity and Opposition in an East African Labour Force* (London: Cambridge University Press, 1973); D. J. Parkin, *Neighbours and Nationals in an African City Ward* (London: Routledge and Kegan Paul, 1969).
30. Wrigley, op. cit., p. 24.
31. W. Elkan, 'Circular Migration and the Growth of Towns in East Africa', *International Labour Review, 96,* part 6 (1967) pp. 581–9.
32. Susan Illingworth, 'Kenyans in Busoga', East African Institute of Social Research *Annual Conference Papers* (Kampala: 1963); S. R. Charsley, 'Population Growth and Development in North-east Bunyoro', *East African Geographical Review, 6,* pp. 13–22.
33. J. S. Nye, *Pan-Africanism and East African Federation* (Cambridge: Harvard University Press, 1966).
34. Discussed in a speech by the then Minister of Communications, Power and Work of Tanganyika, A. H. Jamal, included as an Appendix in C. Leys and P. Robson, *Federation in East Africa, Opportunities and Problems* (Oxford University Press, 1965) pp. 209–15.
35. A. Hazelwood, *Economic Integration: the East African Experience* (London: Heinemann, 1975).

36. S. Eken, 'Break up of the East African Community', *Finance and Development*, *16*, part 4 (1979) pp. 36–40.
37. For further discussion on the question of citizenship and responses to census questions see W. T. S. Gould, 'Economic Aspects of International Migration in East Africa' in K. E. Vaidyanatham (ed.), *Demographic/Economic Interrelationships in Africa* (forthcoming).
38. Uganda Government, *Report on the 1969 Population Census. Volume III Additional Tables* (Entebbe: Statistics Division, Ministry of Finance, Planning and Economic Development, 1973).
39. A. A. Mazrui, 'Inter-African Migration. A Case Study of the East African Community', *The Round Table*, *61*, part 242 (1971) pp. 293–9.
40. African Contemporary Record, *General Amin's Uganda*, Current Affairs Series no. 12 (1974).
41. C. Legum (ed.), *African Contemporary Record, 1974–75* (1975) p. 257.
42. It should be noted that the presence of Sudanese in the military in Uganda is of long standing. See A. Southall, 'General Amin and the Coup: Great Man or Historical Inevitability?', *Journal of Modern African Studies*, vol. 13, part 1 (1975) pp. 86–90.
43. United Nations High Commissioner for Refugees Newsletter, vol. 4 (July/August, 1978) pp. 4–5.
44. J. R. Nellis, 'Expatriates in the Government of Kenya', *Journal of Commonwealth Political Studies*, *9*, part 3 (1973) pp. 251–64.
45. D. Rothschild, 'Kenya's Africanization Program: Priorities of Development and Equity', *American Political Science Review*, *64*, part 3 (1970) pp. 748–61.
46. Y. Ghai, 'The Future Prospects' in D. P. Ghai (ed.), op. cit., pp. 129–52, esp. pp. 136–9; R. Plender 'The Expulsion of the Asians from Uganda: Legal Aspects', *New Community*, *1*, part 5 (1972) pp. 420–7.
47. C. Legum (ed.), *African Contemporary Record, 1976–77* (1977) p. 236.
48. Among the considerable volume of literature on East African Asians that has appeared in recent years the following are most valuable: Yash Tandon, *Problems of a Displaced Minority: the New Position of East Africa's Asians* (Minority Rights Group, report no. 16, 1973); UN High Commissioner for Refugees, *How They Did It. Resettlement of Asians from Uganda in Europe and North America* (Geneva: 1973); Mahmood Mamani, *From Citizen to Refugee. Uganda Asians Come to Britain* (London: Frances Pinter, 1973); Vali Jamal, 'Asians in Uganda, 1880–1972: Inequality and Expulsion', *Economic History Review*, *29*, part 4 (1976) pp. 602–16.
49. W. G. Keupper, G. L. Lackey and E. N. Swinterton, *Ugandan Asians in Great Britain: Forced Migration and Social Absorption* (London: Croom Helm, 1975); M. Bristow, 'Britain's Response to the Uganda Asian Crisis: Government Myths v. Political and Resettlement Realities', *New Community*, *5*, part 3 (1976) pp. 265–89.
50. UNHCR, op. cit.; M. Bristow, B. N. Adams and C. Pereira, 'Ugandan Asians in Britain, Canada and India: Some Characteristics and Resources', *New Community*, *4*, part 2 (1975) pp. 155–66; F. Hawkins, 'Ugandan Asians in Canada', *New Community*, *2*, part 3 (1972) pp. 268–75.
51. For general historical background see M. Wilson and L. Thompson (eds.), *The Oxford History of South Africa*, 2 vols. (Oxford: Clarendon Press, 1969

212 COMMONWEALTH MIGRATION

and 1971), and A. J. Christopher, *Southern Africa* (Folkestone: Dawson, 1976).
52. F. Wilson, 'International Migration in Southern Africa', *International Migration Review*, *10*, part 4 (1976) pp. 451–88.
53. B. Davidson et al., *Southern Africa: the Politics of Revolution* (Harmondsworth: Penguin, 1976).
54. *Africa Research Bulletin* (Political, Social and Cultural Series) *15*, part 2 (1978) p. 4748.
55. P. O. Ohadike, 'Immigrants and Development in Zambia', *International Migration Review*, *8*, part 3 (1974) pp. 395–411.
56. H. Kuper, *Indian People in Natal* (Pietermaritzburg: Natal University Press, 1960); M. Palmer, op. cit.; F. Dotson and L. O. Dotson, op. cit.
57. Wilson, op. cit.
58. H. Heisler, *Urbanisation and the Government of Migration: the Inter-relation of Urban and Rural Life in Zambia* (London: Hurst, 1974).
59. R. M. Prothero, 'Foreign Migrant Labour for South Africa', *International Migration Review*, *8*, part 3 (1974) pp. 383–94.
60. Wilson, op. cit.
61. J. C. Mitchell, 'Wage Labour and African Population Movements in Central Africa' in Barbour and Prothero (eds.), op. cit.
62. Wilson, op. cit.
63. W. J. Breytenbach, *Migratory Labour Arrangements in Southern Africa*, Communication of the African Institute, no. 2 (Pretoria, 1972); F. Wilson, *Labour in the South African Goldmines* (CUP, Cambridge, 1972) and *Migrant Labour in South Africa* (Johannesburg: South African Council of Churches and SPRO-C, 1972).
64. Witwatersrand Native Labour Association, 'Organisation of Migrant Labour in the Southern African Mining Industry', *Bulletin, Inter-African Labour Institute*, *6*, part 4 (1959) pp. 40–9.
65. G. M. E. Leistner, 'Economic Co-operation in Southern Africa', *South Africa International*, *6*, part 1 (Johannesburg, 1975) pp. 35–44, and 'Southern Africa in Transition', *South African Journal of African Affairs*, *5*, part 1 (1975) pp. 5–13.
66. R. Vengroff, *Botswana: Rural Development in the Shadow of Apartheid* (Rutherford and London: Fairleigh Dickinson University Press, 1977); S. Wallman, 'The Bind of Migration: Conditions of Non-development in Lesotho' in S. Wallman (ed.), *Perceptions of Development* (Cambridge: Cambridge University Press, 1977).
67. B. Magubane, 'The "Native Reserves" (Bantustans) and the Role of the Migrant System in the Political Economy of South Africa' in H. E. Safa *et al* (eds.), *Migration and Development* (The Hague: 1975) pp. 225–67.
68. Ohadike, op. cit.
69. *Africa Research Bulletin* (Political, Social and Cultural Series) *15*, part 8 (1978) p. 4948.
70. W. T. S. Gould, 'Refugees in Tropical Africa', *International Migration Review*, *8*, part 3 (1974) pp. 413–30.

Index